*The Making of a Teenage
Service Class*

The publisher and the University of California Press Foundation gratefully acknowledge the generous support of the Barbara S. Isgur Endowment Fund in Public Affairs.

The Making of a Teenage Service Class

POVERTY AND MOBILITY IN AN
AMERICAN CITY

Ranita Ray

UNIVERSITY OF CALIFORNIA PRESS

University of California Press, one of the most distinguished university presses in the United States, enriches lives around the world by advancing scholarship in the humanities, social sciences, and natural sciences. Its activities are supported by the UC Press Foundation and by philanthropic contributions from individuals and institutions. For more information, visit www.ucpress.edu.

University of California Press
Oakland, California

Parts of chapter 3 appeared in "Exchange and Intimacy in the Inner City: Rethinking Kinship Ties of the Urban Poor," *Journal of Contemporary Ethnography* 45, no. 3 (2016): 343–64. Parts of chapter 4 appeared in "Identity of Distance: How Economically Marginalized Black and Latina Women Navigate Risk Discourse and Employ Feminist Ideals," *Social Problems*, forthcoming.

Library of Congress Cataloging-in-Publication Data

Names: Ray, Ranita, author.
Title: The making of a teenage service class : poverty and mobility in an American city / Ranita Ray.
Description: Oakland, California : University of California Press, [2018] | Includes bibliographical references and index.
Identifiers: LCCN 2017019115| ISBN 9780520292055 (cloth : alk. paper) | ISBN 9780520292062 (pbk : alk. paper) | ISBN 9780520965614 (ebook)
Subjects: LCSH: Poor youth—United States—Case studies. | Urban youth—United States—Case studies. | Poverty—United States. | African American students—Education—Case studies. | Hispanic American students—Education—Case studies.
Classification: LCC HV1431 .R39 2018 | DDC 362.7092/69420973—dc23
LC record available at https://lccn.loc.gov/2017019115

Manufactured in the United States of America

27 26 25 24 23 22 21 20
10 9 8 7 6 5 4 3 2

For my sister, Ria, my Dadu Satyendra and my Dida Chanda.

Contents

Acknowledgments

One fine day, a long, long time ago, while I was knee-deep in fieldwork, Andrew Deener casually started referring to it as "the book." All the painful anxiety this book has caused is thanks to him. I am only partially serious. There were many moments of pleasure and gratification that came along with the anxiety. Actually, now that I can allow myself some nostalgia as I write this last bit of the book, I recall fondly the intense joys of solidarity, allegiance to a cause, and unconditional familial love I experienced in Port City. In fact, I relished my fieldwork, and I owe to my Port City friends and family my passion, my words, and my identity as a sociologist. It was with my Port City friends and family that I nurtured intersectional brown solidarity.

I would also like to thank Andrew Deener—his love for the discipline, wide breadth of knowledge, and talent as an ethnographer deeply shaped my work. Andrew always pushed me to reach for things that I thought I could not, and I owe him for that confidence in me. I also owe him for always thinking through my ideas with care, rigor, and a critical eye while also assuring me of its significance. My other mentors, Bandana Purkayastha and Claudio Benzecry, were in my corner from day one— pushing me to write, think in new ways, and meet the benchmarks. They nourished my love for sociology and paved the way for this book in crucial ways. Bandana worked hard to ensure my progress in the program when an ongoing research project fell through due to technical issues and I had to start from scratch, and she painstakingly taught me the ways of U.S. academia, including navigating its exclusionary mechanisms while still finding joy and meaning in my own work. Claudio was always available to think through my ideas and provide new directions. He also often ensured that I was included in academic spaces I would otherwise avoid. A special shout-out also to my mentor Gaye Tuchman, the coolest professor I knew in graduate school who told me the feelings were mutual. (I am only kidding. I might have just dreamt this.) Gaye read my work and was always available to share her intellect and humor.

Clinton Sanders, Manisha Desai, and Davita Glasberg were fantastic teachers and friends in different ways. I am grateful to them for their wisdom—I will carry it with me forever. I owe immense gratitude to my professors at Presidency and Calcutta University, India, Prasanta Ray, Dalia Chakrabarti, and Swapan Kr. Bhattacharyya, for teaching me sociology in ways that I never learned again. I carry them with me. At UConn, I also received the National Science Foundation Dissertation Improvement grant, Dean Ross MacKinnon Award for Excellence in Research, and the Hira Jain Scholarship, which helped me finish my research. My family of friends at UConn, Shweta Majumdar Adur, Chandra Waring ("Ch"), and Koyel Khan, saw me through thick and thin, giving me love, care, laughter, and unconditional friendship, and they have made the journey of life pleasurable. Without them as part of my family, life would not be as fulfilling. I owe them for more than this book. Other graduate school friends and comrades, many of whom had come, by themselves, from different parts of the world, just like I had, including Maxim Polonsky, Francisco Quintana, Sotirios Kentros, Trisha Tiamzon, Miho Iwata, and Lwendo Moonzwe, offered their sharp insights, deep friendships, and support as I conducted this ethnography. More importantly, they turned me into that person who constantly reminisces about graduate school. The wine (and other similar things), the study hours, and the deep tête-à-têtes will always be with me.

I brought this book with me to the University of Nevada, Las Vegas, to dwell some more in the painful anxiety. Georgiann Davis, Robert Futrell, Michael Ian Borer, and David Dickens kept up the pressure, and read proposals and whatnot until I sent it out. Georgiann Davis, Robert Futrell, and Barb Brents allowed me to talk them into reading the 120,000-word manuscript and pushed this book to a different level. I cannot thank Georgiann Davis and Robert Futrell enough for their thorough comments on the full manuscript—for the next ten years I will buy you bourbon at happy hour, Robert, iced tea for you, Georgiann, to pay off my debt. I also benefited from countless other supportive colleagues who offered their intellectual support and friendship, including Christie Batson, Lynn Comella, Manoucheka Celeste, Brandon Manning, Constancio Arnaldo, Norma Marrun, Mark Padoongpatt, and Anita Revilla. My graduate and undergraduate students continue to remind me of the urgency of the work, and together, we continue to nourish the love for ideas and debates.

I am also indebted to esteemed colleagues outside of my university homes for their sharp insights and intellectual rigor, as well as other forms of gracious help with this work. My deep gratitude to Annette Lareau, Kathryn Edin, Randol Contreras, Lorena Garcia, Jessica Fields, Catherine Connell, Timothy Black, and Victor Rios. While I did not know all of these scholars personally, I relied on each of them for support. I have also benefited tremendously from the editorial direction and anonymous feedback I received over the years as I published articles from this work in *Journal of Contemporary Ethnography* and *Social Problems*. It truly shaped the book in crucial ways.

I will forever remain indebted to Naomi Schneider for seeing promise in this book, and offering her incredible insights. Her editorial team at the University of California Press made this a smooth and enjoyable process. Merrie Bergmann corrected my commas, and told me kind things about the book just when I needed it. Thanks to Rebecca Steinitz and Olga Livshin for their help and fresh insights on different parts and stages of this book. Thanks also to Lisa DeBoer for helping with the index.

This book would not exist without the support of my chosen family. There would be no passion, no words, and no book without them. Friends and family have inspired me from near and far, far away. My forever gratitude to Chadi Kari for the laughter, joy, unconditional support, and inspiration every step of the way. I am forever indebted to Georgiann Davis for solidarity, thoughtfulness, and inspiration. My love for sociology began in Presidency College, Kolkata. Nabamita Das, Aanandita Sengupta, Debosree Roy, Bipasha Sen, Joy Gupta, Dripto Sarkar, Sukanya Sarbadhikary, Santanu

Sengupta, and countless other Presidentians made it easy to learn sociology as an eighteen-year-old. In Vegas, Rimi Marwah made me feel at home—the long walks, delicious food, and comforting tête-à-têtes nourished my words and soul. My family of friends continues to grow and to inspire me—thank you again Shweta Majumdar Adur, Chandra Waring ("Ch") and Koyel Khan, Rimi Marwah, Pallavi Banerjee, and Pratim Sengupta. Thank you Pallavi and Pratim for the instant and fulfilling connection. From the very beginning Bandana Puskayastha welcomed me into her home and her family. My ideas and the book would not have seen the light of day without Bandana and Kabulda.

My mom and dad, Raghunath and Debjani, were a pain in my behind right from the beginning. They annoyed me until I wrote something I was somewhat proud of. My uncle (mama), Debajit, embellished my minute accomplishments until I developed enough courage to write this. I owe more than my book to my ma, baba, and mama. This book is dedicated to my sister, Irina, my grandmother Chanda, and my late grandfather Satyendra. Like many other things, this book is for them.

1 The Mobility Puzzle and Irreconcilable Choices

I met Angie in the summer of 2010, when she was an eighteen-year-old high school student. A Latina, she lived in Port City Heights, a housing project located on the outskirts of Port City.[1] Port City, a small northeastern town, has one of the highest poverty rates and lowest four-year high school graduation rates in the United States.[2] Angie's paternal grandparents had brought her as a six-month-old from Puerto Rico to Port City. She said her grandparents took her because they thought they would be able to offer her a better life than her parents could. This happened after her parents split and her mother starting dating a man who was caught up in alcohol. Angie still lived with her grandparents when I met her. Her mother now lived in Philadelphia with Angie's five sisters. Angie's father moved in and out of her grandparents' home. Some nights he came home drunk. One night, as Angie and I sat on her old but comfortable loveseat, enjoying some chicken nuggets, her father banged on the door. Angie looked at me: "This fuckin' fat-ass nigga is scratching my door like he a fuckin' ghost! What alcohol does to people!" Sometimes when her father was drinking, he ate all the food she had made for herself and stole the money she had hidden at the bottom of one of her clothes drawers. Despite the conflicts within her family, it was a place of comfort and support for Angie.

Angie remained focused on her future. She had worked two jobs since she turned fourteen, and although she liked to spend some of her money on nail art, tattoos, and trips to Philadelphia, she saved for college, a car, and emergencies. She planned to get a college degree, find a good job, start a family, and live the middle-class American dream.

A self-described "short and thick" woman, Angie liked to dress well at all times, in colorful blouses and tights, though she did not own many clothes or accessories. Some blouses were torn hand-me-downs with missing buttons or small holes that she would keep closed with safety pins. She always ironed what she wore. Angie also styled her hair differently every day and made sure her nails always shone with artistic polish designs. Like many young people her age, Angie liked to go to parties and dress up, but claimed that it was not to attract boys.

Becoming pregnant was out of the question. Even having sex, especially with the "wrong" boys, Angie said, was dangerous. She had heard from her teachers and employers, her church, and the nonprofit organization that helped with college admission that becoming pregnant or a "gangbanger" was a sure ticket to poverty and that people "like her" were "at risk" of the same. Angie said: "Niggas in Port City only want to talk and think about their baby daddies. That's how they like it. I have my dream man, but he ain't gonna be from this ghetto-ass place." Angie felt that she was different from her peers and on her way to becoming upwardly mobile since she was not a parent or a gang member.

Angie earned average grades in high school and her plan always included higher education. She had heard over and over that she would need a college degree to move beyond the struggles her family faced. But her aspirations were irreconcilable with the reality of her unpreparedness. Still, she remained hopeful, stating, "I don't have the grades for UConn [University of Connecticut] for now, but I'm gonna start at the community college .... I don't gotta take the SAT [Scholastic Aptitude Test], I can take the placement test and later transfer."

After she graduated from high school in 2011, Angie packed her bags and used her savings to move to Florida. Once there she was going to attend Miami Dade College and live with her aunt and two cousins. Her aunt offered her a job at the food truck she owned to help her niece pursue her dreams. Angie explained to me that the food truck was very popular in

Florida because restaurants were crowded and expensive. During the cold, snowy northeastern winter, Angie would imagine a busy, warm day working on her aunt's food truck under the tropical sun. It made her giddy with anticipation.

She was unhappy about leaving her family and friends, but she wanted to be far away from her father's alcohol and drug binges and felt that her best chances for a better life lay outside of Port City. She reasoned: "You gotta work for success and it's hard, people don't wanna get outta here. Like, nigga get outta here."

I stayed over at Angie's house the night before she left for Florida. We awoke at the crack of dawn. I was sleepy after staying up until three a.m. and chatting. But Angie implored: "No, we gonna miss the flight! Get up! Get your ass ready!" We picked up coffee at McDonald's on our way to the airport, which is approximately an hour's drive from Angie's home. "I'm leaving for college!" Angie shouted to the server as he handed us our coffee through the window. So that warm summer morning I drove Angie to the airport and she was on her way to Florida.

.　　.　　.　　.　　.

Two weeks later, Angie called me from Florida the day she filled out her Free Application for Federal Student Aid (FAFSA). She was ecstatic. However, only a few days later, Angie told me her aunt could not deliver on her promise to hire her. According to both her and her aunt, Angie then applied for over ten other jobs, but no one contacted her. A few weeks later, she called me and announced that she had reached the end of her patience and could not continue to listen to her aunt and cousins "talk about [Angie] being lazy." Not long after this phone call, Angie unhappily decided to return to Port City. The defeat and fatigue Angie felt for not making it in Florida did not last long. Soon after she returned home, Angie was surrounded with family, friends, barbeques, and the beauty of the northeastern fall. Life fell back into place. I also regularly visited Angie again, just like the old days—or, as she put it, "before the taste of Florida."

Soon after, Angie and I visited Port City Rivers Community College, and she enrolled in classes and continued to pursue her dream of a college degree. But she had already missed a few weeks of classes, and she often heard about job opportunities from friends who worked at the mall, local bakeries, and hair salons. The work hours in these prospective jobs conflicted with Angie's class times. Angie decided to withdraw for the semester and take on three jobs. She claimed it was an easy decision because she had already missed a few weeks of the semester, was recovering from moving back home, and, most importantly, needed to focus on work to make up for all the money she had spent trying to attend college in Florida. That semester flew by quickly for Angie between her three jobs, what she called "friendship dramas," and family gatherings.

The following semester, Angie seemed to be on top of her life. She reenrolled at the community college right on time, and was determined to acquire a driver's license so that she could get more easily to two jobs that she needed, if not three, while attending classes. But given her lack of funds, Angie found it difficult to gather the money necessary to complete the mandatory eight-hour driving course. In addition, both she and her friends and family who had offered to teach her to drive or let her use their car lacked time for driving practice.

Angie did have some success that semester: she passed her remedial college classes. Although drained by fatigue, she was euphoric: "Success makes you tired, but I'd rather be this kind of tired." Angie's third semester in college also looked promising. She enrolled in her first introductory college-level courses and went over the textbook for Introduction to Sociology during the summer (I had given her a copy) while working three jobs. She persuaded her uncle to teach her to drive that summer, completed the mandatory course, and bought a used car. However, halfway through the semester, Angie's car broke down.

While she tried to manage work and school by asking for rides or using public transportation, everyday exhaustion began to add up. Angie's routine consisted of standing on her feet at work, then attending classes that required substantial in-class assignments and homework. After class, she often tried to go back to work when her employer gave her hours, but bus rides to work were unreliable; promises of rides from friends were often broken. Eventually, Angie accepted that she had to choose between continuing her classes and keeping her jobs: without convenient transportation she couldn't have both. She chose to keep the jobs. This decision did not seem life-changing to her; the manager of the bakery where she worked often mentioned that Angie had a knack for the "food industry" and should attend Cordon Bleu, a well-known culinary school. This seemed like the "smarter" option to Angie given the struggles of attending community college while working, and the fact that a college degree seemed a very distant reality. She announced that she would drop her classes, save up money, and devote all of her energy to her plan to attend Cordon Bleu the following year.

That did not happen. And although Angie eventually decided to go back to the local community college, often enrolling in nutrition classes, she usually dropped the classes soon thereafter, overburdened as she was with school and work and lacking sustained academic support at the community college. She imagined that her work at the local bakery would complement her nutrition classes at community college and ultimately afford her the opportunity to climb up the ladder in the "food industry." Sometime in the summer of 2013, when her grandparents suggested that she forget about college and work at an elderly care center with steady hours and pay above the minimum wage, Angie rebuffed their suggestion: "Ima do it [attend college] again 'cause I done it before . . . . I left Port City to make it on my own . . . . None of these niggas in my family ever done it [enrolled in college]. I am wiping no old people's butt." Moving back and forth between college classes and work was new to Angie and her family: no one in the family had graduated from high school before. For the same reason, however, it also seemed like Angie was upwardly mobile, breaking the cycle of oppression in which her family was stuck.

Angie acquired a variety of resources through several organizations and institutions such as school, family, church, and local nonprofits that allowed her to enroll and continue at community college and participate in the low-wage labor market. Within these institutions and organizations Angie also learned that is was imperative to avoid early parenthood, drugs, gangs, and violence in order to become socially mobile. However, although support for specific goals was available, the mobility puzzle Angie confronted was intricate. Angie faced irreconcilable choices as she attempted to solve this mobility puzzle. She needed a job to continue college, yet work conflicted with school. Her family gave her support and comfort, but her father also created obstacles for her. While abstaining from "risk behaviors" such as drugs, pregnancy, and gangs and attending community college made it easy for Angie to identify as socially mobile compared to many of her peers, the community's preoccupation with preventing risk behaviors often overshadowed the goals of providing educational and occupational opportunities. The promise of a college degree and a white-collar job did not look viable despite Angie's investment toward achieving them.

.   .   .   .   .

This book focuses on the lives of marginalized youth like Angie—a group not captured in academic debates on urban poverty, which foreground drugs, gangs, violence, and early parenthood—who continuously seek to become upwardly mobile. Like Angie, the majority of economically marginalized black and Latina/o youth coming of age in the contemporary United States aspire to earn a college degree and well-paying white-collar job.[3] However, racialized poverty deeply impacts the possibilities of educational success and work opportunities. Children growing up in marginalized households and neighborhoods attend resource-poor schools, while their parents and guardians work long hours at low-paying jobs and struggle to put food on the table and access healthcare. As sociologist Annette Lareau (2003) illustrates, class positions influence life chances starting at an early age. Middle-class parents engage in the "concerted cultivation" of their children. They expose their children to a variety of experiences that develop cultural capital essential to navigating social institutions later in life. They also use elaborate language that fosters reasoning skills, and parents convey a sense of entitlement among their children. By contrast, poor and working-class families that are constrained by their economic position engage in what Lareau calls the "natural growth" of their children. They struggle to provide their children with the basic necessities such as food, clothing, and housing, but allow them to organize their own days and engage in unsupervised leisure activities. Working-class and poor parents also teach children to navigate institutions with a sense of constraint and deference to authority. While neither approach is inherently more valuable, concerted cultivation provides middle-class children with comparative advantages to succeed in school and the labor market, which replicates and rewards middle-class cultural capital.

Marginalized children begin their journey toward college and good jobs at a disadvantage. Yet, as they move into adolescence, like Angie, they begin to learn from their parents, siblings, peers, neighbors, teachers, politicians, nonprofits, and media that they can act on these circumstances to overcome them.[4] Specifically, they learn that they are "at risk" of becoming teen parents, drugs users, and violent gang members who reject academic goals and work ethics.[5] Youth learn that if they work hard in school, cultivate a strong work ethic, earn a college degree, and avoid early pregnancy, drugs, gangs, and violence—that is, if they play by the "mobility rules" and avoid risk behaviors—then they can become upwardly mobile.[6] This at-risk discourse now informs how government agencies, schools, and community organizations orient their efforts to target poverty.[7]

By avoiding early parenthood, drugs, gangs, and violence, enrolling in college, and joining the labor market, marginalized youth like Angie often make what seem like concrete gains when compared to some of their peers. Angie enrolled in college, stayed out of prison, and did not have parental responsibilities. In fact, another youth in my study, Sandra, was even invited to interview with a Harvard alumna. Yet, youth who follow the mobility rules nonetheless often end up as low-wage service workers. The institutions and organizations that youth navigate in their everyday lives act in conflicting ways. They support youth, but simultaneously create impediments.

In the realm of family, which is the subject of chapter 3, some youth create elaborate exchange systems that facilitate their survival and mobility. However, the nature of the exchange between family members is often obligatory, constant, and sometimes one-sided, which may become burdensome and exhausting. This type of a relationship can uncomfortably blur the line between an exchange and unconditional relationships and further constrain youth's opportunities.

Their romances generate support, but are tenuous and emotionally draining under the constraints of poverty as youth often struggle to balance school, work, and relationships. Dominant risk narratives about black and brown youth's sexuality, which construct all women as potential teen mothers and welfare dependents and all men as sexual predators, impact the ways in which youth engage in intimate romantic and sexual ties.[8] The young people often police their own bodies and the bodies of their friends and sisters within heterosexual romantic ties to prevent early parenthood. The young women use their romantic and sexual relationships to construct their own identities as socially mobile, morally superior, and without children, and in the process, they both stigmatize, and distance themselves from, their peers who are teen parents. This creates rifts in their community. I explore romance in chapter 4.

In chapter 5, I show how community organizations and institutions that provide resources to marginalized youth can also constrain teens' opportunities. For example, schools and nonprofits encourage and support teens toward higher education. Yet they also adopt a culture of control,[9] policing youth constantly through haphazard searches, camera surveillance, and punishments for minor school policy violations such as not following dress codes or coming late to class.[10] They regularly instill fear in the youth by implying that they could very easily become teen parents, gang members, or drug users if they do not adhere to the rules of the educational institution. They justify the close policing of the teenagers as necessary to future success, claiming that without it the youth would engage in risk behaviors. These policing efforts are, in fact, detrimental to students' present and future chances of success. They disrupt the very trajectory that schools and community groups are trying to encourage. As I will demonstrate, nonprofits devoted to "youth development" in Port City dedicated more time and resources to training and disciplining "violent" youth and preventing early pregnancy than to assisting with college applications, providing transportation, or addressing food security. In addition, the teenagers internalized this disciplinary emphasis. Instead of pursuing education at four-year universities, some of them joined the military to "become disciplined." These fear tactics lead many youth to equate academic success with simply staying out of trouble. Meanwhile, college assistance programs are inadequate, pushing higher education further out of marginalized youth's reach.

Conflicting choices are also at play in the work world—as I highlight in chapter 6. Marginalized youth work during the school year for extra money, and to cover some of their basic necessities such as food, clothing, and school expenses. Many youth financially assist their families with day-to-day living expenses as well as to buy brand-name clothing, costly prom attire, and new phones, engaging in conspicuous consumption in order to participate in trends and local cultures. The demands of low-wage, part-time work interfere with teenagers' educational trajectories as they put more hours into their jobs than attending school to make ends meet. Employers often encourage young workers to take introductory-level culinary, technology, or fashion classes alongside their jobs at local bakeries and coffee franchises, electronic stores, or clothing stores, based on the premise that they will eventually climb the ladder in the food, technology, or fashion industry. In reality, Port City youth struggled to balance school and work, dropped classes, postponed college for semesters or even years, or moved from four-year universities to community colleges. They reenrolled when their work hours permitted, or when they were able to save money for classes, cars, computers, and food. As youth find themselves moving between low-wage service work and intermittent college enrollment, they construct work as a form of dignity. They also draw on the flexible meanings of emotional and aesthetic labor involved in service work in order to seek some continuity between their low-wage jobs and college aspirations: for example, imagining that working as floor crew at a clothing store while taking a fashion class at a community college will lead to a successful career in the fashion industry.[11]

Conflicting intimacy and institutions shape an uncertain life for marginalized youth. In chapter 7, I show how they navigate their haphazard and uncertain trajectories to adulthood and the everyday struggles of poverty such as hunger, illness, and evictions by internalizing uncertainty as inevitable, and constructing meaning systems that are equally haphazard. Because more privileged youth can count on their basic necessities being met, they are able to plan for the future. Marginalized youth learn to manage their uncertain life situations through systems that are equally unpredictable. This adaptation to unpredictability often hinders them in their efforts to realize their aspirations—sometimes leading them to take, or justify, actions that otherwise did not fit their mobility projects.

Youth may hold on tightly to their aspirations of upward mobility through college education and white-collar work, but many of their efforts toward class mobility conflict with one another, and they never move up. In the process, as I show in chapter 8, youth renegotiate what it means to be middle class. These definitions of mobility are couched within racialized, classed, and gendered discourses that center on framing "hard work"—

which they attempt to demonstrate and accomplish through low-wage work and college enrollment—as a viable piece of a respectable life-course. Youth also assume a middle-class identity through conspicuous consumption practices. In this reframing of mobility, the pursuit of a college degree as a route to mobility is temporarily, at least in their eyes, set aside, replaced by the consumerism that their work enables them to access more easily. In chapter 9, I argue for moving beyond at-risk discourse, and provide some insights into potential local-level policies that could support marginalized youth's educational and occupational goals.

I describe in this book the processes through which marginalized black and Latina/o youth, who try to become upwardly mobile by following the mobility rules and avoiding risk behaviors, end up as low-wage service workers. Drawing on three years of ethnographic observations in Port City, I report on the lives of Angie, twelve other young women, and three young men. I analyze their everyday interactions within various spheres of their lives, including family, romance and sexual relationships, school, and work. I illustrate how these young women and men attempt to put together pieces of a complicated and elaborate mobility puzzle. I argue that the institutions and other agents that interact with the youth on a daily basis generally place disproportionate emphasis on preventing risk behaviors at the cost of providing holistic support for marginalized youth's transition to adulthood, thereby constructing marginalized youth in general as an "at-risk population." The emphasis on risk behaviors ignores structural impediments such as a failing education system, the constraints of low-wage work, lack of healthcare, a failing transportation system, and food insecurity.

Critical race feminist scholars have recognized contradictory moments when constructing a particular group as "at risk" becomes necessary to afford them access to basic resources. In her 2011 book, *Reproducing Race: An Ethnography of Pregnancy as a Site of Racialization,* Khiara Bridges argues that the "revolutionary" (p. 73) moment of universal healthcare is achieved in New York City's Alpha Hospital by designating marginalized pregnant women as so pathological as to warrant the denouncement of a privatized system. This, in turn, reinforced marginalized women as carriers of disease. The material consequences of risk discourse in Port City did not circumscribe any revolutionary moments, but further depleted the resources available to youth, making the mobility puzzle almost unsolvable. The puzzle's general picture is clear—a young individual gets a higher educational degree and avoids early parenthood, drugs, gangs and violence, which will lead to a good, white-collar job, a suburban home, stable family, and life satisfaction. However, some puzzle pieces are incompatible and others are missing. Still other puzzle pieces are misrecognized by the youth as they fail to comprehend the requirements for, and nature of, educational and occupational opportunities.[12] Moreover, putting one puzzle piece in the wrong place can drastically alter their trajectory as the formidable constraints of poverty ascribe great costs to seemingly inconsequential choices and leave no room for minor mistakes. Further, the inordinate focus on risk behaviors also reinforces race, class, and gender structures. It ignores the sociocultural and historical processes through which black and brown youth are marginalized via the problematization of teen motherhood, criminalization of their styles, and overpolicing of their neighborhoods.[13] As I discuss in the next section, youth's educational and occupational experiences and trajectories reflect broader labor structures and educational changes in the United States.

LABOR AND EDUCATION IN THE UNITED STATES

Low-wage workers rarely gain financial security, or health and retirement benefits, and typically are unable to build stable careers.[14] However, like the Port City youth, the wide majority of low-wage workers expect and aspire to obtain a higher educational degree, and many remain enrolled in college.[15] Higher education has expanded on a global scale over the last five decades. Research shows that the expectations of obtaining a bachelor's degree and overall fall college admissions increased dramatically over the last fifty years.[16] Angie's college aspirations were not an anomaly.

As manufacturing jobs started in decline in the 1970s[17] and civil rights movements challenged the exclusion of racial and ethnic minorities and women from institutions of higher education, the "college for all" ethos grew.[18] Shifts in public opinion and new federal policies such as financial assistance based on need (for example, the Higher Education Act of 1965) led to the expansion of four-year universities, an increase in community and online colleges, more federal spending on higher education, and trends toward open admissions in some higher education institutions. These changes allowed some previously excluded groups, including racial minorities, women, and economically marginalized students, greater access to higher education. Socioeconomically marginalized youth like Angie began to enroll in institutions of higher learning, primarily in community colleges such as Miami Dade College or Port Rivers.[19] High schools and other organizations encourage students from wide-ranging backgrounds to attend college.[20] While black and Latina girls have historically held higher educational aspirations than boys, the aspirations of both groups, as well as economically and racially marginalized groups in general, have increased.[21]

The expansion in higher education has been accompanied by the growth of a postindustrial service economy characterized by flexible, contingent, and disposable labor.[22] "Good jobs" in the service economy, for example middle-management positions, are now primarily reserved for those with higher educational degrees. Economically marginalized black and Latina/o youth, like Angie, are usually at the bottom of the service sector. They must often change jobs, remain jobless for extended periods, or work multiple part-time jobs as service sector establishments regularly refuse to offer full-time work and benefits to low-wage workers.[23]

Simultaneously, corporations employing low-wage workers promote the idea that youth who start at the bottom can eventually acquire white-collar professional jobs if they work hard enough.[24] Youth such as Angie are told that working for a low wage at a bakery could provide opportunities for becoming a pastry chef. In reality, within-job mobility for those who start out in frontline service work is virtually nonexistent. For example, low-wage, frontline workers (such as cashiers) make up 90 percent of the fast-food labor force. Only nine percent of workers in the fast-food industry are supervisors at the lower level, and barely more than two percent of fast-food workers hold white-collar jobs in the professional, technical, or managerial occupations.[25] Low-wage workers can, and do, grab on to false hopes of career development. As sociologist Katherine Newman (1999) points out, low-wage jobs indeed require employees to employ valuable and complex skills, and cultivating these skills should ideally allow young workers to build stable lifelong careers. But this is typically not the case as the disposable labor force continues to grow.[26] As I will show, the skillset that the Port City youth acquired never facilitated upward mobility. All the jobs that Angie found were minimum-wage jobs with no security or benefits.

Alongside expansion of higher education and disappearing job opportunities, in recent years marginalized communities have confronted receding public assistance, underfunded public schools, growing eviction and incarceration rates, and deteriorating neighborhood conditions.[27]

TOWARD A FEMINIST URBAN ETHNOGRAPHY: UNDERSTANDING LACK OF SOCIAL MOBILITY

Class inequality in the United States is greater than at any time since the Great Depression of 1928. The richest 10 percent of American households possess 76 percent of total wealth.[28] Forty-three percent of children grow up in low-income families.[29] Inequality is woven into the structure of U.S. society: family resources, community, and economic and political structures make it difficult for the socioeconomically marginalized to attain upward mobility.[30] Many U.S. Americans, however, believe that individual choices largely shape the kinds of lives people lead, and that those like Angie may become upwardly mobile through determination and willpower.[31]

In contrast, social scientists largely agree that a person's location in the social structure shapes their chances of success. However, no consensus has been reached about the respective roles of larger social structure, individual agency, and local culture in understanding the lack of social mobility.[32] Over forty years ago, economists Samuel Bowles and Herbert Gintis in their 1976 groundbreaking book, *Schooling in Capitalist America*, explained why individuals find it difficult to get beyond their parents' class position, arguing that educational institutions similar to Port City High School and Port City Rivers Community College prepare poor and working-class students for jobs at the bottom of the economic order through hidden curricula. They posited that the goals of educational institutions and economic systems align perfectly to turn the children of the rich into white-collar professionals and the children of the poor into low-wage laborers. Adding nuance to this structurally deterministic argument, Pierre Bourdieu contended that students acquire different cultural competencies at home depending on their class positions.[33] Bourdieu goes on to say that institutions such as schools and the labor market value the cultural capital of the dominant classes, which, in turn, increases their chances for academic and job success. Similar theories that highlight the role of large social structures show that neighborhood structures play an important role in determining what kinds of opportunities an individual is afforded, and that these structures shape the intergenerational transmission of poverty.[34]

Highlighting the role of individual agency and culture in sustaining cycles of poverty, micro / interactionist perspectives on the reproduction of class challenge these macro arguments as too deterministic. For instance, in his 1977 landmark book, *Learning to Labour*, British sociocultural scholar Paul Willis wrote about a group of high school students who rejected the achievement ideology offered at school and instead revered manual labor. He concluded that individuals are not mere pawns of the economic structure. Rather, individuals make everyday life choices mediated through local culture: they reject academic goals or adopt interactional styles that reproduce their class positions.[35] In the United States, academia's focus on culture and agency became associated with the well-known and controversial "culture of poverty" debate of the 1950s and 1960s. Those advocating the culture of poverty argument declared that the poor shared a culture different from the rest of America. Anthropologist Oscar Lewis noted: "[O]nce it [the culture of poverty] comes into existence it tends to perpetuate itself from generation to generation because of its effect on the children."[36] It is important to note that some sociocultural scholars from the opposing camp argued that limited opportunities and racial discrimination affected poor individuals in each new generation, and marginalized neighborhoods are culturally heterogeneous.[37] Still, the idea that the poor have a pathological culture influenced policies that reduced public assistance, and it deeply informed the American public's understanding of the poor by creating gendered, classed, and racialized tropes.[38]

Recently, scholars have begun to articulate the interrelatedness of structure, culture, and agency in reaction to the debate around their respective roles.[39] The new argument contests the assertion that poverty invariably reproduces itself across generations due to the values of the poor, despite structural changes in economy and society. Instead, these innovative scholars view culture, agency, and structure as inseparable and avoid using culture as an umbrella concept to explain poverty.[40] They define culture as "narratives," "repertoires," and "values" that individuals are able to mobilize in their everyday lives.[41] Specifically, many of these works theorize the connections between structure and individual agency in marginalized neighborhoods through the mediating role of local cultures. Such cultures, scholars argue, define themselves in opposition to middle-class culture and its valorization of educational achievements, economic independence, and marriage followed by childbirth.[42] These oppositional cultures, often symbolized by drug use, gang membership, early parenthood, and participation in the illegal economy, are understood as a reaction to blocked opportunities. Some scholars go as far as to argue that oppositional cultures often reflect and extend mainstream patriarchal, capitalist, and violent cultures.[43] The emphasis on the relationship between local culture and the reproduction of poverty allows scholars to avoid overly deterministic reasoning while also distancing themselves from the early culture of poverty debates.

Contemporary scholars also argue that portraying the cultures of marginalized communities allows us to counter the idea that the poor are different from the rest of society by showing the prevalence of mainstream values in economically marginalized communities. Offering nuanced, humanizing understandings of the lives of the poor may help dispel myths about the poor as immoral or lazy individuals, myths that have come to strongly occupy public and political imagination.[44] For example, sociologist Mitchell Duneier (along with Hasan and Carter) highlights the complex organization of morality among New York City's scavengers, panhandlers, and vendors—some of the most misunderstood and stigmatized residents of the city—in his 1999 book, *Sidewalk*. Sociologist Katherine Newman highlights the presence of middle-class values among working-class Harlem residents in her popular 1999 book, *No Shame in My Game*. Those in her study face distinct opportunity structures that shape their decisions regarding health, parenthood, and work practices, while their family values and work ethic remain intact and resemble those of the middle class.

In understanding the lack of social mobility, the majority of these portrayals of marginalized communities, however, continue to foreground drugs, gangs, violence, and early parenthood as central narratives. They leave out the trajectories of youth such as Angie, who follow the rules they were prescribed, and continuously struggle to become upwardly mobile.[45] These studies continue to place emphasis on the question of why socioeconomically marginalized individuals either embrace or reject middle-class culture at any given point. In answering this question, scholars simultaneously construct teen parenthood, violence, gangs, and drugs as ubiquitous social problems and risk behaviors in marginalized communities, and privilege middle-class culture, reifying it as static.[46] Rooted in white hypermasculine traditions, such representations, while meant to "normalize" the poor or the "other," work to perpetuate stereotypes. The goal of ethnography, as scholars argue, is not merely to familiarize the "other," but to question what we know.[47] It is then worthwhile to question why urban ethnographers, policy makers, and the public continue to place "risk behaviors" at the center of understanding and targeting poverty without fully acknowledging how populations are constructed as at-risk, whether avoiding risk behaviors will indeed break the cycle of marginalization, and what problematizing certain behaviors means for "at-risk populations."

In this feminist urban ethnography, to tell a different story and ask different questions, I followed a group of marginalized youth who are not part of the negative outcome statistics.[48] They are not teen parents, drug users, gang members, or school dropouts. Drawing on the data I collected, I argue that by focusing squarely on "risk behaviors" such as violence, drug use, and teen pregnancy, and by policing youth, scholars and policy makers are diverting resources that should be invested into addressing socioeconomic disadvantages confronting all marginalized youth. I call for scholars and policy makers to rethink what we know about poverty and how we target inequality. Drawing on intersectional feminisms, I argue that this risk discourse also reinforces oppressive race, class, and gender discourses by privileging middle-class cultural norms, and ignores the problematization of black and brown youth and their cultures. Whether deliberately or unintentionally, such discourses perpetuate a definition of success and mobility that relies on the marginalized urban youth's ability to avoid getting caught up in risk behaviors such as of violence, crime, and teenage pregnancy.

This feminist urban ethnography draws on well-established traditions within women of color feminisms, race scholarship, and urban ethnography. Using the data and analytical tools from these traditions, I provide a feminist analysis that considers the gendered, racialized, and classed processes and mechanisms, as well as the sociohistorical and cultural context that constructs teen parenthood, gangs, drugs, and violence as ubiquitous social problems in marginalized communities. This feminist urban ethnography approach, which draws on intersectional feminisms and questions the taken-for-granted understandings of risk behaviors as central to thinking about poverty, enables us to shift the analytical lens away from either the presence or absence of oppositional cultures and risk behaviors in marginalized communities. This shift, in turn, allows us to gain a set of insights into how marginalized individuals navigate and interact with oppressive and exploitative institutions, discourses, and policies in an effort to mobilize resources and attain upward mobility. I demonstrate how factors such as food insecurity, the lack of access to transportation, healthcare, computers, and the internet, dwindling college support programs, overpolicing in schools, and low-wage jobs regularly and clearly interfere with youth's mobility goals.

I focus on the experiences of black and Latina/o economically marginalized girls and boys as they transition to adulthood. My feminist analysis addresses central questions in poverty research on family, early parenthood, educational commitment, work orientation, and meaning making in novel ways. I move beyond dichotomous answers by either rearranging the questions or reconciling oppositional answers. For example, I move beyond the question of whether the poor have stable/resourceful or unstable families, and beyond their family values, by underlining the complexities of family and showing how elaborate support and exchange between family members *itself* complicates relational work within families.[49] My argument moves beyond the trite question of why it is some youth become pregnant, and what their sexual behaviors and understandings of motherhood have to do with them becoming pregnant, to instead show how the construction of teen parenthood as an epidemic in marginalized communities affects *all* youth negatively.[50] Instead of looking for and describing some version of academic goals and work ethic among youth, I show how work and higher education goals and actions became *irreconcilable* as youth navigate educational and occupational institutions in the college-for-all era and growing service economy, thus highlighting the ways in which educational and work systems interact with one another in the postindustrial era to channel ambitious youth into a low-wage service class.

In asking old questions in new or renewed ways, I relinquish binaries that privilege middle-class cultural norms. In centering on actors, whose stories do not resemble popular representations of drugs, gangs, violence, and early parenthood and are largely ignored in poverty scholarship, I provide an empirical case that, at least partially, challenges poverty scholarship's myopic vision of what and whom to write about. I show how inequalities are produced and reproduced not through their cultural, economic, and social isolation and adoption of oppositional culture, but through marginalized youth's interaction within institutions such as the family, school, and labor market, with middle-class actors, and with dominant discourses that trap them in a mobility puzzle by focusing on risk behaviors instead of structural impediments that confront all marginalized youth.

ENTRÉE AND OBSERVATIONS

A brief story of how I got to know Port City and the Port City youth, their families, friends, peers, and neighborhood is important to understanding what I learned about them. When I was in graduate school, my close friend's immediate family lived in Port City and I sometimes visited them. In the summer of 2010, I started volunteering at several organizations and institutions in Port City with a vague desire to understand how neighborhood organizations collaborate to challenge inequalities in urban communities. One of the local nonprofit organizations (I refer to it as the Port City Youth Center from here on) was thrilled to have me because it was understaffed and in dire need of volunteers to meet the growing needs of city residents who used their services. I decided to devote the majority of my time to this organization.

The broadly conceived mission of the organization was to provide material resources to economically marginalized city residents. It was approximately four years old and employed twenty young staff members. None of these youth expressed a particular alignment with the mission of the organization. They claimed that they worked there because the job became available to them, and most of them moved on to other jobs soon after I met them. Volunteers from the local elite liberal arts college were also there regularly. They mostly came from other cities and states and volunteered because of their desire to "serve the community" or as part of their course requirements for service learning.

The organization rented a space from a public institution with a pantry that they often kept stocked with food—something that the youth appreciated. The building was old and rundown, the chairs uncomfortable and broken. Ceiling and floor fans served us whenever the air conditioning broke down, which happened frequently during the hot and muggy summer.

As I continued to volunteer at the organization, I began to participate in the youth's conversations at work; then, occasionally, I gave them rides after their shifts. We gradually began to encounter various daily events together, and this formed the basis for future conversations, organically leading to general familiarity and friendship. My watershed moment of earning the young employees' trust occurred when I left the organization because the employers had unfairly fired one of the young women (at least according to the other youth).

Eventually, I became close with sixteen youth. Seven of them were black (self-identified) and nine were Latina/o (self-identified), including seven second-generation Puerto Ricans, one second-generation Honduran, and one second-generation Dominican Republican. As I became friendly with them and started to become involved in their lives, watching them apply to colleges and plan their futures, I asked the youth, whom I refer to in this book as the Port City youth, if I could write about their experiences as they transitioned to adulthood. They agreed.[51]

From June 2010 to June 2013, I spent, on average, five days each week conducting intensive fieldwork, spending about eight hours a day observing and participating in the lives of the sixteen young men and women from Port City. Every day, I decided who to spend time with based on the youth's availability, their needs (for example, when they needed a ride or assistance with an application), and the significance of the day's events. I assigned more value to events that I expected would produce the largest payoff in terms of my emerging themes, such as visits to a college or filling out job applications.[52] I also did homework with them, ate with them, spent time in their homes with their families, went with them to visit out-of-town friends and relatives, followed them to organizations and institutions, and talked over the phone and exchanged text messages with them. Sometimes I spent time with the group as a whole, other times with a few of them, and other times yet with a single youth. In group settings, I was always careful to talk less and listen more, and, mostly, not to talk at all unless someone spoke to me. In one-on-one situations this was less possible, so I engaged in conversations where I revealed certain matters about myself—which also served to alleviate my own discomfort about knowing so much about the youth with the intent to someday write a book.[53] I constantly mentioned to them that nothing in the study would be written without their permission.

Becoming part of a group during the course of my fieldwork also meant that I had to participate in internal group politics. For example, Franklin Junior and Angie were part of two different dance teams. One day, when I casually asked Franklin Junior about Angie's dance team and what he thought of their performance the last time we all went to watch them, Franklin Junior began belittling the team and scoffed at their performance as well as their teacher: "Ya, whatever, you like that?" As I tried to come up with a polite answer, Franklin laughed hysterically and said to me, "Ay, you mad awkward now, whatchu gonna say? You can't say shit about Angie but you know I'm good at it and judge well." I kept quiet.

When I met both Angie and Franklin at work the next day, our interaction became very awkward. I walked in and Franklin started speaking loudly, with a grin, as if he knew what he was about to bestow on me. Calling to Angie, he said, "Come here, I got news for you." Not knowing what he was about to say, I waited awkwardly. As Angie came out, Franklin said: "Yo nigga, Ranita told me she thinks you guys no good at all! Ask her, we were talking about you and the dance the other day." Angie looked at me and asked, "Why you guys talking about me?" I had no good way to reply. Reassuring her that I hadn't claimed that her dance team was bad, although we did talk about her, would mean calling Franklin a liar. Angie avoided me that day and the following few days. This incident affected my relationship with her and set back our friendship. Angie often made subtle comments about my dislike for her dance team. I would smile guiltily or tell them that was never what I meant to say, but I might have been misunderstood. But like many other kinds of relationship, it recovered with time and work. I made additional efforts to praise her dance performance and dance team whenever I attended their performance. I even went to their dance practices. It took a few weeks before Angie forgot the incident. Group ethnography thus has its own specificities, and ethnographers often make mistakes navigating internal dynamics.

Navigating group politics while remaining respectful of everyone and attaining some level of insider access was not a straightforward process. For example, Ashley and her sisters, with whom I grew very close, were not fond of Shivana. Shivana read a great deal, and was often judgmental about Ashley and her sisters' perceived lack of interest in education. This irked the sisters, who then made several negative remarks about Shivana, including her "nasty smell." Once after I spent time with Shivana, the sisters snubbed me: "Damn, you smell too, spending time in her house, how do you do it? You can't smell her? Or it doesn't matter to you?" Siete also told me, "[Shivana] converts people." When I inquired, "Converts to what?" Siete responded: "She a lesbian or something." Sometimes, animosity also surfaced in public, when Ashley would make statements such as the following: "Do you wanna hang out with me tonight or her [pointing to Shivana], 'cause we ain't got interest in same things. I like to have fun, not sit at home. I got friends." Given that I grew up in a boarding school in India, where negotiating with various groups was a constant necessity, navigating youthful politics was a skill I had cultivated for years. I would remain silent, change the topic, tell Ashley I would text them both to plan something, or tell them that I was planning to leave early that night. Moreover, the divisions were rarely permanent or severe. For example, by the time I left Port City, Shivana and Ashley started spending their days together, enjoying each other's company.

Over the course of the three years, I also met the youth's families, friends, boyfriends and girlfriends, teachers, and employers, as well as the local nonprofit employees and other people the youth knew. I spent time at local coffee shops and restaurants, attended community meetings, and befriended several youth in Port City. I interviewed forty youth in addition to the sixteen at the center of this research. These interviews helped me gauge the generalizability of my findings to the other youth of Port City; specifically, I was able to evaluate the extent of the educational and occupational optimism among the youth of Port City and their ultimate transition to the local low-wage economy, thus bolstering the credibility of my findings. Over the three years, some of the young men and women and their families became my home away from home. They invited me for the holidays because they knew that I did not have family in the United States, provided me with home-cooked meals, and offered me familial support when I was homesick.

FIELDWORK AND THE ETHNOGRAPHER

Eventually, I formed a strong bond with many of the young people I write about, and this bond offered a distinct perspective on their lives. The insider/outsider debate, however, is a contentious one, and there are advantages as well as challenges in studying a community from both positions.[54] My own, multilayered position was one of a brown woman from the global South who was obtaining a graduate degree at an institution well regarded by the youth. It interacted with their position to produce a particular type of knowledge that Clifford calls "partial truth."[55] The Port City youth revered me for my college education, looked up to me for guidance regarding their own educational pathways, and admired me for coming to the United States to attend graduate school. At the same time, they also felt sorry for me as a newcomer from India, asking questions about how "crazy" it was to live in India and talking about the Indian people they knew from school. They also asked me if certain hard-to-believe narratives about India they had heard from other sources, such as the media, were true. This unique position also allowed for distinct insights. Although many of the young men and women were conscious of, and humble about, their class positions, feeling ashamed to admit that they received food stamps or lived in the projects, I often felt that my background (as a person of color from a presumably poor country) allowed them to welcome me into their lives and homes with less intimidation.

In other instances, it was instructive to hear the youth try to explain various aspects of "American culture" to me. For example, during my first few months in Port City, the then eighteen-year-old Curtis, who is Latino, told me that poor people in the United States did not cook steak at home, but could only afford to eat steak when they were dining out at Applebee's and a deal was available. Therefore, when Curtis cooked steak for me at his place soon after, he was telling me that he belonged to a certain class. Additionally, the youth were curious to learn about my country of origin and drew inspiration from the fact that that I had come from so far away to make a life for myself. Of course, I had not traveled to an unknown, faraway land; I grew up consuming American news and media—for better or worse. My country of origin provided fodder for my initial conversations with the youth. Angie said, "You mad brave for coming here," and Lexus added: "But down there [in India] it's nasty though, right? 'Cause one of the teachers, who I think invented Tylenol, is from India, but he came here 'cause it was nasty there."

While feminists such as Dorothy Smith, Donna Haraway, Sandra Harding, and Patricia Hill Collins have questioned if researchers can or should write about groups they are not members of, my status as a person of color from a different country offered a unique set of advantages. My position both intersected with and diverged from those of the youth, with varying degrees of power embedded in each of our axes of oppression. Some of these differences, similarities, and degrees of power were deployed in daily interactions, while others were identifiable on the structural level. My privilege as a doctoral student who held a greater familiarity with higher educational institutions than the youth intersected with my position as a noncitizen with an accent different from theirs and a lesser familiarity with various aspects of living in the United States than they had. While the supervisors at the nonprofit organization talked to me as if I were one of them, given my status as a graduate student, these interactions were more uncomfortable than welcoming. Most conversations involved their upcoming or past visits to India or their desire to visit India, and the fruitfulness of yoga as a discipline, and the like. They looked to connect with me through white middle-class imaginations of India. Growing up outside the United States also did not make it easy to locate myself in the lives of sixteen youth coming of age in an American city—even though, as a twenty-six-year-old brown woman, I felt more comfortable in their company than in the company of forty-five-year-old middle-class white Americans.[56]

The Port City youth claimed that I looked much younger than my age. Angie and Ashley always told me that this was because I did not have children and was not married, although they expressed bewilderment that I could be "mad old" and yet not worried about getting married and becoming a mother. They often commented on my youthful disposition, claiming that the other twenty-six-year-olds they knew were more "serious."

As a lighter-skinned brown woman with long dark hair who looks younger than her age, I didn't particularly stick out in Port City, even when I spent time with the youth. More often than not, I was mistaken for a local Latina high school student. This meant that I was not generally questioned about my presence among the youth, the youth themselves did not feel self-conscious about my presence, and I was often treated similarly to how the youth were generally treated in the community.[57] I did not immediately receive some of the privileges that fieldworkers acquire by virtue of their position. During one community meeting, for example, I was the fourth person to reach the community center and it was almost fifteen minutes past the scheduled meeting starting time. As I entered the room with Lena and Ashley, an elderly white woman exclaimed (chiding us for coming late and showing her frustration that not many young women had shown up), "See there! This is the most important issue we are facing, youth violence, and you have three old women here. Where are all the young mothers?"— as if she were waiting for us to answer for young mothers. "Maybe more folks will show up, school just got over," I responded. She continued, "Why don't you people show up, are you not worried about your own futures? Why are we here?" Ashley, humiliated and angered by the woman's comments, decided to cash in on my PhD student status:

> We're not parents or pregnant. [Pointing to me] She is a PhD student at UConn and she is writing her paper and everything on Port City kids. So we're not here to learn about everything. She is writing about all this and doing research and whatnot. You should be talking to other kids, not us.

When they were in a group, the youth were often lectured by older people in the community about issues of teen parenthood, drug abuse, importance of education, and violence. However, when the older people learned that I was a PhD student at the University of Connecticut, their tone often shifted. It was challenging for many individuals, who first perceived me as a Latina from Port City, to imagine me as a PhD student. The youth often used my status to redeem the group in public when we / they were faced with blatant judgments.

In restaurants and coffee shops, within organizations, and generally in the city, people would speak to me in Spanish, ask me whether I was from Puerto Rico or the Dominican Republic, what grade I was in, and so on. I also dressed like many of the local youth—I wore tights, skinny jeans, Converse shoes, sweatshirts, and similar clothing. I didn't do this in order to fit into the community for fieldwork; rather, I was influenced in much the same way as we all become influenced by trends around us. I had never dressed in formal clothing in the first place, and at the University of Connecticut I was always mistaken for an undergraduate student. I usually carry a backpack, and some of the youth commented on how "childish" it looked. When all was said and done, I fit in—from an outsider's perspective.

On the inside, however, my time in Port City included several uncomfortable moments, particularly in the beginning—just like in the beginning of any relationship. Age and gender dynamics meant that some of the young men would misread my professional and research interest in their lives and invite me to "hang out" in a romantic or sexual way. This was one of the primary reasons that I became friendly with only three men. Two of the men were very young-looking, more childish in demeanor, and had girlfriends. Curtis initially flirted with me, but then became genuinely interested in developing a platonic friendship. Our interactions were facilitated by my consistent explicit disinterest and his interest in another girl.

I attempted to present myself in the lives of the youth not as some sort of implant from the outside, "objectively" researching them—it would not have been possible to spend three years of my life as a "researcher."[58] I developed emotional and political connections and allegiances. That said, I aspire to limit the role of my experiences, and stories that center me, in this book.[59] Whenever I became concerned about how I might be limited by my own subjectivities, I drew on sociologist Julie Bettie, who states: "The logic of an identity politics in which identity is conceptualized as static and clearly bounded doesn't easily acknowledge the *continuum* of experience, *relative* sameness and difference, and *degrees* of intersubjectivity that allow for emotional empathy and political alliance."[60] In her book *Women without Class: Girls, Race, and Identity*, Bettie points out how her white working-class cultural identity did not always grant her intersubjectivity with the white girls in her study, for example, because of differences based on class identity, something that is not as enthusiastically explored when theorizing reflexive ethnography.

Throughout my fieldwork, I made efforts to be cognizant of my subjectivity, my differences with the youth, and the power relations in which we

Table 1 The Youth at a Glance

Name	Age in 2010	Race and Gender (Self-Identified)	Household Arrangements	Siblings
Lexus Martin	17	Black Woman	Single Mother	3 half siblings
Alize Robinson	18	Latina Woman	Single Mother	4 half siblings
Angie Martinez	18	Latina Woman	Single Mother	4 half & 1 foster siblings
Shivana Abraham	20	Multiracial Woman	Both Parents	1 full sibling
A. J.	18	Latina Woman	Single Mother	4 half siblings
Lena Diaz	17	Latina Woman	Single Mother	1 half & 1 full + 1 half sibling
Cassy Alfonso	17	Latina Woman	Both Parents	2 half siblings
Brianna Green	17	Black Woman	Single Mother	1 half siblings + 3 step siblings
Evelyn Salas	17	Black Woman	Foster Mother	2 half & 2 foster siblings
Ashley Florez	20	Latina Woman	Single Mother	5 half siblings + 1 half sibling
Letisha Gathers	18	Latina Woman	Single Mother	2 half siblings
Curtis Page	18	Latino Man	Single Mother	4 half siblings
Sandra Brown	17	Black Woman	Single Mother	0 + 2 half siblings
Franklin Junior	18	Latino Man	Single Mother	3 half siblings
Donte Branch	17	Black Man	Single Mother	2 half siblings
Gigi Phillips	17	Black Woman	Father + Stepmother	1 half + 1 half & 1 full siblings

NOTE: The number after the plus (+) sign indicates the number of siblings who lived in a different household but maintained regular contact with the youth. I do not include siblings who did not live in the same household or maintain regular contact. Additionally, family arrangements changed frequently. I used a different pseudonym for one of the youth in other publications that were based on this research. Both during and after my fieldwork, Shivana Abraham identified as black and multiracial at other times.

were embedded. Donna Haraway (1988) urges us to practice reflexivity by recognizing the location from which we write. Pointing to the exploitative potential of the myth of "objective knowledge," feminist philosopher Sandra Harding (2015) emphasizes the significance of collecting and presenting data while navigating the possibilities that our research will shape the lives of those about whom we write.[61]

Writing about the lives of sixteen people in a holistic manner can be both rewarding and limiting, as well as, of course, extremely intimidating. It is hard to summarize, conclusively and exhaustively, and then analyze the complexities of life in a particular social and historical context. I have had to abandon various significant and central lines of analysis in an attempt to provide readers with a theoretically and empirically coherent story. One of the central purposes of this book is to provide a multicontextual look at the lives of the young people. Following the works of ethnographers such as David Halle and Elliot Liebow, I write about Port City's young people by separating various contexts that both the youth and our society at large see as central components of daily life, including school, work, family, neighborhood, peer groups, and romantic and sexual relationships.[62]

Ethnographers who write about the lives of those living in the margins of society have to be careful about their representation of marginalized groups because their work risks being appropriated by conservatives for their political agenda. One of the goals of this book is to counter the common representation of drugs, gangs, violence, and early parenthood as central to growing up in urban poverty. I provide an analytically rigorous look at the lives of youth who are deeply invested in higher education, white-collar work, and delaying parenthood. However, writing about coming-of-age experiences in all its complexities means documenting mistakes, mishaps, and various aspects of the young people's lives that may elicit judgments from those who wish to overlook the nuances of my argument, which is that youth growing up in poverty are not afforded the same room for mistakes as their wealthier counterparts. I have not omitted data for fear of judgment, and yet I realize that some of the data could be misappropriated to further perpetuate the stereotypes of marginalized youth that already plague mainstream perceptions.

2 Port City Rising from the Ashes

We often read about those who are struggling to survive in big cities like New York, Chicago, and Boston. As a result, many view urban poverty and suffering as largely a "big city" phenomenon. But economically and racially marginalized youth coming of age in relatively small cities like Port City, which are always under the radar, also struggle to make ends meet.[1] They hope to gain a greater level of educational and economic mobility than their parents and grandparents, who may have moved to Port City, away from big cities in the United States, for a better life. Cities like Port City have confronted forces such as deindustrialization and late twentieth-century urban renewal[2] and the economic recession of the 2000s,[3] and they continue to struggle with food insecurity and to confront the effects of the war on drugs, mass incarceration, underfunded schools, and more. Human pain and suffering as well as the desire to access the American dream are as real in cities like Port City as they are in New York.

Philippe Bourgois cites a plethora of dissertations and theses written over the course of a century as he uncovers the lives of second- and third-generation Puerto Ricans living in Harlem in his 1995 book, *In Search of Respect: Selling Crack in El Barrio*. However, I was hard-pressed to find such historical insights into the everyday lives of the residents of Port City or neighboring cities and towns. A combination of factors, including intellectual traditions and the resources of the region's universities along with the general tendency of social scientists to focus on larger cities, accounts for this lack. My general theoretical contributions are not specifically related to Port City rather than bigger cities, yet the absence of work on smaller cities is a telling trend. I hope this book will shed some light into the lives of marginalized residents of smaller cities.

The Port City youth's educational experiences, work trajectories, intimate lives, hopes, and dreams that I describe in this book must be placed within the ecology and history of Port City. For instance, the reader needs to be familiar with Port City's local labor market, among other economic factors, as it shaped the young people's work opportunities and trajectories. Even if the youth decided to pursue jobs in neighboring towns, they would have to depend on the public transportation system since many of them could not afford cars. Similarly, Port City's institutions such as churches, schools, and colleges, among other forces, shaped their educational outcomes. The histories of their families' immigration to the United States and the treatment of black and brown people in Port City and the Northeast in general also shaped how the youth and their families imagined their opportunities for social mobility.

A PHOENIX RISING FROM THE ASHES, TWICE: A BRIEF HISTORY OF PORT CITY

A fishing city founded in the mid-seventeenth century, Port City was attractive to colonists because of its waterways. The city became central to the state's development. Like other American cities, Port City experienced massive economic growth between the second half of the nineteenth century and the first half of the twentieth century. By the late nineteenth century, Port City was considered one of the fishing capitals of the world. The local municipal historian, who delivers monthly lectures on the city's history, considers the 1938 hurricane as the start of "modern-era" Port City. The city's favorite beach park grew out of the ashes of the city like a phoenix after the hurricane destroyed most of New England.[4] Port City hosted shipping, boatbuilding, and, eventually, railroads. Its participation in various transportation industries made it a desirable destination for Italian, Irish, and Jewish immigrants.[5]

A published survey study reveals that in the late 1930s, around two percent of Port City's population was "colored." The same study indicates that Italians were considered the "most important element in the community" for the coming years.[6] The city also became a summer colony for wealthy families from Philadelphia, Pittsburgh, and other mid-Atlantic cities. Italian immigrants who settled in the city during the early twentieth century gave parts of it a Mediterranean atmosphere. With new, shiny structures that were built after the hurricane, Port City thrived as a shipbuilding base, industrial center, and fishing port, and several local families became wealthy.

Today, the majority of the Latina/o population in Port City are Puerto Ricans. Large numbers of Puerto Ricans began migrating to the United States mainland, settling in New York, Connecticut, and Massachusetts as American corporations made conditions worse for farmers in Puerto Rico. During World War II, some of the Puerto Rican immigrants to Port City fought in the American army, while others worked in Port City's shipping industry to produce war supplies.[7] Manufacturing jobs began to disappear in Port City and neighboring northeastern cities in the 1960s. This decline was followed by the urban renewal projects of the 1970s, which left many of Port City's neighborhoods as casualties. It was not until the 1970s that Puerto Rican women began to immigrate in search of work. Puerto Ricans filled cheap labor demands in the state in munitions factories, textile mills, and other enterprises.[8]

While, today, 20 percent of Port City residents are black, they continue to be some of the city's most marginalized residents. At a town meeting in the early eighteenth century, the residents of Port City voted to object to the emancipation of blacks, preventing them from either living or owning land in the city. In the same year, the colonial assembly made it illegal for blacks or "mulattoes" to reside anywhere in the colony. Blacks were also forbidden to purchase land or conduct business without the town's approval.[9] One of the city's historical neighborhoods, the Johnson Historical District, was developed by local abolitionists in the mid-nineteenth century to provide housing for free blacks. The community that grew there created its own organizations and institutions, several of which survive today. The first black professor was hired at a postsecondary institution in Port City in the 1970s, but he could not find a house to buy in a neighborhood of his choice. The same institution graduated its first black student in 1966. Port City elected its first black mayor in the 1980s. The mayor, who completed a full term, promised to improve the local beach and persuade minorities to participate in city government. Decades later, the first black professor's wife also served as the mayor of Port City.

During the Cold War, Port City benefited from employment in a nearby military research facility. The defense industry downsized considerably after the Soviet threat disappeared.[10] Several of Port City's wealthy residents deserted the city and took many of its resources with them, which also led to absentee landlords. By the close of the millennium, the city was approximately 63 percent white, 19 percent Latina/o, and 18 percent black, Port City's schools were underfunded, the city's downtown was in shambles, and the city was struggling in general, requiring additional funding from the state to maintain its services.

WISER, INC., AND OTHER DRUGS

Then there came a promise that the city would once again rise from its ashes like a phoenix. A pharmaceutical giant, Wiser, Inc., proposed a plan that would transform the almost four-hundred-year-old city once and for all, promising it prosperity and "renewal." Wiser assured the city it would make the abandoned downtown, neighborhoods, and even the rancid sewage plant vibrant, declaring that this transformation would eventually attract startups and other business opportunities, benefiting the city as a whole. However, Wiser wanted millions in tax subsidies and other incentives in order to develop a multimillion-dollar center that would bring thousands of jobs, it claimed. Employees of the company in turn would then buy housing, go to local restaurants, stay in hotels, and send their children to the public schools. The company opened its base in the early 2000s as Port City awaited all the improvements with bated breath.[11] However, Wiser failed to hire many Port City residents, and most employees continued to live in other wealthier cities that surround Port City. One local restaurant owner gave the company a hundred free lunch coupons, but not one was redeemed.

The company also asked for acres of land that belonged to residents of the city. One resident said in an interview published by a local newspaper that the city was lucky to have Wiser, because "drug dealers" and other "undesirables" were renting homes and populating the street corners. Others, however, considered the city safe and desirable, claiming that residents could walk around any time of the day or night and feel safe.

The economic downturn of the 2000s hit Port City hard. As labor data shows, this turn of events gave the city little time to recover and increased its chances of a double-dip recession. The entire region remained in recession for nearly twice as long as the rest of the state. The local casinos that had been among the city's major employers since the 1990s were all hit hard by the recession, leading them to stall various construction projects and downsize extensively.[12] After the decade of tax abatements ended, Wiser also decided to withdraw the few thousand jobs it had created and moved to a neighboring city where it also had a campus, in order to cut costs. The vacant buildings and barren lands the company had acquired by displacing residents with a promise to build condominiums, hotels, and stores were all that remained. A preservationist bought the orange home that belonged to an elderly woman and had been acquired for the renewal project and moved it to another location.[13]

While the city mourned its breakup with the drug company that had picked up and left, another kind of drug trader was less welcome. During my fieldwork, the city's officials and several of its residents breathed a sigh of relief when federal and local agents arrested almost a hundred suspects in a drug trafficking case in their homes in Port City (some of the suspects came from neighboring towns and cities) early one morning. An investigation that lasted over a year expanded from Port City to Puerto Rico and the Dominican Republic and revealed that extensive amounts of heroin and cocaine were being trafficked into the streets of Port City and neighboring towns.

POOR CITY IN A RICH STATE

Today, Port City is about 50 percent white (plus 10 percent white Latina/o), 20 percent black, and 30 percent Latina/o (10 percent white Latina/o). Among the Latina/o, 60 percent are Puerto Rican.[14] Most of the city's wealthy people, who are also white, live in the city's south end, close to the beach. They made up 90 percent of the city council and other important positions, such as the city's financial director and economic development director, until after I left my field site, when racially marginalized residents became the numeric majority serving on the city council for the first time. A local newspaper declared that this was far more representative of the city's diversity.

According to 2010 Census data, a language other than English is spoken at home in approximately 30 percent of Port City's households. Along with the increase in its Spanish-speaking population, the city has also seen an abundance of businesses with Spanish names—although Latina/os continue to face higher degrees of unemployment, underemployment, poverty, food insecurity, and other hardships.[15] As one resident said, "It's hard. I don't think the Hispanic people and the community is part of the Port City community at large."[16] A nonprofit worker who had moved to Port City from Puerto Rico claimed that she was regularly called upon by residents struggling with unemployment who could not meet the costs of basic necessities, including food and rent. Lexus Martin, a black woman, felt that the Latina/os "were taking away our city, moving into the projects, not knowing any English. They were everywhere."

Although the state's median household income is one of the highest in the nation, its urban areas are among the poorest. People in towns and cities across the state live dramatically different lives, despite their shared residence in a very small state. For example, as many as 25 percent of Port City's population was living below the poverty line in 2014. According to a 2005 report released by the Food Policy Council in collaboration with one of the state's public universities, Port City was among the ten most poverty-stricken cities in the state, and it also ranked among the bottom of the state's 169 towns for community food security. Additionally, the report found that Port City was among the five towns that had the worst access to transportation.

Not everyone, however, abandoned or lost hope for the city. Some of its residents continued to take pride in the city and did their best to provide for themselves and sometimes for their neighbors and friends. One resident of a local religious residential community, a white woman in her twenties, planted vegetables and fruit for those without homes (who often gathered in the area outside the residential community, especially at night). Beer bottles would be left lying around outside some mornings, and the same resident cleaned them up. She told me that the chores were transferred to her:

Two brothers, Andrew and Jessup, planted this garden, mainly strawberry trees [plants] and some vegetables, when they lived here as transitional housing. Then they moved to DR [Dominican Republic]. Their aunt and grandmom were so proud, they wanted to help by weeding but ended up taking out the plants and they had to redo. So now I plant some lettuce, which sometimes gets ravaged by animals, and there is no sun, so I planted collard greens or kale in the sun on the outer wall. Anyway, they also liked when the homeless ate some and rested. So I do it too.

There were several nonprofit organizations in Port City. They ranged from organizations that housed educational programs for youth focused on the arts to organizations focused on access to college, nonviolence training for youth, pregnancy prevention, and alcohol and drug abuse prevention. Employees and volunteers in these organizations often hosted movie nights, debate nights, art shows, and the like. While some nonprofits were specifically set up to prevent violence, gangs, drugs, and pregnancy among youth, no matter the stated goals of the nonprofit, all of them made it their central mission to work toward these goals—without it, they claimed, everything else was meaningless.

Port City was also basically segregated. The wealthy and the poor and working classes mainly navigated different sections of the city, as did the white people and people of color. Sometimes the wealthy, who were mostly white, simply did not spend time in the city; instead, they shopped, ate, and entertained themselves in wealthier neighboring towns and cities. Most of the city's people of color, who were also poor or lower middle class, lived near the north end and the center of the city, which also hosted several housing projects. White old-timers in Port City frequently mourned the loss of community in racialized ways. Many times, the youth also claimed that the "wrong people" kept moving to Port City. As Ashley and I were walking to my car from a coffee shop one day, a black man standing next to his motorbike shouted, "Sexy, what's up?" as we hurried along, falling behind a black man and a white woman who were talking loudly.

"Man, how can they not admit me to the class just 'cause I'm a felon? They told me they can't because of my felony and I don't understand why they would do that," said the white woman. Ashley whispered to me, "This is the kind of people you got here in Port City. At least we famous for our pizza. In Boston you got a Port City Pizza."

I also met white, black, and Latina/o residents who found the city familiar and comforting, having developed networks over time. As I was walking with Sandra's mother one afternoon after we did our eyebrows together at the local salon, she said, "Oh girl, I'm sweating, and this is good exercise!" Then, as a young black man and a brown woman walked by, she stopped them and said, "Oh my god! Is that you? Oh, I need a hug, even if it's middle of the street." The young boy and Sandra's mother hugged each other. "How are you? And how's your sister? Can't believe she is due soon," Sandra's mother said. The young man responded, clearly eager to end the conversation. As we kept walking, she told me, "He was probably embarrassed with his girl and all. He was very small when I knew him, and now he goes to Port City High. Now I wanna cry! He has a girlfriend!" "Damn, you know everyone!" I exclaimed. She responded:

> Girl, I been here long enough. I love this city. There are so many nice people. The lady who runs the afterschool center, she moved here from Detroit like thirty or something years back and she loves it. I just was talking to her. It's home, this city, people say Port City this and Port City that, but what's better? Detroit? People [are] dying out there. New York [City]? People killing you out there.

Although there was a semblance of "renewal," it was not much more than skin-deep. The seemingly "in shambles" downtown Port City had a bohemian ambience and contained a few cultural centers, art galleries, museums, and alternative coffee shops that served only organic food. I met several artists who had moved to Port City from bigger cities and other countries, looking to join and revive its art scene. However, most restaurants, bars, and shops were empty at any given time. The Sequence neighborhood, located closer to the ocean, hosted some majestic houses, infused with wealthy white families' histories. This tree-lined neighborhood was mostly quiet, with slower traffic, and had a few restaurants. One did not see much activity here, except for cars driving to the beach.

The first exit from the highway led to a lower-middle-class neighborhood that was congested, with houses built very close to one another, with no backyards or lawns, and with a deserted park that was known to host drug dealers. Working-class and poor residents also lived in apartment complexes a little further away.

Some roads in Port City were rather steep. The public library was located on one such road. If you walked a few miles from the library to the busiest intersection in Port City, you would see several restaurants, gas stations and convenient stores, and laundromats covered with graffiti. Abandoned by supermarkets, Port City is host to numerous fast-food chains like Dunkin' Donuts and a number of liquor stores. You could find one of each at this busy intersection. A little further away, closer to the city center, there was an enormous volume of empty commercial space. The food co-op was located close to the nonprofit where I met the youth. Close to the co-op was a busy road that the youth take to Port City High.[17] Along this road were an ice cream store, a Dunkin' Donuts, a Subway fast-food restaurant, and two used-car lots. One could also take this road to the mall that is right outside the city, but not within walking distance.

For the most part, Port City residents did not frequent local businesses such as beauty salons, coffee shops, bars, and restaurants. The middle class almost always took their business elsewhere, and the poor and working class usually did not have the resources, which I strongly suspect constrained the opportunities for youth in the local labor market. Walking in downtown Port City any time after sunset, one could, with only slight exaggeration, compare these streets to a post-apocalyptic sight. People rarely walked along the streets, and restaurants and coffee shops were mostly empty. Some bars had regular patrons, but even these were scantly occupied. Sandra's aunt had to lay off Sandra from her beauty salon because she did not have enough patrons. Angie was laid off from her brief stint at a local coffee shop because they also did not have enough patrons to merit an extra helper. I imagine that many bars and restaurants had similar situations impacting the number of jobs available to young people.

Middle-class people in Port City usually did not go out to eat or for entertainment in Port City. Many neighboring towns were regarded as safer, and more sophisticated, than Port City. As I will discuss in chapter 5, various incidents led to the construction of youth as "dangerous" during my time in the field. For example, after a young man was stabbed to death outside a restaurant, people stopped going there. When I visited with Shivana Abraham one afternoon, the manager complained: "It's been hard. Business is down, I think because of what happened and I don't blame people. It's our bad luck." Indeed, I was warned by numerous people who grew up or had lived in or near Port City not to go out alone after dark and not to visit the city alone. During one of Port City's largest festivals I urged many of my graduate-school friends to join me. Only one friend agreed to come. Another told me that alcohol and Port City were a bad combination.

The community meetings I attended, informal discussions I had with various residents, and formal interviews I conducted all pointed to the idea that Port City was a dangerous place. For example, several elderly residents who lived near the beach told me about their organization called "Save the Beach." The organization was founded not only to organize beach-cleaning events but also to advocate against a local big business buying the beach: "Most beaches around here are private, and we want this to be a public one where minority people and all kids can come and people from other poor cities can come here and we want it to be open." These elderly people had grown up in Port City and nostalgically reminisced about their childhood: "When we grew up here [the beach] was the only source of entertainment, and we came in the morning and played and then went and bathed because there was no shower then, and came back again and met the boys." One of them added:

> That's not the only thing that has changed. It's not just that, I mean, we just can't go around the way we used to. This used to be a safe place. Now my daughter, she goes elsewhere to take her family for entertainment. It's not safe here. It's not just about the beach being private, but it's like the whole city is going downhill.

Others nodded. One person added:

> Now a lot of inner-city people come here [the beach] when it is hot, and the parking lot was closed a few days ago and it got so crowded, and lot of cars were there and something got stolen. I mean everyone should come, but then there is your issue.

While the elderly women claimed that they wanted the beach to be open to everyone, they simultaneously feared that racially and economically marginalized people posed a threat to the city.

PORT CITY HIGH

Most of the young men and women who are the central characters of this book attended Port City High School (three attended a local technical school). Port City High served around a thousand students and had roughly eighty faculty members. The school district had a flat budget for six years, and it held the state's record for the most years a public school system went without a budget increase. The four-year graduation rate at Port City High is 64 percent. Port City is among the poorest performing school districts in the state, and the state board of education intervened in the Port City school district in 2012 by assigning a "special master" to oversee the public school system. In the years before my study, budget cuts eliminated administrative positions, teaching positions, educational aide and assistant positions, secretarial positions, and custodial positions. The school had insufficient numbers of computers, English as Second Language (ESL) classes, and counselors. Port City High was also designated a "turnaround school," meaning that it was in the lowest-performing five percent of the state's schools. Parents and the youth largely regarded the school critically. Several school officials, youth, and family and community members even thought of Port City High as a "dangerous" place where fights break out and students are "out of control." Port City's white and wealthy residents abandoned its public schools more than ten years before I conducted this study. Eighty percent of Port City High students qualify for free or reduced lunch, and more than 85 percent of the students are black or Latina/o. In 2011, of the sophomores taking the state's Academic Performance Test, only 52.5 percent made proficiency in writing, 43 percent were at or above math proficiency, and 45 percent met science proficiency. Students at Port City High must pass these tests to graduate from high school.[18]

Several school personnel members, nonprofit workers, and parents themselves blamed parents for not actively participating in their children's education through parent–teacher meetings, regular monitoring of homework, and contact with the school. They blamed the students for being out of control. Lexus's mother said to me on several occasions, "These people [students at the high school], they're dangerous. I don't blame teachers, what will they do?" Dinners were often organized for students at the high school—according to the superintendent, the administration was aware that several students belonged to "unsafe homes" where they went hungry and some students struggled with homelessness. The school was also trying to start a program for students struggling with homelessness, although this remained at the "discussion stage" while I was in the field.

The majority of the teachers at Port City High are white, and the majority of the students are black and Latina/o. Some teachers group students based on race and refer to them as "the Hispanics" or "the blacks." Some of the black students claimed that "Hispanics" were taking over their neighborhood, and the Latina/o students claimed that they were bullied because of "their accent."

·   ·   ·   ·   ·

When I disclosed my Indian roots at UConn, my friends there usually responded with, "Oh, I would love to go to India" and "I was there last summer, trekking in the Himalayas." No such responses were forthcoming in Port City. Not only did the youth already have close connections to places that are conceptualized as "poor" and "less desirable," like India, but they also had other more immediate dreams and desires. When I told the Port City youth I was from India, they always expressed awe that I had come so far away from home to "go to college" and "move up in the world." Indeed, I had moved to America to realize the dream of a better life with more opportunities in a postcolonial reality. The young people I met and came to know in Port City also wanted to leave Port City in search of better opportunities, just as their parents and grandparents had moved to Port City in search of a better life. Angie's, Alize's, Ashley's, and A. J.'s parents or grandparents had moved from Puerto Rico to New York City as factory workers in the 1960s and then to Port City in the 1970s and 1980s, as employment dropped by 50 percent in New York City between the 1960s and the 1980s.[19] Curtis's, and Franklin's parents had moved directly from

Puerto Rico to Port City to join their relatives in the 1970s and 1980s. Cassy's parents had moved from Honduras and Lena and Letisha's from the Dominican Republic to join relatives in bigger cities in California and Florida that were popular Latin American immigrant destinations in the United States, but they too subsequently moved to Port City in search of what they called a "cheaper" and "safer" life.[20] Port City youth's families hoped that their decisions would afford their children opportunities for upward mobility. Their families continued to function as a place of support for the youth, but as we will see next, this support was complicated by the predicaments of poverty.

3 Sibling Ties

> You know you're a true family when your grandparents
> don't care about money and change their ticket to Puerto
> Rico so you can celebrate your birthday with them in PR!
> And you know you're in a Puerto Rican family when you go
> to your grandparents' and your grandma washing clothes
> outside. But then also know you're in a messed-up family
> when all these niggas having babies left and right and then
> they don't even come to see them no more, like my own
> momma!
>
> —Angie

In 1995, when Ashley was five years old, her mother relocated to Port City from New York City to escape an abusive boyfriend and to save her daughters from "dangerous" New York City. Ashley told me that her mother, who had moved from Puerto Rico to New York to work in manufacturing, wanted her daughters to experience a "calm life outside city hustle." Ashley also claimed that "New York City would eat you alive." Although their life improved in Port City, as it did for cohorts of Puerto Ricans living outside New York City in the 1990s, Ashley and her family still faced plenty of hardships.[1]

Ashley lived with her mother and sisters in an overcrowded apartment in a Port City housing project, close to the city center and far from the beach.[2] However, life got a little better when the family moved to a home in a working-class neighborhood, which they were able to afford through a bank loan program and the Habitat for Humanity coalition.[3] Some of the sisters still had to share a bedroom, but Ashley had her own room. It had nice satin sheets she had bought from a concession store, framed printouts of family photos, small knickknacks she had collected over the years, a beanbag she got on sale from Target, and plenty of costume jewelry, neatly arranged on the top of her closet.

Ashley's weight fluctuated frequently; she was 5 feet 6 inches or so and anywhere between 180 and 230 pounds. She liked to wear bright red lipstick and mascara and made a mole on the right side of her upper lip. Although she liked to wear makeup even when she exercised at the local gym, on the day of a job interview she decided to not wear lipstick because "red lipstick can look ghetto." Ashley was always looking for (another) job. She imagined that at the very least her "nonprofit experience," combined with an array of other work experience and the high school diploma she had acquired in 2009, would give her a job that did not require "frying food or mopping people's piss and shit." She especially did not want to "clean after rich white people," something her mother did for a living, working at an elderly care center. Her sisters looked up to Ashley.

One sunny afternoon, as several of the youth and I talked about Chinese food, ankle bracelets, and tattoos, Ashley's phone rang continuously with text messages. Ashley ignored them all, telling us she was "done with the drama" for today. After about fifteen minutes, Ashley took the phone out of her purse, raised her eyebrows, appeared to scan her texts, rolled her eyes, sighed, and said, "Families, they suck the life out of you." Many of her daily struggles occurred within her family, so her statement was not surprising. According to Ashley, her mother had intermittently forced Ashley and her siblings to live with their abusive stepfather, and her siblings needed a lot of her time and resources.[4] That day, her older sister wanted Ashley to buy groceries for the family and pick up their younger sister from work. "All they do is use me," Ashley said. She was feeling particularly exhausted with her family responsibilities that afternoon.

Despite these difficulties, Ashley was strongly attached to her family. A few days later, her then-boyfriend Paul found a job in Massachusetts and asked Ashley to move with him. As she struggled to decide what to do, she explained, "I don't know if I wanna leave my sisters, I feel like we're getting torn apart, I don't know if I should go." Ashley considered what it would mean to leave her family behind. After recalling both good and bad memories, she summed up their relationship: "Niggas caused me pain, but we sisters tight."[5]

The nature and function of the family, both biological and fictive, has long been at the center of discussions around the economically marginalized. One of the most significant sites of the social reproduction of class, families provide varying access to economic, social, and cultural capital. As children move into adolescence, peer groups start to become central to their daily lives. Yet family continues to exert significant influence,[6] especially for those growing up under the constraints of poverty. A plethora of scholarship on poor children and youth focuses on the role of parents because it has important implications for making family-focused poverty policies.[7] While some Port City youth were self-sufficient—paying their portion of the rent, and buying food and other basic necessities—other parents supported youth's basic necessities. However, much like the poor and working-class parents of young children portrayed in Annette Lareau's work, the parents of the Port City youth were not deeply invested in the "concerted cultivation" of their teenagers, spending little time keeping up with their children's academic performance, college plans, or extracurricular activities. The parents explained that their educational and economic backgrounds left them unable to provide academic and other assistance to their children. Parents were also not very involved in helping young people find jobs, even though in most cases, everyone over the age of fourteen was expected to contribute to the family's material needs in some way (see chapter 6 for a discussion of the youth labor market).

Even as a system of obligations bound families together, parents thus played a relatively marginal role in the lives of the young people of Port City especially when compared to siblings. Located at the nexus of family and peer group, siblings[8] played a unique role when compared to peers, parents, extended family, teachers, or romantic partners.[9] Sibling relations are a particularly important family arrangement within families that lack material resources and social and cultural capital: in such families, brothers and sisters regularly take on adult responsibilities and make contributions to the household.[10]

As parents were preoccupied with providing for their children's basic necessities and, in certain situations, lacked the capacity or confidence to provide assistance to their children, older siblings supported younger ones with schoolwork and college admission, taught them how to manage interactions with police, and provided them with work opportunities as well as cultural capital necessary for interactions within the workplace. In addition, given the proximity in age, siblings were better acquainted with the local school, work, and neighborhood settings than parents. In other words, when constraints of poverty made it hard for parents to provide various types of resources for their children, older brothers and sisters often stepped in, an arrangement that had both advantages and challenges.[11] Regular and obligatory exchange between siblings, however, often made families unstable.[12]

The majority of the young people of Port City had more than three siblings who lived with them and many had additional siblings who did not, but remained in contact. Siblings are the central focus of this chapter.[13] However, to highlight their role, I sometimes tell stories about entire families. Delineating the interactions among all family members—parents, grandparents, fictive kin, and extended family—reveals the distinct nature and role of sibling ties.

MANAGING PARADOXICAL FAMILIES THROUGH SIBLING TIES: COMMON HISTORY AND SHARED STRUGGLES

When I met them in 2010, thirteen of the Port City youth lived with their mothers, while Shivana and Cassy lived with both parents, and Gigi with her father and stepmother. Some of the young people had lived within the same family arrangements their entire lives. Others had changed living arrangements more than once by their late teen years. The economic precariousness of poor families and neighborhoods leads to several situations that entail instability—job loss, eviction, financial struggles, and even drug abuse. The youth changed homes for a variety of such reasons.

A. J. briefly moved in with her aunt when her mother moved across the country so she could visit her ex-husband in prison on a regular basis. By the time they were in their mid- to late teens, the young people had some say in whether and where they wanted to move, mainly because they could depend on their own personal networks rather than their parents. For example, when Lena and her family were evicted while she was in high school, Lena decided to stay with friends and extended family in Port City rather than move with her mother to a neighboring town. No matter the source of the volatility, unstable family life and living arrangements shaped the young people's lives, perceptions of family, and enactment of sibling ties.

Ashley's experience epitomizes this volatility and tells us what roles siblings can play in managing it, planting roots, and imagining family. One evening, I planned to interview her family, but before I could begin asking questions, the evening turned into an emotional recollection of Ashley and her sisters' childhood (I had permission to record the conversation). Ashley, her sisters, and their mother reminisced about their days in New York over a few bottles of Mike's Hard Lemonade (Ashley's favorite). Ashley sat on the floor looking at old family photos, while the rest of us sat on Ashley's neatly made bed.

"He was real asshole, that nigga," Ashley said, pointing to a picture of a man in his thirties, her stepfather, holding a baby in one hand and a packet of Doritos in the other. "Ranita, he was abusive to us; to tell you the truth, there are things you don't even know he done to us. Siete [Ashley's younger sister] doesn't know much, I think. I have some memories of New York, lot of them were not good 'cause of my stepfather. Nigga almost separated us." At this point Ashley's mother left the room as if to avoid the conversation, while Ashley continued:

Yeah she [their mother] remembers what he done to us. He used to beat us and so she took us and moved to Port City. But then bitch went crazy again and my stepdad ended moving down here with us. Anyway, so my stepdad he was getting drunk and then he would beat people and not adults but kids . . . . One thing I will always remember was that we were in New York and I was little and I needed to take a bath; he filled the tub with cold, cold water and filled it all up and he would shove my head in and take it out and [then] in again so that I would drown and then he shoved me into the freezer and left me out there. My sisters tried to save me but he kicked them out of the apartment and locked it . . . I don't remember who pulled me out but I had icicles in my hair, eyelashes, eyebrows. My childhood is all messed up . . . cause it was so random and we like moved all the time.

At this point Ashley began to tear up and her older sister Maria tried to refocus the conversation by recounting one of the times they fought back against their stepfather:

You [Ashley] was clever too, you was mad mature. Like she [Ashley] would visit my aunts and everything and they would give her like twenty dollars here and ten dollars there . . . But she knew money was important 'cause our mom was always talking about money . . . so I think she [Ashley] wanted to save it up and give it to my mom. And I think she had like eight or twelve twenty-dollar bills and couple of tens or [a] couple of dollars . . . but we didn't even know how to count them, so we was just counting one, two, three, four, five, but it was actually counting a hundred dollars but we were counting like one to five. And then the nigga walks in and he is like, Watchu doing there, nothing, watchu you got in your hand? Where did you get it from? And he put his big hands on my face and was like smothering me, and he enjoyed watching me and I kicked and I was fighting yo!

Ashley jumped in:

I remember alright. . . . Like one night when my little sister [Betsy] was like five, six, or seven she found him drunk on the floor and he was like, "Come here" and she ran and he started chasing and we saw her running and asked what happened and she said, "He is chasing me," and we blocked the door. Then it was quiet for a while and we thought he left and [we] opened the door but he came running. He grabbed and threw Siete and threw her and she fell and passed out and he beat us like real bad and we was bleeding and stuff. Then Maria called the police.

The mood in the room was somber by this time, and Ashley was holding on to Maria's hands and looking straight into my eyes with a stern look:

They came, they took pictures of my face—blood everywhere, cut over my eyebrow, my nose was bleeding, and I had a cut on my lips and all over. My sisters had cuts and bumps on their heads . . . my mom at the end of it she told us to say that we are the ones who started it and she wanted us to lie that we started it so that we won't get split by DCF [Department of Children and Families]. . . .We could've died and you want us to say that we made him mad. We did it . . . because we didn't want to be splittin' up so we lied and whether DCF believed her or not was up to them. And me and my sisters made up runaway bags so that if they [DCF] were going to take us we would run away and our coats were waiting for us . . . It was like any time we could be [separated], you know what I'm sayin'.

Growing up in a precarious family cemented sibling bonds between Ashley and her sisters based on a common and very intimate struggle.

Sisters fought to protect one another in the face of their stepfather's abuse. Ashley alluded to the belief that the common, traumatic experiences that the sisters in her family shared, and their commitment to protect one another, meant that the bond between them was indestructible. (Their mother never discussed this decision with me or in front of me, and I do not know the specific circumstances that led to her allowing her husband to move back in with them.) The sisters were critical of their mother in retrospect, and Ashley was particularly proud of the strong connection between the siblings in her family, and found it to be a constant source of support as well as a way to remain rooted in the face of daily instabilities.

SUSTAINING AND THREATENING FAMILY BONDS

In the face of instability, siblings often collectively preserved the family. Sometimes, the young men and women worked to maintain family symbolically by engaging in holiday celebrations or tattooing names of family members. When new members threatened the family bond or old members left, siblings supported one another and collectively invested in maintaining and imagining the family.

Celebrations: A Time for Family

Ashley and her sisters felt that now that they were adults, they needed to engage in what they perceived as "normal" family activities as a way to balance out their family's instabilities, and create distance from stereotypes of "broken families" that their teachers and community members often referenced as a problem in Port City. The intimacy between family members needed to be performed and preserved through giving gifts or celebrating holidays.

Ashley's favorite family activity was celebrating every holiday with her younger sisters, mother, two adopted siblings who joined the family when her mother's sister died, and her older sister and her family. She especially loved celebrating Easter: decorating eggs, hiding them for her two nephews, and eating a big dinner with her family. In April 2011, Ashley spent all her money on her family's Easter celebration. She cooked an elaborate dinner, bought presents for her family members, and even bought new outfits for her nephews. Ashley invited me to the celebration and asked me to bring any family members, saying, "Bring who you like. It's nice to have family together." The day of the dinner, Ashley and her sisters pulled two small plastic tables together, covered them with a white bed sheet, and set a place for each guest. She wanted to create a table like the one she had seen when she was the dinner guest of a friend she met during her time at Public Allies (a popular nonprofit organization that is part of an AmeriCorps program). Ashley commented: "It was real nice. Like everything was same and their family was real nice too." However, her family did not have enough dishes to use the same pattern of plates and bowls for each guest. It was a mostly quiet and uneventful dinner where the guests, including myself, were busy enjoying the delightful meal that the family had prepared.

While the Easter dinner was expensive for Ashley and her sisters, it mostly lived up to their vision. Occasional performance of family did not make up for the everyday instability. However, it allowed Ashley and her siblings to experience family in ways they witnessed being enacted in white middle-class homes—albeit at the cost of resources that were already constrained, and symbolic violence experienced in attempting to enact this unattainable white middle-class picture of the family.

I Tattooed Your Name

Like Ashley, Angie experienced a great deal of family instability. During one of my first extended conversations with her, I noticed a tattooed name spread across her arm. "It's my mom's name," Angie explained when she caught me staring at the tattoo as we ate at the local Applebee's. "She's the most important person in my life; my family is important 'cause they're the only ones that are really there," she said when we discussed our family histories.

Later that month, when I visited Angie at her home for the first time, I learned from Angie that her mother had "abandoned" Angie and her siblings, disrupting their living arrangements a number of times to "move in with boyfriends." Over the years, Angie and her siblings lived with several guardians, including their grandparents, father, uncle, and a foster mother, and they learned to embrace their family in the context of this instability. Angie's half sister Monique was visiting from New Jersey that day, and as the two reminisced and showed me old photos, Monique said: "Our mom, she loves us but she's not the type to spoil us. She does what she wants." Angie explained:

> Sometimes I don't know, but I feel like she doesn't care. This family of ours, it's crazy but that's how it is . . . . If you met my mom, though, you'll love her. She's a good person. My grandpa brought me with him to Port City back when my mom was living with this nasty-ass nigga in Puerto Rico; she sacrificed to let me have the good life.

Angie imagined that it had been hard for her mother to part with her little daughter, while she stayed back with an abusive partner. This view allowed her to believe that her mother had sacrificed a great deal for her. Moreover, Angie believed in what she called "family pride." She believed that families were to be loved and respected no matter what they gave you in return. For example, she once called me in an emotional state:

> It's so hard to hear my mom cry through the phone, and because of my sister, yeah, my mom hasn't really been there for all of us as much as we would want to, I always told you that but she's still our mother, don't you think? None of us wouldn't be here if it wasn't for her. Everyone makes mistakes and no one's mom is perfect, but no matter what, she is still my mother and I wouldn't change her for the world. They're [her sisters] young and fucking ignorant now, but when mom, God forbid, isn't here anymore, they'll wish they said 'I love you' to her. 'Cause that's what family is for me. That's how it is for us.

The next day, Angie sent her mother and sisters a picture of her tattoo (her mother's name) with the text, "I love you Ma, you in my heart," seemingly to remind both herself and her mother of their deep attachment. The same day, to reciprocate the gesture of love, Angie's mother convinced her sister to let Angie stay with her and her sons in Florida and attend college there, something Angie had wanted to do. Angie and her mother exchanged a series of text messages throughout the day in which Angie's mother updated her about her conversation with her aunt. When the aunt finally agreed to let Angie live with her, Angie received the following text message from her mother, "You in! You made it to college." Angie explained that this was a big step in the right direction because her dream had been to move to Florida.

A few days later, Angie and her sisters decided to use their savings to fly their mother to Port City to celebrate Angie's big step toward college. This was the first time I met her mother. On the way to the airport Angie announced, "I'm gonna be a spoilt girl to my mother," like she believed daughters should be. She added, "Ima annoy the shit outta her." Angie had a good time when her mother visited. I went to Applebee's with her and her mother to celebrate Angie's future; Angie paid for her mother and herself while I paid my share. She expressed her gratitude to her mother: "Thanks to my mom, Ima be out of this ghetto-ass place and be hundred miles away in Florida." Later the same night, Angie told her grandmother (who often criticized Angie's mother's parenting) that her mother had in fact come to her rescue and would do the same for her other sisters, and that's what family was about.

Siblings often collectively constructed their own stories to navigate the stories of their families that did not resemble the images of what "good" families look like, and to alleviate resentment of abandonment.

Mothers' Lovers

A few days after the Easter celebration at Ashley's house, Ashley and I were sitting in her bedroom in the evening when Siete came in and announced that she was hungry and hadn't eaten since breakfast. Shouting, so that her mother and her mother's boyfriend could hear from behind locked doors in the next room, Ashley complained:

> Niggas got money to feed each other but not see [to] their girl. I'm tight. I don't wanna do anything for these assholes [her mother and her mother's boyfriend] ever, they don't care about us. Don't keep your girls hungry to please your man, that's low. He don't even speak good English and she wanna bring him in.

When Ashley's mother came out of her room, she turned to me and commented, "She [Ashley] use all [her] money for Easter and then we have no food so she complains." Indignant, Ashley protested: "But I did it for this fucking family though, not for some outside nigga. That's what normal families do, but you wouldn't know . . . It's about who you done it for. She doesn't get it. I don't mind giving everything to my sisters, but not to random niggas."

Ashley and her sisters were afraid to leave their home when their mother's boyfriend was there. They claimed that he stole their food and misplaced things. They also tried to avoid being in the house alone with him. Ashley missed work for multiple days so Siete would not be alone with her mother's boyfriend when she was home with the stomach flu. Ashley also claimed that he was using things in common rooms, such as toilet paper, and their mother never bought more to replace it. "People gettin' paid, but no one wants to spend a few bucks on things we need like toilet paper! I didn't get paid yet this month and I buy what we need, but since people want to be greedy, you can wipe your ass with your hand," Ashley griped in front of her mother one morning.

One day her mother's boyfriend stole her mother's money and ran off. At first Ashley insisted that we call the police. But because both she and her mother were driving without a license at the time, they eventually decided not to involve the police. They looked for the boyfriend in every possible place he might hang out, while I stayed with Ashley's cousins, since Betsy and Siete were both at work. They never recovered the money.

When they returned to the house, Ashley's mother was in no mood for conversation and promptly retired to her room. Ashley and I sat and talked about all the signs of the boyfriend's disloyalty that had been obvious to Ashley but overlooked by her mother. Ashley focused on his lack of respect for the bond the family had forged as a result of their collective difficult experiences:

> First off, he didn't even like us. Like, with us, if you wanna be part of the family you gotta love the family. Like that's what's most important to us 'cause we sisters been through a lot together and you can't just come in and be like I'm in [the family]. What have you done for us, you know?

Not only did the arrival of newcomers threaten the established family, but the departure of established family members could fracture the family structure. Sometime in the winter of 2012, I received a frantic call from Letisha: her mother was missing. Letisha and her sisters had been calling her mother all morning but she had not responded. Even though it was her mother's day off, Letisha checked in at the elderly care center where she worked, but she wasn't there. I went to the family's house with another friend, Elizabeth, who had also briefly worked with Letisha's mother and knew the family. Elizabeth suggested that we call the police after waiting for a while, but Letisha and her sisters did not want to appear foolish, reflecting their feelings of constraint in navigating institutions. Letisha exclaimed: "I'm not calling no police! The bitch could be anywhere. Like she don't even speak good English, the other day she texted me like it was mad funny: 'Daughter you come buy patata [potato] when you come.'" Everyone laughed, enjoying a brief moment of relief from anxiety.

We spent the whole day trying to figure out where Letisha's mother had gone. Letisha called relatives and friends to see whether they knew where her mother was, but she had no luck. Next, she spent a few hours trying to discover her mother's Facebook password; she was finally able to reset the password and log into her mother's account. The account revealed that her mother had been chatting with a man from Miami who had bought her a plane ticket to come visit him, and had even invited her to make a home with him in Miami.

Letisha's mother finally called around 8:00 that night and informed her family that she was indeed in Florida and had taken a few days off work the following week so she could give the new relationship a try. Her mother said she left directly after her night shift and explained that she decided not to contact her family until she reached Miami because she did not have any phone minutes. Letisha, however, suspected her mother did not call earlier because she did not want her family to persuade her to not go. Letisha ended the conversation with her mother by saying "You do what you want alright, I'm not gonna say nothin'. You just think about what you doing here."

Letisha had conflicting reactions to her mother's disappearance. She questioned how her mother could have left with no notice: "How she leave us like that? I don't even understand." However, she also sympathized with her mother's reasons for leaving: "Port City is mad ghetto, so I would hope she finds someone somewhere else, that's definite." The family struggled over the mother's departure for several days. At first, they questioned how she could have left them so abruptly. Then they reasoned that they were indeed grown up (Letisha was already a little over twenty at the time and her siblings were older), and that their mother had worked very hard and taken care of them all her life and was lonely now that they had their own lives. Later, they recounted all their mother's failed relationships and hoped that they didn't end up alone like her. They wondered whether their mother had just needed a break or whether she truly hoped to start a relationship with the man. At other times, the family tried to joke about the situation, making comments such as, "At least we got a place to go." Letisha and her sisters felt betrayed as they tried to come to terms with the fact that their mother had abandoned them—emotionally if not materially, since they were young adults, but they also attempted to understand their mother's decision.

The trip did not result in a long-term relationship. Letisha's mother returned the following week. I never talked to her mother about the incident or asked the family any direct questions about her reasons for going or for returning, and after her mother returned Letisha and her sisters never discussed their mother's absence. They did not call certain relatives or friends who they thought would insult their mother or question their family. "I'm not gonna say nothin' to Aunt Carla 'cause she think of us in bad ways already," Letisha told her older sisters, who agreed.

Youth had to negotiate their family paradox, in which their understanding that their family members hurt or betrayed them was combined with their continued belief that their family members were good people who cared for them. Ultimately, as the youth transitioned to adulthood and became aware of hardships associated with family life and relationships, they appeared to accept instability as a part of life.

In the face of parental failure, which is of course situated within larger structures of oppression, the siblings dealt with family conflict by protecting each other and the family dignity, as well as by creating shared narratives about the experience that allowed both betrayal and care to coexist and legitimized the stories of their families that did not fit hegemonic stories of "stable" families. Additionally, siblings provided crucial resources for survival against poverty and for upward mobility, as will be discussed next.

SIBLING TIES AND RESOURCES

Siblings are aware of both intimate personal details within the family and various external contexts that youth must navigate on a regular basis such as school, workplaces, and neighborhoods. Below I show how the youth in my study both received and provided a wide range of resources on a regular basis, creating a complex system of exchange among siblings. Some of these resources supported daily survival. Others, such as help with college admission, were aimed at facilitating upward mobility.

School

Port City High had one guidance counselor per more than five hundred students. Appointments with counselors were difficult to obtain unless a student's parents were personally acquainted with school personnel. One evening Ashley and I were picking up Siete after a financial management workshop that Ashley had insisted Siete attend. We ran into a student named Anthony who gloated about how easy it had been for him to schedule an appointment with the guidance counselor. Anthony explained that his mother and the guidance counselor had attended college together; his mother now worked at the youth center and he had come to pick her up. For most students, however, meetings were difficult to schedule, nerveracking to attend, or both.

When parents couldn't help, siblings proved to be a crucial source of access. When A. J. managed to obtain a meeting with the guidance counselor during her senior year in order to finalize her graduation plans, she also used the time to find out which classes her younger sister, also a high school senior (but not slated to graduate with her), needed to graduate the following year. She explained: "If I don't ask then she'll never know, 'cause it's hard to see the guidance counselor like that."

Having a sibling, especially an older sibling, was an important support for academic success. Cassy regularly helped her younger sisters with their homework; she remembered many of the things her sisters were learning since she was still in school. The process of helping her sisters improved her learning, too; she often made comments such as "Oh, I learnt some algebra stuff while working on Shiela's homework last night." Older siblings did more than just supervise homework. They also knew helpful tricks—for example, Lexus's older brother taught her how to avoid all-day detentions, which were given when a student missed an after-school detention (for policing of youth, see chapter 5), and return to her classes. The youth also helped younger brothers and sisters prepare for college. Ashley told her sister how to obtain SAT and college application fee waivers through the school—information that they did not learn from their guidance counselors. She had learned this information from an employee at the city's youth services that I had befriended.

Julie Bettie, a sociologist who has studied the educational experiences of working-class young women, also identifies siblings as an important source of support in the lives of poor and working-class women. Specifically, she found that siblings were helpful for young women who sought to take college prep classes in high school. While neither Bettie's data nor my own can detect whether sibling support eventually leads to upward mobility through white-collar work, we both found that such support grants at least temporary access to several resources.

Parents noted the significance of older children's help in their younger children's educational careers. Donte was almost like a father to his younger sister. His mother often described times when Donte was young yet acted responsibly, and wished the siblings were in school together:

> He would ask me when we left the ATM: "Ma, did you take the card?" or "Ma, did you lock the door?" Guess they grow up when there is no other man, but with his sisters he is more like that, he is keeping an eye on her all the time, I think it would be nice if they were more of same age, so he would be in high school when she went. He is so responsible—like when we leave the house he asks five times whether I locked the door.

Work

All of the youth in my study intended to hold one or more jobs at all times. Siblings functioned as a central source of support for those seeking work and navigating the work environment. Brothers and sisters exchanged resources that they may have acquired from a variety of sources such as friends, co-workers, nonprofits, and community members, including information regarding available jobs, guidance concerning how to please employers, and transportation to and from work.

Not only did Ashley drive her sisters to work, but when she got a job at the Port City youth center, she convinced the managers to hire her sister Siete as soon as there was a vacancy. She vouched for her sister, convincing the supervisors that Siete was a very dependable, honest, and earnest person. Ashley broached the topic when I was in the room, asking one of the supervisors: "I know you lookin' for someone, right? We gotta put flyers in the school and whatnot?" Her supervisor responded, "Yeah. We need someone soon," and Ashley suggested that they could hire Siete: "If you don't wanna [put flyers] for now, and like want someone for now, then my sister can probably do it. She mad devoted to shit. Ask Ranita. She knows her [nods at me], right?"

Ashley coached her sisters on how to interact with employers, instructed them to remain on employers' good side, and chided them when they were late to work. When Siete missed work one day, Ashley talked to her about how to negotiate days off and told her which reasons worked best when explaining a day off she had to take: "Tell him [Siete's employer] that you took Ma to the doctor, not that you had to get her the pills, 'cause hospital looks more professional." She also often offered general advice about how her sister should behave at work, imparting lessons to manage discrimination: "Don't wear those tights to work," "Don't be sayin' nigga this, nigga that at work all time."

My visit to a local after-school care center to inquire whether they had a job for Shivana's sister further revealed the extent of sibling influence in the realm of work. Four of the ten employees at the organization were siblings. Of the sixteen youth in my study, seven had found at least one job through a brother or sister. Siblings were familiar with the places that were most likely to hire youth—local fast-food joints, retail stores, and youth organizations—and were often aware of job openings available to young people at these places. Brothers and sisters were keen on assisting one another in work-related matters because helping a sibling find a job led to additional family income.

Police

In the current era of mass incarceration, young people growing up in marginalized communities have frequent contact with police, and lessons on navigating these interactions are important, especially for young men.[14] A young athlete who believed in God, Curtis lived with his terminally ill mother and four siblings in the same housing project as Angie. Their home was lively and always appeared busy. One brother's girlfriend always visited and cooked for everyone. Curtis was indifferent about most things in the house, except for his Jordan sneakers, of which he was very proud. When one of his older brothers had a baby boy, Curtis was ecstatic with joy but also pitied his brother: "Damn, nigga has no life now!" Curtis often got into trouble in school, although it was never serious. One of his brothers tried to involve Curtis in selling marijuana. "It's not even nothin' crazy," his brother would say, but Curtis was not interested.

One evening in 2010 the police visited Curtis (then eighteen years old) at his house to interrogate him regarding a homicide that had occurred the previous evening; after talking to him briefly, they requested that he accompany them to the police station to answer further questions. Curtis had two older brothers, but neither of them were home that evening. His mother cried frantically, unable to comprehend the situation, while the cops led him out of the house. After the interrogation, Curtis called his brothers from the police station and asked them to pick him up. Upon receiving the phone call his brothers went straight home to explain the situation to their mother, and then drove to the police station to collect Curtis.

The next day, as Curtis narrated these events, his relief was palpable; he said that the lessons his brothers had passed on to him facilitated his inter-actions with the police. He explained that his brothers had taught him that if he wanted to avoid trouble when he was confronted by the police, he must try to prove his honesty in any way possible and do whatever the police directed him to do. Curtis assembled his brothers' advice, and when the police asked him about his whereabouts on the evening of the murder, he confessed to smoking marijuana: "'Cause, like, if I tell them I did some-thing illegal, like something small you know, then they be like 'Oh this nigga honest' and whatnot. My brother taught me that." Curtis went on to say that his brothers reacted to the incident by inquiring about the inter-rogation and offering detailed opinions on what went well and what did not. For example, they advised him to mention their mother's terminal ill-ness and his caretaking responsibilities to the police in future interactions, in order to demonstrate that he is not a "gangbanger."

Both peers and siblings taught the young men in Port City about the role of the criminal justice system in their lives and offered strategies for dealing with police contact. However, siblings who shared a household were more likely to provide and receive focused, immediate advice that incorporated intimate details. As we will see in chapter 5, navigating policing practices inside and outside the school, including detentions, suspensions, or other more serious encounters, had serious implications for youth's educational and occupational opportunities. Educational performance could be influenced negatively by something as small as missing classes and falling behind due to all-day detention or suspension, as well as more serious offenses such as engaging in physical violence, which could lead to encounters with the juvenile justice system and dropping out of high school. Siblings taught youth how to manage encounters with the law. Ashley told her sisters to provide her phone number so that school authorities could call Ashley directly if the siblings were at risk of losing grades due to truancy. Others, like Curtis's brothers, provided lessons on interaction with the police.

Role Models

In addition to engaging in a direct exchange of resources, older siblings often served as role models, while younger siblings idealized their behaviors and adopted their moral repertoires. During my time with the Port City youth, I noted two particular areas in which the influence of siblings was evident: managing scarce resources and understanding early pregnancy.

One sunny summer day, Franklin, Ashley, Lexus, and I were heading out for pizza after work. As we passed a senior living center, we saw an elderly woman putting some used books outside the building. As we walked past, the woman yelled, "Hey, if y'all need books, I'm getting rid of these." Franklin immediately took out his phone, called his older brother, and asked, "Yo, there is some books here—we can sell, right?" Then he turned to us and said, "My bro told me never to pass up free shit, no matter what they be." Gigi also relied on a sibling's financial advice. While we were at a shopping mall, she struggled to decide whether to purchase a twenty-dollar hair drier: "You know, 'cause my sister told me, like, you gotta save when you can, 'cause you don't know when there's no job. She'll be mad if she knew I bought this. She saved mad money and that's how she got her prom dress too." Heeding her sister's advice, Gigi decided not to purchase the hair drier that night. Older siblings passed on lessons in frugality that facilitated survival in the context of extreme deprivation. They frequently supervised their siblings' conduct, reprimanding them when they did not act with sufficient caution.

Some of Ashley's friends had children during their teenage years. Although Ashley frequently complained about feeling "out of place" or "left out" because her friends had families of their own, she took every opportunity to affirm her conscious decision to postpone childbirth (a topic I discuss at length in chapter 4). Her older sister and brother in-law played a significant role in Ashley's understanding of the issue. Maria and her boyfriend Johnny had been together for almost ten years and had two young sons, but were not legally married. I visited Ashley at Maria's house one day when the couple's younger son Jojo was two years old. We were sitting in Jojo's room when Jojo came in, jumped onto his bed, and screamed, "You want some water? You know I'm not kicking their [his friends] ass at school no more." Both Ashley and I laughed hysterically and Ashley exclaimed, "You can have a full-blast conversation with this little man! He is very smart because both Maria and Johnny had him when they were fully mature, and when mature bodies have babies, they're real smart. I keep telling Siete, 'Girl, you'll have babies before me.' 'Cause she got no control like Maria and me!" Within Ashley's family the older sisters preached to the younger ones that waiting until later in life to have a baby results in children who are smarter.

During the three years I spent time with Ashley and her family, early pregnancy was discussed often and extensively at their house. When the friends of any of the younger sisters became pregnant, Maria would once again remind the sisters about the advantages of avoiding early childbirth. On one occasion, I heard Maria haranguing her sisters after they found out that their sixteen-year-old cousin was pregnant: "See, it [childbirth] don't bring no value to who you are, that's all bullshit. Your ass is just gonna be broke and you can't even give nothing to your child. All baby daddies ain't gonna stick around just 'cause Johnny did. It's good for your child if you have them late; they grow up smart too."

For many of the young men and women of Port City, siblings were an important influence when it came to matters of romantic relationships and pregnancy; however, the specific lesson a young person would take from a given circumstance was difficult to predict. Sometimes they copied the actions of their siblings, while at other times they did the opposite. Curtis did not fare well in school but played on the basketball team. He did not know exactly what was required to go to college, and when I first knew him, he never expressed a serious interest in attending college. In the spring of 2012, one of Curtis's brothers, who was in his early twenties, had a child. The arrival of the baby affected the entire family—there were financial and emotional consequences as well as alterations in everyone's daily schedules. Soon after the baby was born, Curtis told me, "I wanna go to Miami, to college there. I don't wanna stay in this ghetto-ass place and raise no babies. I'm done with this shit and I gotta get my shit together." Curtis followed through on his plan and applied to a community college in Miami to get away from his family. In this instance, Curtis's brother did not offer specific advice, but his actions served as an example of what not to do.

Because of the nature of the support needed and the timing of requests, certain types of assistance were available only from siblings. For example, most of the young people regularly babysat for siblings who had children; sometimes they got paid, but when money was short they watched their nieces and nephews at no charge. When babysitting was needed during inconvenient hours, siblings were often the only available source of child-care. For a few months, Lena's older sister Astor, a twenty-something single mother who lived with her teenage son, had been living with a pregnant friend to save rent. Her pregnant friend had no family in Port City. One winter night in 2011, the friend's water broke and Astor had to assist her as she went to the hospital and gave birth. Astor called Lena at one in the morning and asked her to stay over and send her son to school the next morning, which Lena agreed to do. At the time Lena was working at the local after-school care center and when I met her there the next day she was half asleep. We began chatting and she told me:

> I had to send him [her nephew] to school. I was sleeping like a log when she called, but mom's not well and she can't trust no one else to get into her house at one [in the morning] and then be with her kid and whatnot. She is paranoid but I get it, though. She pays me, though, so I don't mind. It's less money for her 'cause babysitters are mad money. The one girl here, she babysits— ask her! Yeah, so I make some money and it's a good deal for Astor.

In these kinds of emergency situations siblings often served as the first line of support.

Emotional Care

Short, self-declared "thick," and always dressed shabbily in sweatpants and goofy T-shirts, Cassy took pride in being a "nerd" who had no interest in clothes and other such things that teenagers valued:

> I like video games and zombie movies and comic books and basically all the things opposite to the other girls you see here in Port City, I don't care I'm fat—I'll do karate, but 'cause it's cool, not 'cause I wanna look a certain way, you know what I'm sayin'.

Unlike what some may imagine as the traditional "nerd," Cassy liked to color her hair frequently. She dyed it purple, bright red, and navy blue.

Cassy was proud of who she was and firm in her aspirations: "I wanna go to college and become a psychologist, I want to help people and not be like my parents, just frustrated about money." Cassy was especially motivated for her sisters. Once, tired, hungry, and exhausted while working after school, she said to me: "Fuck, I don't even know what's worth what, I just wanna go to college and work hard for my sisters so they know what to do." Most of the time, however, Cassy was jovial, enthusiastic about life, and full of ambitions. She had very clear moral grounds about what young people should and should not care about: Kim Kardashian and Justin Bieber were on her "no-no list," as she called it. Cassy frequently let loose her guttural laugh, played video games during her leisure time, went to the pier with her boyfriend and friends, and did her homework with different levels of enthusiasm on different days.

Although Cassy was proud of her Honduran heritage and very critical of her teachers who did not allow students to speak Spanish in class, she criticized people for not speaking "proper English." One day, after we went to a tattoo artist who gave Cassy an eyebrow piercing, we went to eat at a Chinese buffet, her favorite food. Three of her schoolmates sat at a nearby table and giggled. Cassy commented:

> God, they [the schoolmates] make me mad, you know. It's such a waste, they think it's cute how they act and talk. Speak in full sentences, please. I

didn't have any friends through middle school and most of high school 'cause it's like I don't want to speak like that: I think I found my confidence in high school in my Spanish class and in cooking classes with this teacher who was also Spanish.

Cassy's friends thought of her as somewhat pretentious or too much of a hippie. One of the youth, Evelyn, claimed that Cassy was "gay and like hippie white people." Many of the others pitied Cassy. One of the young women, Gigi, told me, "She always hang out with weird-ass ugly niggas. I think she can look pretty 'cause there are pretty fat people, but she needs to stop doing her hair blue on purpose."

Cassy's parents had moved to the United States from Honduras. Her father was a custodian and her mother stayed at home—the family income was modest. Both parents had limited fluency in English. Cassy lived in a sparsely furnished two-bedroom apartment. The living room had a few plastic chairs, two sets of plastic drawers, and a queen-size bed where Cassy's sisters slept. Her room contained a mattress; her parents' room, a mattress on a bedframe. When times became hard, Cassy's father sublet the living room to a cousin and his wife. Her sisters, who often lovingly called her a "nerd," had to move into her room. While this led to small fights, Cassy and her sisters knew that the family could use the extra money and did not complain very much.

In the spring of 2012, Cassy was unable to pay her phone bill, as was frequently the case for many youth when they lost a job or had to use their money for other purposes such as rent or food. She decided to use her father's cell phone while he was asleep to call her boyfriend in another state. After speaking with her boyfriend, Cassy perused her father's text messages and found out that he had exchanged sexually suggestive text messages with another woman, whom she appeared to have met on a dating website. Instead of discussing the matter with any family members, Cassy decided to keep an eye on her father's phone, and hoped that the two would discontinue their relationship sooner or later.

Her father was still exchanging messages with the woman almost a month later. Cassy confronted him and threatened to disclose everything to her mother. Her father promised to discontinue his relationship and conceded that he had committed a grave mistake, yet when Cassy and I discussed the matter, she acknowledged that he would not stop. She also confessed that her threats were rather empty because if she did reveal her father's emotional infidelity to her mother, her younger sisters would bear the brunt of the consequences. Cassy felt that although she was mature enough to endure the emotional turmoil that would accompany the fall-out, her sisters' lives would change for the worse in multiple ways. If her parents decided to separate, it would only add to the already mounting struggles her sisters endured on a daily basis. Cassy explained:

> I'm not really gonna do anything anyway. I'm just bluffing my dad. It'll be rough on my sisters, they're little you know, they don't do that well at school and they don't even have many friends and it's not like they don't have other things to worry about. Like we're broke as hell, I'm like their mother, I feel . . . . I don't know, I'm really like a mom to my sisters, they really listen to me and it's like if not for anyone else, I want to go to college for my sisters 'cause they look up to me, you know. I told my mom that she should learn to drive because it would make her independent, but she doesn't listen and she hasn't worked in the last five years, so she got nothing.

Cassy and other older siblings in my study performed the labor of shel-tering younger ones from parental quarrels and other family distresses. The practical and emotional burden of keeping the family together often fell disproportionately on the shoulders of older siblings and came at the cost of their own emotional well-being. Cassy claimed that she wanted to protect her sisters, because a wedge between their parents could mean that the sisters would be left to fend for themselves and for their mother who barely spoke English and could not find a job.

Cassy's decision to keep her father's secret came at a price: she was overwhelmed by the burden of the secret she was carrying and dealing with her father by herself, and unsure of whether this was the correct way to handle the situation. She wondered if she was doing wrong by her mother who deserved to know. Cassy was distraught over this experience: it made her anxious regularly, she sometimes missed work and school, and her general jovial disposition was dampened.

Cassy parented her siblings by filling in the gaps left by their parents, even at the cost of her own well-being. In the next section I show how, in the context of limited resources, her care functioned in paradoxical ways and sometimes had a negative influence on her little sisters.

THE DESTRUCTIVE SIDE OF SIBLING TIES:
PARADOXICAL INTIMACY

Sometimes siblings passed on lessons in surviving poverty that paradoxically led their younger family members into trouble. Cassy, who supported
her sisters in myriad ways, also passed on knowledge about how to shoplift without getting caught. She encouraged her sisters to shoplift when
they desired small luxuries they could not afford such as shampoo, lip
balm, or a snack. Cassy taught them how to remove security stickers,
watch out for undercover shoppers (hired by stores to surveil aisles for
shoplifters), be aware of which products don't have security beepers, open
CD covers in the bathroom, and determine which aisles do not have cameras. One day, I spent time with Cassy as she colored her hair and applied
lip makeup, including lip liner, lipstick, and other products. She was fas-
tidious about her hair and skin and used many products to take good care
of them. Her younger sisters and I were asking questions about the products she was using. When one of her sisters said she wanted some straw-
berry-flavored lip balm like Cassy's, she replied:

> You can get 'em when you're older. Dad won't give you money but I'm gonna
> teach you how to get it. If you hungry and there's no food at home you can
> just go to the store and get some, or like, if you want a CD or something. I
> took you one time, remember? When I asked you to see for like people just
> walking and walking around aisles? I gotta teach you, 'cause I can't do this
> for you all the time.

Cassy also taught her sisters what she saw as the moral boundaries of
stealing: "Like if I find an iPhone, I'll even give it back, like if it's someone's. But who cares about Walmart anyway? Don't steal from no one that
bought something with their blood money."

A few months later, Cassy's younger sisters were caught stealing. The
girls had made a list of things they wanted to shoplift. They stole some
food, lip balm, and a bottle of shampoo that cost eight dollars. The girls
looked around for cameras and saw none, but they missed one directly
above them. Cassy had trained them to avoid any behavior that might
appear suspicious and they thought looking straight up would be suspicious. As they left the store, an employee checked their bags and found the

shampoo; the store manager called their father and eventually charged the girls a $300 fine, which their father paid. Cassy gave him $250 because she wanted to take responsibility for imparting these lessons to her sisters, but she was not happy about parting with her money. When we discussed the stealing incident at her house one day, she confided that she often shoplifted and then offered her sisters further instructions:

> My dad was like, "Is this how I raised you?" I steal from stores all the time. I stole forty CDs one time. I am honest in that I say I stole it [looking at her sisters]. You just put the CDs in your bag and then go to the bathroom and you carry a knife and then just tear the plastic and any of the censors and then put it in your jeans and then leave. I even stole the PlayStation games and I have all the games and everything. My mom burned everything one time when we had a fight though. I am honest though, 'cause I won't steal from people.

Cassy taught her sisters lessons that led them into legally troublesome situations, which might negatively impact their educational and occupational opportunities. As the sisters become older they may continue to get into trouble: shoplifting is a serious offense in the state and racially marginalized youth are likely to receive harsh punishments.

Curtis also received both beneficial and detrimental guidance from his siblings. While his brothers passed on important lessons about interacting with the police, they also offered him incentives to quit his job and sell marijuana, which could have negative consequences for his educational and occupational opportunities in the time of a racialized and classed War on Drugs. Curtis left his job at a local nonprofit organization to spend time with his brothers and learn about the drug trade. He was not happy with his pay at the nonprofit, which was low and irregular and depended on grants the organization received. Curtis wanted money to pay for his phone, contribute to his family, buy some new Jordans, and "have some money to feel safe."

A few weeks after quitting his job, Curtis approached Ashley, who was still working at the organization, and confessed that he desperately wanted to return to his old job. He revealed that he had felt somewhat coerced into leaving so that he could hang out with his older brothers and their friends. However, his involvement in the drug trade was proving to offer neither social nor financial benefits—his brothers and their friends were not "treating him right" and he was not "making any money." Later, Ashley remarked that Curtis "likes to work but Paul [Curtis's brother] and them always trynna gangbang."

Having a sibling with a tainted reputation often proved to be damaging for the other children in the family. When one sibling was stereotyped as a "troublemaker" at school, teachers often treated other brothers and sisters with caution. Lexus and her half brother, Leon, attended the same high school. Leon was known for his involvement with a local gang. One day he was arrested for bringing a knife to school. Lexus had to be overly cautious in school because anything she did drew attention from the school staff. Her teachers often made comments such as, "I know who you are; you better be careful." Lexus was discouraged by the trouble her brother's reputation caused her; she lamented, "I'm not my brother you know, I really feel bad when they say things like that 'cause then my friends look down on me too."

Work opportunities were also sometimes jeopardized by connections to notorious siblings. When Franklin Junior's brother was arrested for a serious offense, Franklin found it harder to land a job. He felt ashamed and constrained by his brother's reputation, telling me, "I know it'll follow me around. Both my brothers are involved in gangs—there is no way someone will believe that I am not." Several of my acquaintances in Port City expressed concern regarding my association with Franklin Junior, even though I almost never spent time with his brothers.

The influence of siblings supported academic success—and yet, simultaneously, created educational barriers. This was the case for poor youth who already doubted their academic skills and whose older siblings performed poorly in school or college. Even though Ashley was only a few years older than her sisters, she was their idol. However, this idealization sometimes decreased her siblings' expectations and ambitions. After graduating from high school in 2009, Ashley enrolled in community college, but struggled: she repeated the same two classes for multiple semesters. Siete later enrolled in a nursing program at the same community college but dropped out within the first few weeks of the semester. Siete insisted that Ashley's inability to pass her classes indicated that she [Siete] would never be able to succeed at the school: "She is so smart, you know, she is the smart one. She can paint and talk like she be the shit." Younger siblings witnessed their older siblings facing significant constraints and often imagined their own probable futures (and life chances) within the same limitations.

Shivana lived with her parents and her younger sister, Brittany. Shivana had been contemplating enrolling in college ever since she graduated from high school in 2009. She struggled with depression, anxiety, and a learning disorder, and had received therapy periodically for years. When Shivana failed to attend college, Brittany's desire to graduate from high school evaporated. Brittany argued that because Shivana "did nothing amazing" upon graduating from high school and had worked minimum-wage jobs ever since, Brittany should not have to graduate from high school. She dropped out and enrolled in a GED program. Brittany planned on working at the hospital where their father had worked for the past twenty years at a minimum-wage job. When Shivana attempted to explain the importance of graduating from high school, Brittany often responded: "What do you know? You didn't even do nothing with all the fancy high school degree." Both Siete and Brittany looked to their sisters' experiences for guidance and doubted the value of pursuing any further education.

While sibling relationships had a distinct importance, they also had contradictory effects. While sibling ties generated resources for the youth, they also entailed negative influences, simultaneously fostering and jeopardizing the youth's chances for survival and upward mobility. And while siblings offered a sense of shared history that served as a supportive foundation, the youth also imagined their futures within the constraints set by siblings, whose experiences sometimes represented the limits of economic marginalization.

CONFLICT AND INTIMACY

Scholars such as Viviana Zelizer have noted that exchange and intimacy are not antagonistic but rather connected and complementary because individuals who are intimately related to one another successfully exchange a variety of resources on a regular basis.[15] When this exchange occurs within the constraints of poverty, it impacts the way in which youth enact and imagine sibling ties. The experiences of Port City's young men and women shed light on the relationship between exchange and intimacy when resources are constrained. Exchanges between siblings in Port City were frequently one-sided, indispensable, and obligatory. Because they shouldered significant responsibilities and offered indispensable resources, the older siblings in this study were granted sizeable influence over how their households functioned. In turn, they demanded loyalty and gratitude by making overpowering decisions for those dependent on them, engendering resentment, emotional conflict, mistrust, and hostility. Older siblings also incurred emotional costs, overburdened and weary of the various responsibilities for their younger siblings. Younger siblings often came to resent the extraordinary amount of authority their older brothers and sisters exercised, as well as their own vulnerability in the face of this. The obligatory nature of exchange also meant that siblings were often unable to make the distinction between the sacred filial bond and the exchange of resources. They became skeptical, doubting whether expressions of love by brothers and sisters were essentially selfish acts meant to secure future resources.

Love and Need

Both Ashley and Siete worked at the organization where I met them. After Ashley was fired, Siete often had to walk to work because Ashley refused to offer her a ride. Siete claimed that Ashley refused to bring her to work because she was jealous, and Ashley admitted she was irritated that her sister maintained a cordial relationship with their employers even after Ashley was unfairly fired. One day when I was at the girls' house, someone called the house phone and their mother answered: "Who this is? Who you want? You don't know any manners? You should say who you are and ask for who you want, no? How you got my house number? You want Siete?" Their mother turned to Ashley and gestured, indicating her frustration. Ashley rolled her eyes and said, "Just hang up on him, Ma." Their mother returned to the caller and said, "Yeah, she will call you back." Ashley then turned to me and explained, "She [Siete] prolly didn't pay her phone, but she doesn't pay no phone bill for the home. She always be talking to boys anyway." Betsy [one of Ashley's younger sisters], who had witnessed the entire conversation, narrated the event to Siete when she returned from work, and a huge altercation between Siete and Ashley ensued.

The two argued, breaking down and weeping several times, as Ashley's mother and I tried to contain the fight. Siete claimed that Ashley had no right to make decisions regarding who could call their house phone. Ashley claimed that Siete was dependent on her, and hence she did not care what Siete thought. Siete retaliated by telling Ashley that her boyfriend had been seen in a car "getting some" from another woman ("getting some" could mean any sexual act). Ashley and Siete did not speak to one another for two days after the argument. Ashley told me she was mostly hurt because Siete decided to insult her by revealing her boyfriend's betrayal during the course of the fight, rather than expressing concern for her emotional well-being. She complained: "Nigga didn't even tell me nothing before the fight, she didn't care for me or nothing or she would've told me. She just wanted to get at me, that's what hurt me, honestly."

Siete eventually apologized to Ashley, but Ashley confessed to me that she was certain Siete apologized merely because she needed rides to work, and not because she genuinely cared for Ashley. Over the course of the following weeks, Ashley often told me she had finally realized that her sisters probably did not "love her as much as she thought," but only wanted to "use her." She doubted whether they would be there for her if she was ever in need. I reminded her of the unconditional support Maria [their oldest sister], Betsy, and Siete had offered on many other occasions— sometimes this reassurance seemed to alleviate her doubts but other times it did not. Eventually, the hurt feelings subsided and resurfaced only during arguments, but not before Ashley and Siete both experienced extensive emotional turmoil. The family, as a whole, went through an extended time of constant bickering and unpleasant quarrels.

Of course, such bickering is far from uncommon among siblings and peers. As Zelizer points out, actors who are intimately tied to one another, such as siblings, successfully exchange resources such as care and gifts. However, exchange and related arguments take on a different significance in the face of poverty. While care-giving and gift-giving are often optional in middle-class and affluent families, and can be easily understood as a form of love, the obligatory nature of exchange between siblings in Port

City structured their perceptions of their relationships: they often struggled to distinguish between filial love and exchange. For example, since Siete absolutely needed to depend on Ashley for rides, Ashley could not tell whether Siete had apologized out of genuine care for her or merely because she needed rides.

Uneven Exchange and Demand for Deference

Siblings, especially older siblings, often grew exhausted due to their responsibilities, both emotional and material, toward their younger siblings. Those who fulfilled many responsibilities concerning their younger siblings desired respect, loyalty, and deference in return; this was particularly the case when exchange between siblings was not reciprocal.

Lena Diaz and her two younger siblings lived with their mother, who was fighting a serious illness. Lena's older sister, Astor, lived with her son in the same city. Because Astor was the only one of all the children who drove a car, she was responsible for taking their mother to her medical appointments. In addition, she regularly drove her younger siblings to school and work. Astor resented this obligation: she felt overwhelmed trying to balance work, child-rearing responsibilities, and care-giving responsibilities toward both her mother and her younger siblings. Consequently, Astor often felt entitled to make demands of her siblings. One day when Astor was particularly frustrated after having to miss work in order to take her mother to the hospital, she yelled: "You know I'm sick of this shit. It's too much to take. It's like, why do I gotta go through this shit? Why can't Lena get a fucking license?" I asked, "But she doesn't know how to drive: she needs lessons first, no?" Astor looked at me with an expression of frustration and helplessness, and said, "Well then the bitch [Lena] better fucking appreciate this and respect the shit outta me."

When Lena became romantically involved with a young man, he began to spend most of his time at the house where she lived with her mother. Astor eventually grew weary of him and complained: "That nigga be spending all his time at my mother's house. I told her [Lena], 'Bitch, you get that ugly-ass man out of the house.' I don't want no stranger living with them." When Astor asked Lena to "get rid of the ghetto-ass boyfriend from the house," Lena argued that it was not Astor's house to begin with, and that her boyfriend was not inconveniencing anyone. She claimed that perhaps Astor was jealous because Lena had a "man" and she did not. However, this argument further infuriated Astor, who replied, "Well, I'm the one who takes them places, gives them stuff, my sister even has me buy her tampons. That bitch'll be dead if she spoke to me like that one more time. I'll see where she'll be without me." Declining to concede to an older sibling's demands for loyalty and obedience could cost dependent young people the resources provided by their siblings. Losing these resources was seldom an option because the young people typically had no alternative way to obtain these resources. In this case, because Lena feared her sister would stop giving her rides or lending her money, she was forced to ask her boyfriend to move out.

Lena was unhappy about the situation and complained to me regularly, but decided not to go against Astor's wishes. She explained, "Astor is trynna show me that I'm her bitch 'cause she feels like she gives me shit, so *I am* her bitch." As illustrated by Lena and Astor's relationship, when exchange places overwhelming demands on one person, they may respond with a power play, causing further conflict between siblings. For the Port City youth, the strongly hierarchical nature of sibling relationships and their feelings of exhaustion as well as helplessness in the face of regular, obligatory dependency often led to disdain and hostility and thus weakened ties between brothers and sisters. This resource-respect dynamic also had the potential to jeopardize youth's well-being due to their burdens of managing relationships and emotional turmoil.

The Emotional Price of Mandatory Exchange

After Ashley was fired from her job and failed her classes at the community college, she spent all her time either at home or at the beach. Her older sister Maria and her boyfriend Johnny felt she was wasting her life (and gas by driving to the beach) and decided to take away Ashley's car keys. I went to visit Ashley at her home during the time they had her keys. As her mother was cooking dinner we started talking and her mother offered to read my tarot cards, something she did to earn a little extra money. We went to the dining room to continue when Johnny came in looking for Ashley's car keys. He asked, "Ma, you know where car keys are

---

Table 2   Costs of Exchange on Intimacy

Characteristics of Exchange under Constraints of Poverty	*Consequences on Intimacy*
Recurring	Blurred line between need and filial love
Obligatory	High dependency on providers
Indispensable	Hierarchy
Providers are overburdened with responsibilities	Providers demand loyalty

---

at?" Ashley's mother suggested that he ask her whether she had taken her car anywhere. Johnny replied, "No, no, how she gonna do that? It's outside, I took the power out, she not going anywhere. She got no job or school, what's she gonna do driving around?" When Ashley had a job interview a few days later, it was raining heavily and Johnny drove her to the interview. Unfortunately, there had been a miscommunication, and two minutes into the interview Ashley learned that the position required a bachelor's degree. Johnny had already left for work and Ashley walked home in the rain because she was too embarrassed to stay at the site of the interview.

Ashley called me, screaming and infuriated, after this incident. When I suggested that the best option was to discuss the situation with her sister and brother-in-law, she agreed:

> Look, Ima tell Ma and tell Maria that Johnny don't have no say in how I run my life. I lost my job and I'm looking for another one, that don't mean that I should sit at home—that is not good for me. And who is he to say that it is right? I will tell them that I will pay for my own gas and I always pay for my own shit, so I should not have to be humiliated and run around in the rain and go through this.

We agreed that Ashley would calmly present her argument to the whole family. The hope of a fair argument alleviated Ashley's anger and provided some reparation for her damaged self-worth. However, after she reached home, Ashley called and informed me that her mother and sister were opposed to the idea of her challenging Johnny because he was the "only man" in the house and his support was essential. When I met Ashley that evening at her home, I thought she would be furious at Johnny, but she was not. Johnny was at the house, and although I could feel some tension between the two as we sat and chatted, Ashley said nothing harsh. I thought I might be imagining the strain between them, but later I saw Ashley tearing Johnny's face from a family photo in her room. The bond and cooperation among Ashley, Johnny, and Maria had suffered a massive blow with significant consequences for their family: for example, Ashley retaliated by declining to babysit her nephews. After the fight, she often adopted an aggressive disposition toward Johnny, and he did the same in return.

This close analysis of kinship ties among Port City youth challenges the simplistic view of the preoccupation with exchange of resources (or absence thereof) within kinship systems by recognizing the *costs* of exchange on intimate relations (see Table 2), as well as accompanying emotional work. In resource-poor families, members including siblings were often compelled to negotiate both material and emotional investments, engaging in complex and nuanced relational interactions. Exchange of resources within kinship networks often strained kinship ties, making them simultaneously resourceful and hostile. There were, therefore, costs of exchange on intimacy. Sibling relations entailed resentment, obligations, appreciation, love, anger, loyalty, mistrust, and trust.[16] Family dynamics played out in paradoxical ways, providing support for upward mobility and acting as sources of hostility and conflict.

As Port City youth navigated the ups and downs of family life, they also dreamed of their future, attempting to create and imagine families of their own. As we will see next, romantic relationships were central to the lives of young people in Port City.

4 Risky Love

When nigga treat his girl well, that nigga got class.

—Lexus Martin

On a sunny Saturday afternoon in May of 2011, Sandra, her boyfriend Alex, and I were sitting in the two-bedroom apartment Sandra shared with her mother, waiting for her mother to come home so we could all go to Dairy Queen for ice cream. Sandra and I sat on her bed while Alex lounged on an old armchair covered with a clean sheet, the sunlight from the window forcing him to squint. We chatted, moving swiftly from one topic to the next, including my hometown and boarding school in India, plastic surgery in the Dominican Republic, our employers, and girls at Port City High. While discussing their high school classmates, Sandra commented:

> That's what they be singing at school. Yeah, they be singing "All girls are hos yo mothafuckin' bros," I swear, the high school boys are mad ghetto and all they care about is getting laid. Alex is cool though, he is mature and not like the guys that he be hangin' with; he respects me. He plays ball and does his shit you know, and don't gangbang all the time. I mean sometime he make me mad though, you know, like foolin' around [generally, among the youth "foolin' around" ranged from sexual flirtation to some level of sexual intimacy]. I don't like when he does things like that. But there are bitches that like shit like that, you know, talking about baby daddies and sex and their inflated belly .... That's how so many women end up like this, with nothing.

Alex listened closely as Sandra sung his praises. His eyebrows moved up and down as they did whenever he gave something his undivided attention. He seemed embarrassed but could barely hide his smile, and I could tell he was extremely proud that Sandra did not lump him with the "gang-bangers." Sandra and Alex thought of themselves as different from some of their peers whose lives, they thought, were likely to be ruined by sex and pregnancy.

Romantic and sexual relationships are central to the coming-of-age experiences of youth everywhere. However, popular culture and media, public policy, and academic scholarship[1] alike have pathologized the romantic and sexual relationships of economically marginalized youth of color by constructing their sexualities as "risky."[2] These risk narratives present teen childbirth as inherently problematic and an epidemic in cities like Port City and treat black and Latina women like those in my study as sexually precocious, likely to drop out of school, and future burdens on the state.[3] They also construct black and brown men as predatory.[4] However, although a few of their teenage relatives and friends had children, none of the sixteen Port City youth became pregnant or were parents by the time I concluded my fieldwork in 2013 or when I checked in with them in 2016.[5]

Nevertheless, Port City youth subscribed to dominant narratives that cast early parenthood as an epidemic in marginalized communities.[6] Simultaneously, having been born in the 1990s, just like their middle-class counterparts, Port City youth were (explicitly and implicitly) influenced by feminist ideologies in their everyday lives.[7] Specifically, the young women strategically used the feminist ideals of independence, self-development, and self-respect to construct their own identities as agentic, careful, ambitious, and independent women who are morally different from and superior to the few of their peers who were young mothers. In the process, youth also sought the kinds of relationships they imagined would facilitate self-development and upward mobility, and symbolize self-respect. As a result, they tried to avoid men they imagined would be jobless or in jail, and they evaluated the men in their communities and their own chances of becoming pregnant in racialized and classed ways. In this way, they distanced themselves from the risk narratives about their sexuality and from their pregnant or parenting peers. While this distancing allowed the youth to construct unproblematic identities and manage risk narratives about their sexualities, it also created rifts in their community and disrupted relationships with their sisters and friends.[8]

Feminist ideologies, thus, intersected with risk narratives in complex ways in the everyday lives of Port City youth. In the end, enacting romance under constrains of poverty and risk narratives meant that while romantic and sexual relationships generated resources, connections, support, and transcendental emotions of romantic love for the youth, relationships were often hard to sustain and efforts to nourish the ideal relationship often jeopardized the youth's pathways to social mobility.

EARLY PARENTHOOD AS A SOCIAL PROBLEM

During my first month at the Port City Youth Center, an employee claimed: "Forty-eight percent of the youth here have STIs [sexually transmitted infections]. That's like [a] little ways from it becoming declared as an epidemic by CDC [Centers for Disease Control and Prevention], and half of them end up pregnant." She made this claim enthusiastically, as if offering me a thrilling topic: one that encompasses the potentially titillating subjects of teen sexuality, disease, and motherhood. While teen birthrates have remained higher in the big cities of this northeastern state than in the rest of the state, the teen pregnancy rate in urban areas has actually declined in recent years.[9] Still, in Port City, the local community, families, and the young people themselves collectively constructed pregnancy and early motherhood as a force keeping young women from leading rich and productive lives.

At Port City High, the school's sex education program utilized scare tactics that conflated sex, illness, and pregnancy. For example, in 2012, an HIV-positive woman was invited to present a lecture on the perils of sex and teen pregnancy. Angie's voice shook with fear and anger toward those who did not take the message seriously, as she summarized the talk: "[The presenter] looked like a fucking zombie, that's whatchu get for being a ho' ... and they [those who become pregnant] still don't get it." The same year, after Planned Parenthood distributed condoms in the school without the principal's approval, students were asked to return the condoms they had taken. The youth used humor to communicate their confusion about the incident. Curtis said, "I don't know why they took [them], though."

Several others nodded their heads in agreement. Then A. J., distancing herself from potential mothers, asserted that she thought the school asked students to return condoms "'Cause, yo, niggas never gonna know how to use that shit [condoms], and then come up with huge-ass bellies with their baby daddy in jail. Better not have sex if that's how you gonna end up!" Curtis agreed: "Yeah, yeah." In the absence of other explanations, the students reluctantly accepted this explanation.

The conflicting practices with which the school regulated youth's sexuality turned out to perplex the young people: they learned that sex, or unprotected sex, is "dangerous," then they were offered condoms through which to practice safe sex, and finally they were required to return the condoms, which was interpreted as an indication of authority's mistrust in youth's ability to practice safe sex. My conversations with school personnel on various occasions reflected these conflicting understandings about youth's sexuality. For example, during one "Beach Cleaning Day" in Port City where one high school teacher and I volunteered regularly, she told me, "Ahh, it's not just teaching, it's having to constantly make sure they don't go do things like get pregnant because then school is over . . . and I just don't get why they get pregnant. They know what sex can do, and, I mean, they can have sex. Then, if you end up pregnant, though, then maybe just protect yourself and don't do it [have sex]." The teacher acknowledged that youth have sexual desires and the right to enjoy their sexuality, but she also believed that they are not responsible enough and may end up becoming pregnant. Since the youth were deemed free but irresponsible, the only solution seemed to her to be constant vigilance to rein in the irresponsible behavior.

Other neighborhood organizations and institutions were similarly concerned with teen pregnancy and took measures to regulate youth's sexualities. Multiple neighborhood organizations in Port City working toward a variety of goals, including art training programs, college admission programs, antiviolence training programs, and an after-school care center, all intentionally and regularly repeated the significance of avoiding early motherhood to young people. During one community meeting, an older white lady who ran a nonprofit organization that provided antiviolence training for youth urged all organizations to collaborate in their efforts to facilitate marginalized youth's transition to adulthood through the avoidance of teen pregnancy. "If you make it to twenty without a child, you've achieved something, and to teach that should be all our goals, because if you're giving them skills, you have to give them opportunity to use skills instead of becoming mothers," she said. Other attendees of the meeting nodded their heads in agreement. As if becoming a mother automatically precludes any other possibilities.

To help teens avoid pregnancy, on the one hand, organizations offered access to information about birth control as well as the perils of early motherhood; on the other hand, they policed interactions between heterosexual romantic partners. One summer, a worker I had befriended at the Port City Youth Center asked me to accompany a group of high school students on a field trip organized by a nonprofit organization that focused on "youth development" in conjunction with the youth services. The accompanying adults were asked to remain alert for young men and women interacting outside of their supervision. The group leader asked me to look out for five specific young people and it seemed that each adult was assigned to watch a few specific youth. Initially, I did not fully realize what this supervision encompassed. As I ate lunch with one of the nonprofit workers and two youth, a student ran up to us and complained that a young couple had gone off behind the bushes: "They ran away there," she said, pointing. The nonprofit worker left her lunch on the table and hurriedly followed the young student to look for the couple. Ten minutes later, trying to catch her breath back at the lunch table, the nonprofit worker exclaimed, "Ah, can't let them out of sight, Ranita, or you end up with teen moms."

Organizations and institutions in Port City placed inordinate stress on preventing pregnancy among youth of color. They did so not only at the cost of recognition for other aspects of sexuality, but also by forgoing many other aspects of support for marginalized youth's transition to adulthood, including access to education and work.[10] Teachers, community leaders, and policy makers who embrace the teen parent epidemic idea overlook young women's multifaceted needs and desires.

REPRODUCING RISK NARRATIVES

The creation of a risk narrative concerning teen pregnancy was not restricted to external organizations; families and the youth also reproduced it, and often attributed their own misfortunes and struggles against poverty to early childbearing. Port City youth internalized local and national discourses that conflate sex with disease, pregnancy, and lack of self-respect.

Older siblings and mothers routinely warned the young women to avoid pregnancy. As shown in the preceding chapter, Ashley and her family created a discourse in which women who waited until after their early twenties to have children had smarter children. Families and youth negotiated dominant teen motherhood discourses precisely by creating narratives of their own while also reproducing dominant narratives.[11]

Those who became pregnant were often the subjects of concern and sympathy, but were also ridiculed by other young people. Some of the Port City youth also expressed their scorn for young women who might be thought of as "potential" teen mothers. One day at work, Lexus and A. J. caricatured a girl they thought was likely to become pregnant, acting out the following hypothetical situation:

A. J.:   Yo, I'm five weeks pregnant, ooooh [in a high-pitched voice], I'm going to tell my mother after Christmas or I won't get no presents; you wanna see my ultrasound pictures?

LEXUS: [laughing uncontrollably] I'm tellin' it in math class tomorrow everybody, but I don't know who's my baby father, oooh!

A. J.:   [laughing hysterically] Stop! Lexus! Relax, you making me get cramps, it's the baby moving, ouch!

LEXUS: 'Cause I'm really pregnant by my man, damn, oooooh! [abruptly stops laughing] For real though, it's crazy how all these girls get pregnant.

When I asked Lexus whether the friend they were impersonating was indeed pregnant, she responded: "No, but she will be. You don't know her. She a slut: she dates these gangbangers and don't even do work. Like she's always getting mad grades taken away [referring to losing grades for truancy]." A. J. added, "Like she even got a job at the mall where my cousin works, and she even got fired 'cause she was always wearing these tight-ass clothes and coming to work late."

The Port City youth participated in stigmatizing not only young parenting and pregnant women, but also the "potential" teen mothers: young women who spent time with bona fide "gangbangers" and did not display an interest or ambition with regard to educational achievements or commit to regular work. They constructed young women who did not desire to become socially mobile through higher education and financial independence—that is, those who did not adopt a middle-class "self-development"-oriented identity—as likely "victims" of early motherhood. The youth interpreted inequalities reflected in discriminatory practices at school and work as indications of potential "victimhood," explaining structural inequalities through personal shortcomings and reproducing dominant risk narratives.

Why did the Port City youth believe that some young women were more likely to become pregnant than others? Some claimed that their peers who became pregnant did so to gain attention. To an extent, this claim reflects a position that scholars have long maintained: a life that lacks meaning leads young women to seek status and fulfillment via motherhood. Meaning, for those making the judgment, can be achieved through ambitions. As we watched a Port City High basketball game, Gigi pointed to a girl from her class and said, "She is one of them who wanna talk about baby daddies and show off her pregnant-ass belly in gym class like it's some sorta fashion. These bitches be stupid!" Then she started laughing loudly. Sandra commented:

> They be thinking, "Oooooh, Ima show off and talk about my baby daddy to you in gym class," and I'm thinking "Yeah, bitch, yo ass gonna be poor for long!" They got no self-respect, that's what it is. It's not always that they don't know how to use a fucking condom [in reference to our earlier discussion about condom use]. They be teaching you that shit with [a] banana on YouTube. Sometimes they want to show off their baby daddies. There are some who don't know things, but most just don't have self-respect.

Gigi responded, distancing herself from the fate of young parents, "For me, I wanna do my nails and my job and college. Here I am planning for college and all these girls wanna do is change diaper[s]. Like what the fuck you want that for?"

During one of our days at the mall with several of the young women, I asked what they meant by "self-respect." Sandra answered, "When you have, like, ambitions and you wanna do something with your life." Alize added:

Like, these girls, they getting pregnant all the time 'cause they don't got work or money. Like, I can't get pregnant 'cause I'm busting my ass trynna make it in the world, you know, like move up in the world. Some them niggas don't mind having their baby daddy in jail and just like them [the young mothers] sitting on their ass changing diapers. When you have respect, you wanna make your own life.

The pervasiveness of racialized and classed interpretations of the early parenthood "epidemic" was reflected in the youth's understandings of young parenthood as blocking mobility opportunities, as well as in their account of those confronting limited opportunities as potential teen parents. These young women thought that early motherhood was problematic because it created daily constraints to socioeconomic mobility and distanced the prospects of a better future involving college degrees and white-collar jobs, and even precluded them from "enjoying life."[12] Although scholars have demonstrated that postponing motherhood is not as socioeconomically beneficial for economically marginalized women as it is for middle-class women.[13] As we will see later in this book, when the Port City youth found themselves in a socioeconomic position similar to their peers who had children, they constructed postponing childbirth (along with other racialized and classed markers) as an indicator of mobility.

MANAGING THE PREGNANCY PANIC

Policing the Bodies of Loved Ones

In the spring of 2012, Ashley's fear that one of her sisters would give birth in her teen years increased when Siete and Betsy began to engage in what Ashley considered inappropriate behavior. Siete had started seeing a young black man named Donald. There were bad feelings between the two families: Donald's mother disliked Siete and Siete's family disliked Donald. Donald was known for selling drugs and having been arrested a few times; he had dropped out of high school a few years earlier. Because neither of their families approved of them spending time together, Siete started to skip work to spend time with Donald. Then Betsy started skipping school to see a friend of Donald's. Siete called the school pretending to be their mother to excuse Betsy.

The girls continued in this way for a few weeks before Ashley found out about it through one of her acquaintances from a previous job where Siete now worked. In order to find out the truth, Ashley went through her sisters' phones one night while they slept. On Betsy's phone she found a video of Betsy and her boyfriend (that Ashley didn't approve of), as well as texts Siete and Betsy exchanged about plans to skip school and work. When I called Ashley to chat the next morning, she whispered over the phone, "Shit is about to go down. You better come here."

While the girls were at school and work, Ashley discussed the situation with her mother, older sister, and me, and the family decided to confront the two girls that evening. Although I was close to the family by this point, I decided to not stay at the house during the confrontation. That night, Ashley called me crying and furious and told me that things had gotten out of hand—her sisters were very unapologetic and had to be "jumped and beaten a little." Siete and Betsy packed a garbage bag full of clothes, shoes, and makeup and ran away. The family did not hear from them for the next three days. Ashley worried about her sisters' safety but was also angry that they had the audacity to leave home.

Three days later, the family discovered that Siete and Betsy had been staying with a friend and her father. Then Siete started calling the house phone and hanging up when someone answered. She told friends that she missed her nephews and was very eager to return home. The sisters also asked for permission to return. Over the following days, most of my conversations with Ashley and her family revolved around the incident.

A few days after she learned where her sisters were staying, Ashley and I were driving through downtown when we saw Siete walking. Ashley slowed the car, put her head out the window, and told Siete, "You know they're [her nephews] starting to forget you, 'cause they're small and everything"; she then drove off. She turned to me and said, "She gotta feel bad, you know, but I know she does already. But Betsy is the bitch, she's not repenting. I bet this is gonna make her feel like shit." I asked Ashley whether she would ask her sisters to return home. Somewhat irritated at my lack of moral condemnation of her sisters, she commented, "You know Betsy was sleeping around with guys? Including this guy called Nick, who sleeps with everyone and goes around saying, 'Oh, I banged Betsy right after this other girl who just came over,' alright?" I looked away embarrassed as Ashley grew angrier about my reluctance to openly side with her. She continued:

> You know Betsy tries to act all saintly, like she is on a pedestal judging all other girls and calling them hos, whereas she has been sleeping around and fucking everyone all this while, behind our back. And girls hate her, not because she is some hot shit, but because they know she can fuck their man anytime. Johnny [Maria's boyfriend] used to tell Maria he suspects her but they fought and many times broke up over this. Sometimes Johnny feeds her [Betsy], taking away from his own sons' mouth and she [Betsy] almost made them break up . . . . we have to pay if she [Betsy] ends up with a baby and some gangbanger baby daddy.

After another two days passed, Ashley told me that she and Maria decided not to let Siete and Betsy in their house for another week. I asked how her mother felt about this decision, and Ashley responded:

> How could Betsy do this to Maria and Johnny? They do so much for them and Siete? How could she do this? Because of your [her sisters'] selfish act you want to put our family down? Do yourself a favor and be a woman and talk to us instead of sending messages and pretending you are an angel. You're far from that. I hope you get everything coming to you.

When I spent some time at the family's house later that week, Ashley's mother tried to convince Ashley, Johnny, and Maria to let Siete and Betsy return home.

ASHLEY'S MOTHER: Ranita, you think it's good for young girls to stay outside home?

[I blushed and looked down at my phone or the floor.]

ASHLEY: [looking at her mother] Look, you want them to learn something about life? If you want them to end up like you with [a] hundred baby daddies then it's up to you. But if you don't wanna take care of grandchildren then you better fuckin' teach them something alright.

ASHLEY'S MOTHER: No one's gettin' pregnant before their time in this house.

MARIA: Your fear will come true if you don't tell them that you mean business. Their ass gettin' kicked to the street because they deserve to end up on the street. That's where babies and mamas without daddies and money end up.

Here Ashley and Maria defined their sisters as pregnancy risks. They drew on race, gender, and class hierarchies that define "good" girls as those who avoid promiscuous sexual activity, especially with "bad boys." Because her sister was sexually active, Ashley claimed that she risked early motherhood.[14] This incident illustrates the significant measures the young women were willing to take to manage the risk of pregnancy, punishing those—even (perhaps especially) loved ones—who they believed were "at risk" of making poor decisions. Siete and Betsey returned home a little over two weeks later at the behest of their mother and sisters, who began to miss them. Paradoxically, the construction of an early parent archetype, even through a benevolent desire to protect opportunities for upward mobility, sometimes threatened relationships between individuals and made them hostile.

Abortion

Lorena Garcia, in her 2012 book *Respect Yourself, Protect Yourself: Latina Girls and Sexual Identity*, discusses, among other things, young Latina women's agency in practicing safe sex. In Port City, too, many young women desired to use birth control to prevent pregnancy, and were sometimes open to abortion.

Seventeen-year-old Jona, a friend of Siete's, became pregnant by her seventeen-year-old boyfriend Mike. Ashley and her sisters considered Jona a member of the family. Ashley had once mentioned that her family liked Jona because she was a "loyal" person and had "done a lot for them." Jona was terrified when the home pregnancy test was positive, and when Ashley gave me the news one cold winter afternoon at work (we both worked at the Port City Youth Center at that time), she said that Jona was adamant about not having the baby. Ashley spent her entire shift that afternoon on the phone with Jona, telling her not to worry and offering to schedule an abortion. She reassured Jona, "Don't worry, Ima take care of this for you." Neither of us was scheduled to work for the next few days, and when we returned, Ashley told me that when she visited a Planned Parenthood clinic with Jona, Mike, and Siete, Jona was told she would need to present proof of income to obtain an abortion at minimal cost.

Jona was afraid to tell her mother about the situation because she feared her mother would be furious and might throw her out of the house. Jona's boyfriend earned minimum wage at a part-time job at a retail store. Ashley told me, "I gave her some money and Mike gave some; my mom put in some too, 'cause she [Jona] don't need a baby right now." Much later I learned that Jona's mother had found out about the pregnancy through another friend of Jona's and did not react in the way everyone had anticipated: she even agreed to pay Ashley back. Jona's story shows that many young women of Port City were very serious about avoiding early childbearing. This desire was not limited to talk—they often acted on their belief that teen pregnancy placed formidable constraints on a young woman's well-being and future life prospects. A network of support formed around getting Jona an abortion as everyone rallied for her.

Self Policing

The young women not only policed other women's bodies and acted to reduce their own risk of pregnancy, but they often understood pregnancy risk in racialized ways. A. J. decided to go to Planned Parenthood to obtain birth control and asked me to drive her there. I casually inquired what type of birth control she had planned on getting and she revealed that she wanted "the rod"[15]:

A. J.:   Ima get the rod 'cause one of my cuz [cousin] she got it too. And I don't want it to come out of my lady parts like whenever. I want the most sure-shot one.

RANITA: Oh, okay.

A. J.:   I'm dumb, 'cause like Gio [her boyfriend at the time] he crazy, that nigga! I'm not even getting' laid! 'Cause he be wanting to take it slow and it's like I'm trynna get into his panties, he got [a] fuckin' chastity belt on, that nigga! I told him the other day, I wanna have sex, but apparently he wants to take it slow and sex means a lot to him and whatnot! I don't even know why Ima have to get birth control, but I told him I will get it anyway 'cause he be like, "No get it" and all. But I don't wanna take no chances and end up with a baby daddy . . . . All these bitches in school with no-good boys. Like, I'm mad scared of that shit, honestly, 'cause I think that's what's wrong with our community, like [the] Latino community, all these girls gettin' pregnant and we stuck in the ghetto.

RANITA: But your sisters are not pregnant.

A. J.: Yeah, they'll be soon, you'll see. It's crazy how it is. Like we [are] like rats giving birth. That's why I wanna get this rod thing in my body so you know this shit can't happen to me like with condoms and pills and whatnot. 'Cause you don't even know if they're wearing it or not.

When we reached Planned Parenthood, A. J. checked in while I waited in the seating area. About forty-five minutes later, she was called in by a nurse's aide; she returned to the waiting area without the birth control she had wanted. She explained:

The lady doctor she just told me I can use condoms and come in later for the other thing 'cause I don't have my mother's Social Security and her proof of income and whatnot. They need that. And my new job they might give me full-time and health insurance, I'm gonna use that then.

The young women who policed their own bodies in order to prevent pregnancy understood their risk as mediated by several factors. For example, they imagined that membership in certain communities automatically put them at risk, and sometimes even expressed that pregnancy was "in their stars" (fated to occur). The young people likely drew from larger organizations and institutions in understanding the risk of pregnancy. Schools and nonprofits spoke in racially coded ways about how young women in some communities were more likely to give birth; for example, a teacher once told Angie that women like her would probably become mothers before they went to college.

ROMANCE AND SOCIAL MOBILITY

For the Port City youth, finding a partner meant looking for someone who would lower their chances of early parenthood and raise their chances of upward mobility.[16] Judging who this elusive "right person" could be was a complex process, based on gendered, racialized, and classed ways of understanding indicators of social mobility.

Looking for Good Boys

Like young people elsewhere, several of the youth in my study were involved in romantic relationships. The Port City women stated that they viewed marriage as a pathway out of poverty. Therefore, serious and long-term relationships were reserved for men who appeared to be respectable and committed, men who seemed less likely to be absentee fathers or husbands, and more likely to have decent jobs and college degrees. When the young women were in relationships with men who held jobs, earned at least average grades in school, and aspired to attend college—factors that made them desirable dating partners—they devoted a reasonable amount of effort (which was straining on them, as we will see later in the chapter) to sustaining the relationship and imagined that they were less likely to get pregnant. In contrast, when they were with men who did not meet these criteria, the women remained cautious, viewing their partners as predators.

Alize was not very confident, but hoped for the best and liked to go where life took her. She took immense pride in being Latina. She never had a well-thought-out plan for the future, but she took advantage of every opportunity that came her way when it came to "moving up in the world." Alize liked to listen to music and sing out loud. "I know I'm no Rihanna but I don't care whatchu think," she jokingly said to Curtis one day when he asked her to stop singing at work. Alize did not like to dress up like the other girls; she hardly wore makeup and mostly wore only a pair of skinny jeans and various sweatshirts. Occasionally, she would also wear a cap. However, for her prom night Alize went all the way to New York City to buy a dress, and she spent $400, her entire savings at the time with some additional borrowed money. After prom night, she decided that she had been the "prettiest one there with the nicest dress" and said that she had finally outshone the others at least in this one thing.

Alize had been dating Ben, a young black man who was very invested in attending college, for just two months, but already talked frequently about their future together. She described a life that included a house, a car, full-time jobs, and children. As we drove to her mother's home one day, Alize pointed to a big white house and told me, "Yo, Ima marry him [Ben] and live in a house like that!" Alize and Ben spent a great deal of time together after school and even on the weekend. Alize's mother was very fond of Ben and often gave them money to go out for lunch or dinner or invited him to the family's home. Although Alize considered Ben a desirable partner, when Ben moved out of state to attend college, the relationship fizzled out and eventually ended because neither of them had enough money to travel to see each other frequently.

Almost nine months later and a few months after she had graduated from high school, Alize took a full-time, minimum-wage job. Around this time she started dating Mike, who was two years older than her, had dropped out of high school, and was an aspiring b-boy or break-dancer. During a conversation about this relationship, Alize commented, "Nah, I'm not gonna give my cherry [have sexual intercourse] so easy! Girl's gotta protect her thing, you know. I'm no ghetto girl who sleeps with wannabe nigga rappers, and just be stuck in the ghetto. I wanna do my nails, not change diapers." That winter, as we sat on the stairs of her home, which were covered with snow that had turned to slush, Alize warmed her hands with a cup of coffee and reflected on her love life: "It was something else with Ben, he was serious, know what I'm sayin'? Like about his future and whatnot. Not like Mike." This was the typical attitude among other young women in my study. All of the women at one point or another acknowledged the importance of having a romantic partner who "had a future and was not ghetto." The risk of blocked opportunities depended on the kind of men they were involved with.

Yet Alize and some other young Port City women often formed relationships with men they perceived as less desirable. Alize remained with Mike because she sometimes felt lonely, and liked to have someone who cared for her. Yet, in the thick of relationships, young women tended to weigh the value of these relationships against their goal of having a stable, two-income family. To sustain these relationships they took on added burdens that impacted their mental and physical health as well as performance in school and work.

How to Judge Commitment

For the young women, an ideal romantic partner was someone who asked them out, arranged and paid for dates, and gave them gifts—fulfilling the traditional gendered role of a provider.[17] The successful performance of the male provider role was considered a mark of a "cultivated" individual, and young women imagined that being with such men would increase their prospects of upward mobility.

The young women thought of Port City men as greedy and potentially penniless, and of women as being vulnerable to being used by men who saw them as a way to gain material goods. For this reason, women often advised other women to gauge a man's level of devotion and commitment by the gifts he gave them and whether or not he paid for their dates. When Ashley's mother started dating a man from the neighborhood, Ashley immediately warned her about the importance of "feelin' him out." She told her mother to make sure "he's not just having fun" by evaluating the kind of gift he gave her on Valentine's Day: "If he like you, he gonna give you something nice or do something special." When the same man stole money from the family, Ashley reminded her mother of the warning.

Engaging in courtship rituals was an important way to ensure a man's worth and commitment, which was crucial for the future security of the romantic relationship. The young women often maintained that their friends, families, and neighbors faced specific economic constraints because they had chosen the "wrong man"—someone who would end up without job and money. At one of the basketball games, Gigi pointed to a girl from her class from a distance and said, "She is one of them who wanna talk about baby daddies!" Sandra added, "They be thinking, 'Ooooh, my boo this, my boo that. Girl, your boo don't even get you Subway! I'm sayin' if he don't even care for you or treat you right now, how you expect him to be a good baby daddy?" Gigi replied:

> Yeah, most of these niggas don't do what they supposed to do, you know? Like take me out for [a] movie and dinner and whatnot, I don't even pay no mind to you otherwise. I'm gonna pick my man right, I'm not getting stuck in Port City while his ass in jail, and I'm feeding his baby.

The young women of Port City believed there was a direct link between a man's current behavior within a romantic relationship and his potential as a secure provider, and they judged this based on gendered roles as well as racialized and classed stereotypes.

Women who gave their boyfriends too many material things, on the other hand, also risked being viewed by other youth as "needy" (needing too much attention) or even "slutty" because they, in some ways, fulfilled a man's role (the provision of material resources and gifts). One day as Lexus, her friend Chanel, Siete, and I spent time together after work, Chanel complained incessantly that her boyfriend did not acknowledge their relationship in front of his friends and only paid attention to her when they were by themselves. Lexus and Siete remained quiet, offering only the briefest of replies and subtly indicating their disinterest in the conversation. After Chanel left, however, the two had much to say about the situation. Lexus commented:

> If you buying a nigga clothes, hats, and whatnot and you don't even go out, then of course he gonna keep you around just so he could get more stuff. 'Cause if he really liked you, wouldn't he wife you up? So he probably don't like you that much, he just like that he getting stuff from you. But it's your fault if you buying him everything. She mad slutty though, she wants attention.

The Rare Puerto Rican Good Guy

Other young women in Port City took on long-term burdens when they imagined that shouldering these responsibilities would strengthen their romantic ties with the men they considered desirable. Ashley and her boyfriend Paul had been seeing each other for almost two years and only interrupted their relationship when Paul moved to Florida to live with his father and stepmother. Paul's brother Frank, who was fourteen years old at the time, moved to Florida as well. The boys' father and stepmother did not send Frank to school after he arrived in Florida.

Paul contacted Ashley and asked whether his brother could stay with her family and attend school in Port City until Paul could make other arrangements. After arguing with her mother about the issue, Ashley agreed, and Frank returned to Port City to live with Ashley's family and finish high school. Caring for Frank proved burdensome for Ashley, who was taking two classes at the local community college. Because her mother

did not approve of Frank living with the family, Ashley was solely responsible for meeting his needs—she picked him up and dropped him off at
school, and bought his clothes. Despite all the obstacles to maintaining a
stable relationship with Paul, Ashley found it difficult to break up with
him. Explaining why she continued the relationship in the face of such
extensive demands, Ashley told me:

> Port City is full of ghetto-ass niggas. You seen how it is? He [Paul] is nice
> and respects me, and my family, you know? I'm just showing him that I'm
> valuable, so he know my worth . . . . In Port City, otherwise, you gotta find
> white guys 'cause all them Puerto Rican ones are useless. People like Paul [a
> desirable Puerto Rican young man] are rare.

One weekend Frank and a friend went to another friend's mother's
house in a neighboring town so that their band could practice. Frank did
not return, and neither Ashley nor Paul could reach him all weekend. Paul
called Ashley and told her his honest opinion, blaming her for Frank's
disappearance. Ashley lamented: "Ranita, what am I gonna do? I can't
find him nowhere and Paul thinks I chased that nigga out of my house
'cause I didn't want him here no more, but you know what I done for him."
I was at Ashley's place that night when she called Paul; I told him we were
looking for Frank and that Ashley was very worried. No one heard from
Frank until Monday night, when he returned.

I was at Ashley's when Frank knocked on the door and then walked into
the house without saying anything to anyone. Ashley screamed: "I wanna
talk! Get yo ass down here!" (he had gone upstairs); Frank shouted back,
"You come up!" Ashley began to rant, saying that she had done him a favor
by letting him stay in the house, and accusing him and Paul of taking
advantage of her and her family just because she loved Paul so much. After
about fifteen minutes, Frank came downstairs and began to talk in a calm
yet stern voice:

FRANK: I wanna do whatever I like and that's what I been doing all my life, and
         now I gotta dress up in the bathroom and can't even walk naked, and I
         don't even like the food you cook here and I got no room.

ASHLEY: [cutting him off] You don't put [in] no money and you a guest here.
         Women lived here originally and you and my cousins are guests and

there is a mattress in the living room, live there or do something with the basement. Put a TV in, you can't not put anything in the box and ask. I give you piece of my bread so you can go to school and all that.

Frank quickly went back upstairs and Ashley said [turning to me], "Nigga woulda busted some comeback if you were not here."

The next day Ashley told me that Frank had thrown a tantrum and tried to beat her up. When Ashley had called Paul, Frank called him names and hung up on him; after that, Ashley kicked Frank out of the house. Frank had no choice but to return to Florida, although his brother had warned him the household was not peaceful. A few days later Paul broke up with Ashley, saying he did not see himself returning to Port City any time soon. Ashley first tried to make plans to move to Florida permanently, and when that did not work out, she attempted to plan a trip to visit Paul, but these plans also fell through. Ashley reflected on this series of events:

I dreamed of getting bit by [a] spider [a] few days before all this shit went down—like you remember when the shit went down with Frank? It [the dream] means someone will start hating you. I known all this time that bad things will happen to me and now Paul's gone. I am going down.

Ashley drew on racialized ideologies, imagining an "acceptable" Puerto Rican life partner as rare and thinking she would be hard-pressed to find another partner like Paul. Her attitude added emotional and resource burdens on her. She explained to me that she wanted to marry a Puerto Rican man who "understood her culture," but "all Puerto Ricans in Port City [were] ghetto" and she "did not want to end up like ghetto girls who like to get pregnant." Port City's school personnel and nonprofit workers also perpetuated dominant narratives as they continuously constructed young men of color in the community as potentially violent and not invested in the labor market. For example, as we will see in chapter 5, the youth center staff and other nonprofit workers often organized "nonviolence" training, claiming that Port City youth needed to learn discipline before they could acquire and maintain jobs or go to college. These attitudes filtered through to the young women themselves and their views about their community's young men.

BEING A GOOD GUY UNDER THE
CONSTRAINTS OF POVERTY

While Port City men desired to fulfill traditional gender roles by arranging dates with their romantic and sexual partners, picking them up, and paying for them, it was hard to enact romance under the constraints of poverty. The men did not have cars, money, or phones and their financial situation impeded their ability to demonstrate that they were suitable partners who loved their girlfriends.

Gigi was approximately five feet and seven inches tall and well-built. She liked to wear makeup, especially mascara and eyeliner: "eyes are what make you," she said. Gigi did her homework most of the time, and she went to work. Gigi had lived with her mother in New Jersey until she was about thirteen, before moving in with her father, stepmother, and younger half brother in Port City when her mother's drug problem worsened. Her stepmother was a nurse's aide at the local hospital, and her father cooked at a small local restaurant that had five tables and made three entrees. When her parents worked late, Gigi took care of the household and cooked food for the entire family. She shared her room with her brother in their two-bedroom house, which was in a shabby neighborhood near a housing project. She affectionately called her little brother "fatman." The Port City youth thought of Gigi as somewhat childish. Sandra said, "She can be mature if she wants to but she is always talking in a baby voice and like being mad loud and obnoxious," and the other youth nodded in agreement. Alize added, "She kind of cute and she knows it and that's why she acts like that." Gigi made strong judgments against those who became pregnant or did not work, but others also judged Gigi for being too loud and judgmental and "sitting on a high horse," as Ashley put it.

One afternoon, as Gigi and I were doing homework at her house, we drifted into a discussion of romance, love, and pregnancy among the young women in her school. She agreed to let me record some of our conversation; the tape recorder was lying on the bed between us. Gigi's stepmother, father, and brother had gone to Six Flags, a local amusement park, and then planned to visit her grandmother (her father's foster mother) in a neighboring town.

Gigi stayed home primarily because she had a date with Chris, a boy from her school. They had started seeing each other a few weeks earlier but until this point had mostly spent time together at school. This would be their first formal date. Gigi showed me what seemed like a hundred pictures on her cellphone while I struggled to remain focused. I had met Chris only once before, when I was at the high school to pick up Siete who had introduced us in passing. I put some finishing touches on Gigi's nails, which she had carefully painted herself the night before. I confessed my incompetence but she guided me thoroughly and efficiently. Then Gigi put on false eyelashes, applied lipstick, changed into her favorite blue tank top and black leggings, put her hair up in a bun, and took a number of selfies while scrutinizing her outfit and makeup.

"When is he picking you up?" I asked. Gigi responded in her usual high-pitched, enthusiastic, and endearing tone, "You ask mad questions, I don't know." She continued, "I don't know, but we gonna go to the movies and then ice cream and then to the pier. Can't believe it's raining though. But he picking me up near his place. You gotta drop me there." "Yeah, sure," I responded. When Chris hadn't contacted Gigi after another hour, she called him and left a message, "Babe, can you hit me up soon please." Chris called back about ten minutes later and I recorded Gigi's side of the conversation:

I'm fine, I just wanna know what time you want me to go out there 'cause I'm home and Ranita is waiting to drop me off.

[Chris's response]

Well, it's not pouring and I don't really care but if you don't wanna go anywhere 'cause of the rain then I will just see you another time, babe.

[Chris's response]

Whachu think?

[Chris's response]

Okay, where you gonna meet me and what you mean leave at the time?

As Gigi hung up the phone, she seemed angry and turned to me, complaining: "What the fuck? He is like 'Oooh, you still wanna come here? It's pouring.' Like I can see it's pouring, nigga, but if you don't wanna see me just say it. He is like 'Oh you gotta transfer [on the bus] on your way back and this and that.'" " So are you seeing him or no?" I asked. "Nigga betta call me back. I don't know, he said if Carrie scoops him up we can go to the mall, but how we gonna go otherwise, I don't know," she responded. Gigi remained angry and upset the rest of the evening as we listened to some music and she painted my nails. The plan did not work out.

A few days later, I ran into Chris at the Port City Youth Center where he was attending the college prep program. "Hey, I'm Gigi's friend, what's up? What're you doing here?" I asked. "For the college thing," he responded. After chatting briefly, Chris told me why their planned date had not worked out the night I was supposed to give Gigi a ride:

> It's not like that. None of my boys were even free then and it was crazy out. You seen it that day? I was gonna drive her around. Nigga is supposed to do that for his girl, no? But I got no car, and none of my boys were free then, what was I supposed to do?

The experience of being unable to maintain a relationship because of a lack of resources was ubiquitous among the young men of Port City. When Franklin Junior was unable to call his girlfriend from work one day, he expressed his frustration about how his lack of resources constrained his relationship: "Damn, man, I feel like an asshole. Wish I had a phone, then things can be easier. Why do I have to be like this? What the fuck?" On another occasion, Donte called me to ask for a favor: "Can you help me 'cause I'm tryin' to leave my crib to see my girl and I would really be grateful if you could help me an' give me a ride to Rockville. I really wouldn't be askin' if the buses ran on Sundays." "Sure, I can get there in an hour or so," I said. "Ehhh hmm, my girl gotta babysit later though, but yeah, that's cool. Hit me up when you here though," he responded. As the young men of Port City sought to fulfill the role of the provider in courtships, they faced significant resource constraints. These limitations gave rise to seemingly trivial and yet regular, visible, and ultimately significant challenges within the everyday enactment of romantic relationships. While Chris and Gigi were able to move past this incident and his seeming digression from his "manly" duties, these regular, if minimal, paradoxes of sustaining a romantic relationship in the context of traditional gender ideologies led to individual-level frustration and even anguish, and often had a cumulative effect of eroding romantic ties as minor annoyances made relationships unstable.

WOMEN SUSTAIN LOVE AND DREAMS

The young women of Port City wanted to attend college, work, and become socially mobile while looking for romantic and sexual partners who were on a similar path. This aspiration was far from simple. Normative gender beliefs in the United States have long held that women desire love, romantic relationships, and marriage; Laura Hamilton and Elizabeth Armstrong call it the "relational imperative." Over the past several decades, an additional norm surrounding women's behavior has emerged: women's increased participation in higher education and the labor force has been accompanied by a societal commitment to the independence and economic empowerment of women. The presence of these conflicting norms means that women must now navigate two conflicting cultural messages in the relationship sphere—they are expected to pursue their careers and engage in what Laura Hamilton and Elizabeth Armstrong call the "self-development imperative," but also to get married and form families. These contradictory forces have influenced the daily lives of the Port City youth. The young women struggled to complete college-level academic work and to balance school with part-time or full-time work while attempting to form and nourish meaningful romantic ties both at the individual emotional level and as a context within which to secure a better future. Under the constraints of poverty, women often experienced significant strain in their daily lives.[18]

We were sitting and chatting in Angie's grandparents' home one evening. Exhausted yet enthusiastic, Angie decided to "do her nails" after all. Her grandparents were old and had health problems, and housekeeping was entirely Angie's responsibility. As was the case most evenings, Angie had come home from school and work exhausted, but she was a "clean freak"— so she washed the dishes, mopped the floor, and dusted the little furniture they had, and then she organized her closet. Then Angie began to contemplate whether she should dress up to see her boyfriend. The young man she was dating at that time had many of the qualities she wanted in her "man." He was "ambitious, worked hard, and didn't gangbang," she said. Angie was exhausted that night, so it took her longer than usual to complete her chores and get ready to go see her boyfriend. She had started work at 8:00 a.m., went straight to the local community college after work, and attended classes until 6:00 p.m. Most days she took an almost two-hour bus ride to meet her boyfriend, who did not have a car, and spend time with him. That morning, an exhausted Angie had called me and apologetically asked for a ride, detailing the many stresses she faced:

Ah, I feel so needy. And you know I don't like to do this but can you please, please give me a ride? I feel like shit; went to work early today 'cause my boss gave me extra hours and then been here [the community college] all day and I didn't even eat nothing. Think my gastric thing is acting up again. And now I gotta go meet him [her boyfriend]. Like, I wanna go home and pass out, but I promised I'd cook for him, and I don't wanna not do it 'cause you know, he real nice to me too.

When I had picked Angie up, she continued to explain and expressed her guilt for asking me for a ride. She said, "I gotta get a car. 'Cause if I wanna like work and do all this shit, I can't even do it. Like my body won't let me."

Angie's relationship with her boyfriend would eventually become unstable as the demands of work, school, and spending time together became overwhelming. Both the relationship and her studies became burdensome. When Angie could not pay her phone bill and her phone was disconnected, setting up a time to meet her boyfriend became a significant annoyance. Not having a car meant relying on the bus and friends for transportation. Angie complained jokingly one day: "Yo, like I'm in class and thinkin' of my boo and then like I'm eating ice cream with him and thinkin' how I'm gonna get my ass to class tomorrow. Real talk, real talk. Angie got a hard life." Even though Angie's penchant for humor eased the strain of addressing these obstacles, her relationship did not survive. Angie and her boyfriend broke up after having countless small quarrels on a daily basis.

As young women sought to reconcile the often conflicting demands of school, work, and romantic relationships by forming relationships that were well suited to their own future educational careers, they were frequently stigmatized and shamed for focusing on stability and upward mobility rather than emotions. Gigi's case provides an illuminating example. Gigi was involved with a boy from her high school who occasionally cheated on her and did not treat her with the respect she desired. He often got into fights with other boys in school, publicly discussed their sex life, and was reluctant to use condoms—things that bothered Gigi. He dropped out of high school to sell drugs and do odd construction jobs. When Gigi discovered that he had begun seeing an older girl, she was devastated that he had cheated on her yet again, and she ended their relationship.

A few months later, when Gigi became involved with Chris, his aspirations to attend college influenced Gigi. Every time I was with them, Chris spent most of the time talking about college or working toward college acceptance by studying for the SATs, writing his college essay, and seeking information about financial aid and scholarships. Gigi was able to access crucial information, such as how to obtain fee waivers for college applications and where to take SAT practice tests, from Chris. She modeled her own college preparation on Chris's well-constructed plan and they eventually attended the same college.

When Gigi's ex-boyfriend asked her to rekindle their relationship, she explained to him and her friends that Chris was a better influence on her. In response, Gigi was criticized for being "selfish," "slutty," and "opportunistic." Drawing on normative gender beliefs that women must desire love, one of her friends argued, "Love comes first. Why you care who goes to school, that's crazy." Gigi also sometimes thought of herself as selfish and wrestled with feelings of guilt:

> You know, Ranita, sometimes I feel some type of way about this thing. What if he [her ex-boyfriend] does love me? But I don't wanna be stuck in this fucking ghetto-ass place for life. Like, I don't want my ass to be broke as hell like my parents. I gotta go to college 'cause there ain't no work that's good if you don't go to college.

Whoever the young women chose, plans of mobility often did not work out due to larger socioeconomic constrains they themselves faced. Gigi continued to work on campus during her first semester at the same college as Chris. However, she was unable to keep her scholarship after her first semester and therefore returned to Port City. Gigi started talking about enrolling at Port City Rivers Community College, and went as far as to visit the campus. Then one day, Gigi met and started dating another boy at Port City Rivers who was planning on moving to Texas and said to me:

> I'm about to move to Texas, Ranita. I keep tellin' everyone: "Guys, if you move to Texas, I promise you won't have to work two jobs! CT is way too expensive, when will anyone understand that?" And, my friend is like, I would love to move there, but my boyfriend won't ever leave. So I'm like, don't let anyone hold you back from a better life, that's not love. And having a hundred babies is not love.

Gigi moved with her new boyfriend and took on two jobs in Texas: "I got a good GPA and I did all AP classes and I got a high SAT score, more than all these niggas and they at Port City Rivers. Ima make some money and then I can fucking do what I want and go to whatever colleges (I discuss this complex relationship between school and work in the next chapter), like who feels like going through this shit now, when I can be making like eight dollars an hour, and I love my man, so Ima support him," Gigi told me and a few others one night before leaving. She now lives in Texas with her boyfriend and works a minimum-wage job at a bakery franchise.

The Port City youth attempted to negotiate the conflicting demands of romantic relationships. On the one hand, they tried to use them to forge a better future. On the other hand, their choices of a partner sometimes conflicted with their individual feelings of romantic love, as well as traditional gender ideologies which underline that men should be active agents directing the relationship and providing for women, and women should be passive recipients. Even as youth strategically navigated these conflicts, the lack of economic resources made it hard to balance school, work, and romance.

LOVE, A BROKEN HEART, AND A THORNY PATH FORWARD

Love can be an uncontrollable emotion. Romance may not be reduced to the end result of a series of cognitive decisions, but includes what anthropologist Charles Lindholm described as the "subjective idealization" of the partner.[19] For the Port City youth, romance was undoubtedly a site of strong emotional connection and passion, and building romantic relationships under the constraints of poverty sometimes led to heart-break and devastation.

Franklin Junior was a great dancer. Somewhat shy but always ready to bust a move, Franklin was well liked by his peers for his jovial disposition. Called both Franklin and Franklin Junior, he was passionate about his dance team and determined to make it as a b-boy. His laugh was contagious, and he fell in love easily. He was afraid of his mother's temper, and he had a kind and gentle disposition. For example, when Cassy said she "felt ugly" when her boyfriend did not contact her for days, Franklin listened patiently and tried to convince her of her beauty. He often borrowed money from his friends but was also quick to pay it back and help his friends in need.

Franklin Junior's girlfriend Leslie broke off their relationship in September 2011. Two weeks later, Leslie started seeing an older boy. He had a car and dropped her off at school, work, and other places she needed to go. Leslie's cousin worked with Franklin and related all the details of this new relationship. Leslie told her cousin that things would never work out with Franklin because they lived so far apart and her parents did not like him. She concluded that there was no point in having a relationship when they rarely saw one another. Moreover, her new boyfriend solved many of the problems she was facing: when her mother's car broke down, she was able to get around town easily because he drove a car.

Franklin was miserable about the breakup, and although we tried to cheer him up in many ways over the next few months, he remained depressed. He was visibly unhappy and unwilling to study, no longer danced (his only extracurricular activity), and sometimes skipped work. Franklin described himself as a "useless nigga—can't give nothing to the one I love," and condemned Leslie: "Bitch be trynna take advantage of that nigga, and [she is] with him [her present boyfriend] 'cause he got a car." Toward the beginning of 2012 Franklin and Leslie got back together, claiming they had missed one another too much to remain apart. Because Leslie's mother still did not have a car, Leslie started taking the bus and Franklin Junior began trying to get a license and save money for a car. Both Franklin and Leslie were visibly happier and worked hard to sustain their relationship. While youth often looked for relationships that would facilitate daily survival and upward mobility, often, love did appear to conquer all.

While heartbreak is an ordinary adolescent behavior, it was harder to overcome under the constraints of poverty. Often, small derailments caused by heartbreak meant a long-term impact on youth's mobility goals. Cassy and Aaron (a nineteen-year-old black man) were another couple who felt a deep love for one another and struggled to stay together in the face of logistical and financial burdens. They had been involved in a romantic relationship for six years, and even though they occasionally fought with one another, their love was palpable. They even went to school together until Aaron dropped out of high school due to some family problems. During most of Cassy's fights with her mother and struggle over mental health issues, Aaron provided Cassy with much-needed support. "Thank God I have someone in my life though, right now," Cassy often said.

Toward the end of 2010, Aaron was forced to leave Port City, as his mother's drug addiction had become worse. He had to move to Ohio to live with his father and stepmother. This news devastated Cassy, and she cried for days. She missed school several days in order to spend most of her time with Aaron in an abandoned house in Port City. She stole small pouches of powdered beverage flavors, Cheetos, and candy from the local retail store and met Aaron at the house. She made sure that the letters of absence the school sent did not reach her parents.

While Aaron was away, Cassy frequently worried that he would start seeing someone else. When he did not call for weeks, she imagined that he had already forgotten her. Having no way of contacting him, since he would not respond to social media messages either, Cassy remained depressed for several weeks. She barely ate, missed work often, and mostly played video games at home. We talked on the phone and I dropped by three times, yet I did not see her for almost two months. I thought that I would probably not be able to remain in touch with her. However, Cassy called me one day to let me know that Aaron had finally called her and told her that he did not have money for a phone and that his father did not have internet at home, and so he was unable to get in touch. Cassy did not seem very cheerful over the phone and narrated the story to me somewhat sarcastically, but I did not want to probe further. However, when I eventually met her almost two weeks later, she seemed quite cheerful: "I finally get to see him! I am so excited." Cassy had saved one thousand dollars for college expenses, and she spent most of it on Aaron's trip back to Port City to visit her.

Meanwhile, her final year in high school was over and she had not taken her SATs or worked toward college admissions. After spending days talking solely about Aaron and the future of their love lives, Cassy finally asked me to come over to her house to help her fill out the FAFSA application: "I decided to go to Port City Rivers for now 'cause I don't even know what to do, it's too late. I wanna enroll in Port City Rivers. I know I'll get in there." According to Cassy, the admission process for Port City Rivers was not hard because she knew a girl who was "much dumber" but had just enrolled last semester.

When I arrived, her sisters let me know that Cassy and her mother were fighting. I did not know what to do, but they had both seen me, so I could not walk out. Cassy was sitting with her back toward the door, howling, while her mother chided her in Spanish. Then her mother told me that Cassy was paying too much attention to boys and had spent all her money on a boy named Aaron who was now in jail and calling her on their home phone. She also told me that she did not think that Cassy would make it to college; she was just not all that smart. It turned out that Aaron had gotten into a physical fight with his stepmother because she had used his Social Security number to take out a loan.

Cassy decided to take the placement tests at Port City Rivers, where she had to write an essay on boredom. When I met up with her to celebrate, she said, "If it was on like politics or economics or something, I think I would've done better but I don't know about this one." Nevertheless, she passed her tests and was placed in college-level introductory courses.

TEEN PARENTHOOD

Although the majority of the youth in this study did not have children, I came to know a few young women who became mothers at a young age for a complex set of reasons. While the Port City youth were critical of those who became pregnant or had children, for both those who gave birth and the young people around them, motherhood was not associated exclusively with one emotion, but rather a combination of complex emotions.

Cassy's best friend Lona gave birth to a daughter a year after graduating from high school. Cassy and I were at Cassy's house one evening; she played video games while I lay on her twin bed reading *The Hunger Games,* which she had insisted I read. Cassy and Lona had dyed their hair blue a few days earlier. Mothers-to-be often got pedicures and manicures to treat themselves right before the baby came, but Cassy told me the girls decided to dye their hair instead of getting a "mani-pedi" because Lona's only source of income was the child's father's work as a grocery bagger. Because Cassy wanted to gift the experience to her friend, she stole the dye, color guard shampoo and conditioner, and a special hairbrush from a local store. Later that evening, Cassy received a message that Lona was in labor. Cassy was very excited about the impending birth. She double-checked that she had packed her camera and a poem she had been writing for the baby, whom she considered her niece.

Lona wanted to give birth at home with a midwife, some of her friends, and the father of the child. When we reached her apartment the midwife, two friends, and the father were already there. Lona endured a few more hours of labor before giving birth in a bathtub with her child's father at her side; the baby was a light-haired girl weighing eight pounds. The couple had decided to name her Persephone after the Greek goddess. Cassy took a lot of pictures, held the baby, cried, and told her friend over and over how beautiful the baby was. She was so in awe of the miracle of human birth that she wondered whether she, too, should become a mother. At the same time, she joked that she could barely dress, feed, and clothe herself, never mind a baby.

As we drove back to her house in the middle of the night, Cassy mused, distancing herself from Lona's impending life: "I want a bright future." The sight of Lona and the baby's father close to one another, basking in the glory of new parenthood as if all the pains of poverty, the dead-end jobs they hated, and their hopelessness about the future had disappeared, was indeed joyful and uplifting. It offered a temporary escape from immediate troubles. But Cassy aspired to become a psychologist someday, or, at the very least, to work many hours at the coffee shop and "make mad money."

Because Lona and Cassy were almost inseparable, I came to know Lona well during the time I spent in Port City; we had had many deep conversations during her pregnancy. Lona assumed that because she was going to be a mother, she was more mature than her friends and perhaps her "mental age was [my] level." After Lona got pregnant, she was briefly happy:

she looked forward to motherhood. She often said that she thought things would change after the baby came. During the pregnancy, Lona was pampered by her friends and the child's father. Cassy stopped by every day, bringing her food and gifts, and I visited her frequently too. She worked for the first few months, then quit her job.

When Lona went into labor, she called all her friends and invited them to come; their presence eased her anxiety over having to raise the child all on her own. She was not even twenty years old and had no family to support her. The presence of her friends during the birth was comforting: it showed her that people cared. Friends arrived, bearing gifts, and some gave her money. They all told her how lucky she was to have a child and that being a mother would change her life.

Parenthood presented a paradox for Lona. Despite all of her community's good wishes and her own joy, she mourned lost opportunities. Lona lamented the constraints she faced in her future and wished for a second chance, saying, "Sometimes I just wanna go back and do stuff without worry and get many hours and maybe take classes." She told me she was envious of Cassy's chance to work, make money, and go to college: she always thought Cassy was bright and would go far in her future. Lona wondered if Cassy would go to college, if she pitied Lona, and if she thought Lona had made a bad decision. When Cassy later enrolled in a community college in Port City instead of a four-year university, Lona was both surprised and somewhat relieved. She was glad her friend would remain close, and her jealousy of Cassy's future prospects waned.

Many young women in this study had networks of support for abortion, accessed birth control information and birth control itself through these networks, were in romantic relationships with men on the way to college, and had older siblings who framed pregnancy as a road block to social mobility. They denounced and avoided pregnancy as a way to indicate that they were socially mobile individuals.[20] The lack of resources held Port City youth back despite their success in delaying childbirth and forming romantic relationships that seemed to advance their mobility projects.

5 Saved by College

In Port City High . . . it's, like, dangerous.

—Alize

During the first few months of fieldwork, Curtis asked me what exactly I did. When I explained, he shared that he wanted to attend college in order to become a computer technician. I asked him what his GPA (grade point average) was, and Curtis responded with embarrassment and excitement: "I know, I know what it is! It is grade point average, now I know. How did you know I didn't know? This one teacher told me few weeks back, he is the coordinator for something at school." Realizing a bit late that Curtis had only recently come to know what "GPA" stood for, I said quickly, "No, no, I mean how much is your GPA, like, grade." Curtis responded with embarrassment: "Damn, you must be thinkin' this nigga some dumbass, how's he gonna get to Florida!"

Curtis looked forward to entering the labor market full-time, often wishing he could work for money during the hours he spent in school. One day when we were at work, Curtis was wearing a pair of brand-new sneakers and our supervisor asked him when he purchased them. Curtis responded: "You know I didn't get them! My brother did. I don't make no money! You don't give us weekend hours and I barely get hours over week." "But you have [to attend] school," the employer responded. "I know, shit sucks but gotta do what we gotta do, I guess," Curtis said.

Undergraduate students from a prestigious liberal arts college in Port City often came to Port City High to talk about college life in order to fill in their volunteer credits. When Curtis got to know a student named Joanna, she invited him to have coffee so that she could tell him about colleges. He said, "She real nice. She's Latino too but she look white though. One of her parents, white I think, but promised to get me in, though. Please give me your car, I wanna pick her up!" When I told Curtis that I could not because I myself needed to get back home to teach a class, he replied: "Damn, see, if I worked mad hours I wouldn't be asking. I would buy a Jetta and I would be in time everywhere if I had my own car!"

A few months after I befriended Curtis, his neighbor and friend who was also a student at Port City High was recruited to play college baseball in Florida. "My boy gonna play in the MLB," Curtis told me proudly one day at work. "If you wanna make it, you can," he said, turning to Ashley. Curtis also played baseball with devotion and hoped that it would take him to college. This belief kept him motivated: he was adamant about following in his friend's footsteps. "I'm outta this miserable place as soon as I'm done with school, my boys in Florida waitin' for me," Curtis declared after he visited Florida for a baseball tournament. He was ecstatic: "All these niggas freezing in here and I was sweating in Florida," he joked with us when he returned. However, playing baseball did not quite work out for Curtis: he was not recruited by scouts. He was still determined to move to Florida: "If you ask me what I do for success, it's struggle. You gotta get out of here to make it. All my boys in Florida. It's not as easy as it looks but you gotta do it the hard way."

"I'm on my way up in the world now," Curtis declared after he and his friend bought one-way tickets to Florida with the plan of staying with his friend's distant cousin who had promised them his living room for a week until they enrolled at Miami Dade College and found jobs. They planned their trip for summer, and then all that was left between Curtis and "moving up in the world" was high school graduation, he said.

Finally, it was graduation day at Port City High and Curtis's time had come. His mother asked one of his brothers to bring a cake with "Congratulations" written on it, and we decided to cut the cake before the ceremony. We cut the cake and Curtis asked me about Angie: "Yo, she in Florida, right? Damn nigga is focused on goals. I always knew she would make it." Curtis's mother kissed him on the forehead as everyone drank beer to celebrate.

As we made our way through the neatly organized open space where the graduation took place, the excitement of hundreds of seniors was palpable in the air. I met and chatted with many people I had gotten to know, and people congratulated one another. One young woman said to Curtis: "Yo, you believe we made it! Damn!" The energy was so contagious, I could barely contain my own excitement. Before students walked across the stage and shook hands with administrators as they accepted their diplomas, speeches were in order. One commencement speaker at graduation, Dr. George Sanchez, welcomed the graduating class by stating:

> They told me I can't, they told me I can't graduate from high school, so I went to college; they told me I can't get a college degree, and so I went and got my PhD. You can do whatever it is that you want to do with your life. It has just begun here. You can make a difference in our community even though you are not bound by it. You must go outside of Port City and see the world.

He ended his speech with the names of a dozen successful Port City High alumni, announcing that they went on to become doctors, professors, basketball and baseball players for national teams, teachers, and officers in the military. The audience clapped after each name, parents cried, and Curtis asked me to feel his arms to show me he had goose bumps.

The principal thanked the teachers and other staff members and acknowledged how crucial they were to the students' success. The superintendent then especially honored students who had overcome personal tragedies such as illness, death, "broken homes," and language barriers to obtain their degrees. "You have come this far and have a taste of success; now you must go forward," he said. As Curtis walked across the stage, his mother cried and cried. Afterwards, Curtis's cousin asked him how it felt to get his degree, to which Curtis responded: "At first, when I heard my name it was disbelief, and then when I was walking across the stage everything was, like, blurry and like nothing else was there. It was unreal, man." His cousin joked and said: "That's what it takes to make niggas happy these days." "That and weed," another friend added jokingly. "And God," said Curtis, ending the conversation. By the time we returned to their apartment, everyone had left. Curtis's mother stayed, sitting in the chair in her neatly kept living room, watching a Spanish-language TV network, and sipping tea. She looked very content and did not speak much.

Cassy came over that evening after her video game session at her friend's place. She came to congratulate Curtis and spend time with him at his house. I said my back was hurting. The two friends knew that I had a small back problem due to excessive driving, not enough exercise, and a diagnosis of "uneven legs." "Yo, that's crazy how you got legs like that—weird," Curtis said jokingly. Cassy looked at him with scorn and responded: "You don't know what it feels like to be in pain." She proceeded to give me a shoulder massage, and then she said in laughter, "Plus, she is mad old." We all burst into laughter. Cassy continued:

> But I'm a good massage giver, though. That's what I think I might do 'cause one of my aunts—like not my real aunt, my blood sister's aunt—she has this massage place and she told me I can get, like, a certificate and I can work in a place like that. They make mad money and I am good with my hands. I used to give massages all the time to my mom and sisters. You like it, right?

Cassy looked at me inquisitively, peering over my shoulders. "Oh man, it's awesome," I said. Curtis responded proudly:

> You gotta stick to your plans, nigga, you can't be goin' around like that. First you gotta do things and not just say this and that like most of these motherfuckers here in Port City. People ask me what I did to succeed and it's just hard work. Now I'm outta here! It took planning.

Cassy countered: "I know, I'm gonna transfer from here [the community college] once I have all the classes 'cause I don't wanna pay all the money and here it's cheap."

Curtis added, thoughtfully, with his legs crossed on the arms of a worn-out but neatly kept sofa: "Life is too short and I'm waitin' for no one to come give me something. I wanna get out of this place, if I've come this far I gotta go." By his graduation, Curtis had indeed been worn out and ready to leave Port City in order to begin a better life. Holding a job, struggling in school, taking care of his ailing mother, being harassed by police, and his inability to get around, in their totality, eroded Curtis's enthusiasm and patience.

Curtis was due at a new job at a pharmaceutical manufacturing company in Port City, since his work at the school as a computer technician helper was over at the end of the semester. He had the third shift, which meant that he worked from 10:30 p.m. to 7 a.m. The job required a high school degree, literacy, proficiency in Microsoft Word, and the ability to lift sixty pounds. His experience at the school computer lab looked good on his resume when he applied. However, Curtis was somewhat embarrassed about the job and asked me to keep it a secret. When Cassy asked him what the plan was until he left for Florida, he responded, "Chillin' with my niggas, and then I'm movin' up in the world."

After we left Curtis, I drove Cassy home. We stopped to eat at the Chinese buffet, where Cassy expressed her disdain for Curtis's ways. She told me that she did not understand what he would do during the coming weeks if he did not work. Cassy also wondered why he needed to go to Florida for college when he could stay in Port City with his mother and save money: "I mean, I would've loved to leave but like, that's just not smart. You have to be careful and plan ahead. I am gonna leave in the next year, but I wanna rack up some class credits before I leave."

In this chapter, I highlight how youth attempted to mobilize the resources they acquired from school, at work, and through nonprofits and churches in order to facilitate their transition from high school to college. These institutions generated resources, which facilitated specific goals, but they also impeded youth's mobility opportunities. The Port City youth understood that a high school diploma did not carry much weight in the job market. In their day-to-day life, however, such a diploma was often a goal that could be undermined by the immediate allure of low-wage work (in the next chapter we will see how and why), as well as organizations' and institutions' inordinate focus on policing the youth. As the young men and women struggled through school and college, they continually weighed low-income work against their educational goals and moved back and forth between prioritizing work and school. Work was sometimes necessary to remain in school. Having to balance the demands of school and work regularly overburdened them, making it difficult for them to succeed in either school or work. This chapter leads to the next one, which focuses on how the youth found low-wage work and reconciled their aspirations for college degrees and white-collar work with their employment at the bottom of the service economy.

HOPE AND AMBIVALENCE IN PORT CITY

Port City collectively embraced the belief that all students can attain soci-oeconomic mobility through college. In this, it is not alone: high educational ambition among youth is a national trend.[1] Many Port City High students are granted access to institutions of higher education such as community, online, and for-profit colleges, which features an open admission policy regardless of students' level of preparedness.[2] This open-admission trend, combined with the increasing commodification of higher education that constructs and treats students as consumers and clients, implies that students can now "consume" college at the pace and time they prefer.[3] They are allowed to defer college graduation while taking arbitrary classes, so that they may feel connected to their aspirations of obtaining college degrees.

Encouraging College

Port City High School personnel encouraged students to pursue college at every opportunity.[4] Dr. Snider, the school district superintendent, gave a speech about the significance of a college education to a group of high school seniors right before their graduation:

> You can go beyond Port City. Don't let your life end here—go out and reach the stars. You have to dream big and only then can you achieve something. If you don't dream big, you will never get ahead in life. Take my daughter, for example: she was one of the first women at her job as an engineer and, you know, she wore a bulletproof vest and just fought. She was the only woman in her class, as well. She is now a top-ranked employee at a big place. You just have to think beyond Port City. Go and see what is out there for you. College is the way to do it.

Dr. Snider started out as a high school teacher and was deeply involved in the school integration process in Los Angeles. In our conversations, he made every effort to avoid stereotyping his students. He was also quick to acknowledge constrained resources, such as a six-year flat budget, as a negative influence on the chances of success among the students. Because Dr. Snider could not perceive how exactly such, as he put it, "big scale" issues are to be resolved, he stressed the importance of individual motivation in student success.

At the national level, Presidents Clinton and Obama made similar speeches in 1998 and 2010, respectively, reflecting a national mood that constructs college education as a reachable goal for anyone who has the drive to succeed. The Port High principal and teachers also regularly mentioned college expectations in their daily interactions with students, making informal remarks such as, "What're you going to do when you go to college, [where] you have to do homework or grades will suffer, but no one will force you to do homework—but if you don't, then that's it" (as narrated by Curtis while recalling his day at school). During counseling meetings, guidance counselors advised students with a wide range of academic performances to attend college, regardless of their readiness. For example, at least three students with a GPA around 1.5 sought my advice regarding admission to a community college because their guidance counselor had suggested that they continue on to lower-ranked colleges and improve their performance.

Not only were students given words of encouragement, but juniors and seniors at the high school also received resources such as a fifty-page information booklet containing names of potential colleges and universities across the United States, scholarship opportunities, and standardized admission test (SAT) information. When Curtis showed up at work with the booklet, he explained:

> They give you all this shit and now if you not gonna do shit with it and sit on your ass then don't complain that this place [Port City] sucks and I can't get out 'cause there's a way, right here [lifting up the booklet]. Principal Kelly be tellin' us, it's not for show in your room, make use of it. Everyone here be livin' in their homes till they're like mad old and raise their babies. There is all the information, niggas just lazy. I'm lazy too—I'm not sayin' I'm not, though.

Several community organizations and local institutions such as churches in Port City provided college-related resources. Path Through College (pseudonym), a local nonprofit, was established in 2010 with the mission to support five to ten students at a time, from high school through their first two years of college. Be A Star (pseudonym), another nonprofit organization, provided Port City adolescents with a physical and metaphorical space to meet other people of similar ages and build a support system for talking about their predicaments at school and sharing resources related to college applications. Another organization provided weekly access to computers and the internet, assistance with online college applications, college essays, and financial aid applications, as well as information about college life.

A local church organized an annual "debutante" competition in which local high school students competed on the assumption that the tasks involved would help them to prepare for college admission. For example, each student had to write essays and do a special project that constituted community service, along with showcasing a talent. The first, second, and third places were awarded $6,000, $3,000, and $1,000, respectively, toward their college funds. Another local nonprofit organization that worked to provide food security offered youth $2,000 toward their college funds if they remained employed at the organization for two consecutive years. Organizations spread the word about their initiatives by posting information flyers in schools, workplaces where youth were heavily employed, coffee shops, and the like. They sent representatives to schools, presented at community meetings, and reached students through their personal networks within the community. I regularly volunteered at one organization that assisted with college applications twice a week, and an average of ten to twelve students showed up at each session. While some students came regularly, there were many new students on any given day, and other organizations reported similar trends when I talked with their employees. Many students never showed up twice, discouraged by their unfamiliarity with the process, time, and energy required. Devoting a slot of time to college application every day or week meant fitting it into work and family responsibilities and transportation availability. This was a chore in itself.

Every youth had at least one family member who consistently expressed support and enthusiasm for them to obtain their college degrees. Brianna's mother borrowed money from one of her coworkers to buy Brianna a laptop when her secondhand laptop broke down. Sandra's mother and grandmother came to every community meeting to find out which organizations offered assistance for college applications. The constancy of the message that valorized higher education and the plethora of college-oriented organizations and activities manifest the power of that message.

Together with normalizing college expectations, this message stressed the importance of personal responsibility in academic success. Students like Curtis internalized individual responsibility from school personnel and nonprofit workers. Students believed that because certain types of resources were available to them, their failure to attend college could only be explained by individual or cultural deficiency. They did not know the possible power of the resources that were not available to them: as Curtis said, it all boiled down to "laziness." This internalization of responsibility amounts to what Pierre Bourdieu calls symbolic violence, which erodes self-confidence and results in hidden trauma and psychosocial suffering among the youth.[5]

The personal responsibility discourse internalized by the Port City youth was also rooted in racially coded messages about affirmative action in higher education. Evelyn heard from a coworker at Chuck E. Cheese, where she worked most days after school, that extracurricular activities were among the most important criteria for college admission:

> This woman who works with me, she read on her Facebook, I think, someone posted an article and it said how it was important to be in things like clubs and radio stations and newspapers and whatnot to get into college, but now I have like no time 'cause I've been working all the time after school. Port City High I don't even think has nothin'. But I don't know. Ima just tell them I wanna do all this in college.

A.J. was listening to our conversation, and when I glanced at her it appeared that she was eager to add her point of view. When Evelyn relinquished the floor, A.J. added with great enthusiasm:

> They [the college admission committee] like to hear about your life! So whatchu gotta do is tell em' you from the ghetto and mad niggas getting' shot in here and all the things that happen in Port City! Tell 'em you went to inner-city school, you should write about how you saw pregnant girls and all the bad stuff and how you worked and what-all you saw, they dig that!

A.J. told me that she had heard from her teachers and some friends that it was relatively "easy" for black and Latino/a students who had had "hard" lives to get into college. Donte received a similar message from his teachers who urged him to apply to regions that have fewer black people as it would heighten his chances of getting admitted.

Port City youth not only imagined themselves as less than worthy, but also relented to inherent deficiencies beyond any salvation in order to explain their inability to achieve what school personnel and nonprofit workers constructed as achievable. By adopting individual responsibility, youth unwittingly absolved schools of the responsibility to provide timely, sufficient resources. As scholars of education have noted for many decades, in a meritocracy such as the United States, open access to institutions of higher education creates the illusion that all students have equal access to education and that ours is an open society.[6]

Reality of Port City High

The year I began my fieldwork, fewer than 37 percent of Port City High students had scored above proficiency level in the state's compulsory mathematics and English academic performance test. There was one guidance counselor for every five hundred students in the high school. Because of a flat budget for six years, two college preparatory programs were on the verge of being discontinued. In 2012, the state appointed a "special master" to improve the school district's performance. Despite all of this, relentless optimism and vague imaginings of a future consisting of a prestigious white-collar job were common among the youth of Port City.

In 2010, Ashley wanted to become a marine biologist. Having graduated from high school without the minimum GPA required to enroll in the state's public universities (according to Ashley herself), Ashley was hopeful that she would have a chance to improve her academic credentials at a local community college before entering a public university for her bachelor's degree. Describing her aspirations, Ashley told me: "Like, everyone at work, my boss and like the teachers too, they're talking about the BP oil spill and whatnot, and my guidance counselor, she told me marine biologists make mad money and they're needed. I'm not cleaning nobody's ass, Ima tell you that much."

While Ashley was adamant in her ambitions, the ebb and flow of encouragement during Alize's final years in high school baffled her. She was simultaneously told that she could not even construct a line in English and that she must apply to community college and work toward her aspiration of becoming a nurse. English classes were a constant source of trepidation for Alize and many of the Port City youth who grew up in Spanish-speaking homes because the public school system had inadequate English as Second Language programs. Toward the end of high school, when the students were required to write their senior year essay, Alize stared at her empty Word document. She commented: "My English teacher, she told me I can't do nothing about it now 'cause it's late, but I can't write well, my English is all fucked up, so I gotta work on it." But then, the guidance counselor told Alize that she must enroll in the local community college because that was the only way she could make something out of herself:

ALIZE: 'Cause I wanna be like those people who check your baby when you're pregnant, you know? Radiologist, I think? 'Cause I love caring for people. When my aunt was sick, I took care of her. I wanna work for people. The guidance counselor was, like, I should do the Port City Rivers nursing program 'cause you don't even need to write if you wanna do that, that's why she told me, I think, to apply... I'm gonna go to college, I made my mind. Like if my English is not good, I'm just gonna go to like Puerto Rico, but I'm gonna go to school every day, I'm not missin' school no more.

Ashley and Alize were not exceptions. All but one of the 16 youth in my study and 39 out of 40 I interviewed wanted to obtain a college education and were optimistic about their chances of doing so. Institutions, organizations, families, and individuals in Port City espoused the idea that good jobs come through college education and that college is the single most effective and feasible way out of poverty.[7] However, only 64 percent of Port City's students graduated from high school and only 4 percent of Port City residents between the ages of 18 and 24 and 11 percent of those 25 or older held a bachelor's degree or higher in 2012.

While a high school degree was a point of pride for the Port City youth, it was also common knowledge that a high school diploma was not worth very much unless they acquired some form of higher education. Port City youth harbored high aspirations and expectations, but there was a major disjunction between the youth's aspirations and the reality of the work world. Expectations, aspirations, and outcomes did not align.[8]

Yet, ambitious youth felt that they were upwardly mobile because they had managed to escape the fate of those peers who had entered the criminal justice system.[9]

POLICING AND EDUCATION: CONFLICTING GOALS

While Port City's high school and other youth-focused organizations and institutions were occupied with educating youth, they also—and sometimes more importantly—disciplined and policed them.[10] Indeed, this policing agenda often posed an obstacle to the youth's opportunities for higher education. Even though the school and community constructed the policing of youth as necessary to prepare them for a bright future, existing and scarce resources had to sometimes be allocated for the policing and disciplining of the youth, as well as facilitating educational success. Although the youth in my study did not enter the penal system, at the time when the criminal justice system looms large in the lives of marginalized youth, these youth saw their educational and occupational accomplishments and aspirations in relationship to their friends who were in jail or fleeing the police.[11] Media, politicians, and academics often construct black and brown youth in racialized and classed ways as inherently prone to violence, and violence as an epidemic in their communities.[12] As Port City youth were policed inside their schools and out in their neighborhoods, avoiding prison, like steering clear of teen parenthood, became a preoccupation and an indicator of mobility among them. This preoccupation with avoiding the criminal justice system, and the imperative to redefine mobility as avoiding the criminal justice system among all youth, demonstrates how the growing culture of control negatively impacts all students.[13]

School as a War Zone?

Many of the young men and women of Port City High regularly get into trouble, end up in detention or are suspended, lose credits, or enter juvenile detention centers. For example, a study conducted in 2014 by a local nonprofit organization and parent advocate group revealed that 42 percent of Port City High students lost credit due to absences (because of illnesses, sibling responsibilities, and the like) and almost 70 percent of these students were not given their class course credit due to accumulated absences, despite having passed the class in every other category. Almost 70 out of 3,000 students were arrested across Port City public schools during the 2010–11 academic year, the first year of my fieldwork. In the same year, there were approximately 670 in-school suspensions in Port City High alone. Arrest and suspension rates for Port City public school students remained steady over the next three years.

During the first few months of my fieldwork, I did not visit Port City High very often. But life inside the school was frequently discussed among the youth, and my field notes contain mentions of the school as a dangerous place where students got drunk, fights in the hallway involving weapons were common, and teachers had no control over students. I noted an undercurrent of the "dangerous youth" narrative when I first entered my field site in Port City. Several people, including the employers at the nonprofit organization where I first volunteered and a schoolteacher I had gotten to know through a friend from graduate school, warned me about the young people of Port City. One said: "You gotta be careful with these people here. Port City High is like this breeding ground for violence. They don't care for their life or your safety."

Ethnographers who have spent time inside urban schools depict violent interactions between students. In his 2013 comparative school ethnography *Toxic Schools: High-Poverty Education in New York and Amsterdam*, Bowen Paulle argues that violence was hardly intentional among young people in the inner-city schools he observed in New York City and Amsterdam. The students in his study displayed a conventional desire for structure. However, the deep-seated and structural dysfunctions of schools in economically marginalized neighborhoods require students to manage chronic stress, which, in turn, shapes their behaviors and peer dynamics.

At Port City High, various agents such as school personnel, parents, media, and community members constructed the school as a war zone on the basis of some students' violent outbursts. Drawing on narratives embraced by institutions, the Port City youth also deemed their peers as dangerous. One afternoon at work, a conversation unfolded after one student who bought a machete was expelled from school:

SANDRA: [speaking with a morose tone that suggests she may have given up on her school]: It's a hard place, like, it's dangerous, Port City High. It wasn't like that, but now it is.

CASSY: In our school [a technical school that Cassy attended] we had this reputation that Port City High is bad and I was scared the first time I
came, but there are good students, it's not all that bad.

ASHLEY: . . . In public schools teachers get paid much more money than at other
schools. Like, in [the neighboring city's] public schools, the teachers
get paid more money 'cause they call it at risk. The teachers are at risk,
they're putting themselves in danger because they're with a whole
bunch of kids who are uneducated and in poverty and dangerous.
'Cause niggas be in war zone, right? . . . There is a lot of crime and violence and they are in danger all right. Just so, like, when you look at
Port City, the school is old, it hasn't been remodeled for God knows
how long. My cousin has been there and gone out of it, and she is
almost thirty and the school was there before her and people before.
There are cockroaches there, the stalls in the bathrooms don't have
doors, the glasses [windows] are broken, there is not enough books
for every student in the classroom, not enough chairs, not enough
teachers for students in classrooms, and you don't get enough attention if you don't understand, you know. I spoke to a social learning
teacher one time and he said that for every student that was going
there the school was getting seven thousand dollars for it, all right,
where is all the money? Where is the remodeling? I don't know, there
are some teachers who are getting paid tons of money, but they are not
really doing anything. They are not teaching, they are just there for
their check they are making. They have remodeled the whole football
field, there was dirt and they put turf and it is proven that players who
run on turf, it messes their knee . . . But, like, niggas done nothin' for
me . . . Like it's all about how many awards they are getting through
the sports and not through the intelligence of the students that are
there, really smart and everything.

CASSY: I agree though but it's not always that, 'cause sometimes some students
are plain ghetto [silent for a minute]. I'm just being real, and you
know it.

SANDRA: I don't even care no more. I just want a degree and I'm on my way to
college and a better city 'cause these motherfuckers [are] everywhere.

CASSY: That's my point, though, if you want you can just do your work and get
out.

ASHLEY: I'm just proud that we [Ashley and her sisters] all made it out of there!

The local newspapers produced and sustained the image of Port City
High as a breeding ground for crime, STIs, sexual assault, and teen preg-

nancy. One author lamented that the school was having discussions about starting a program that would provide individualized support for safe sex practices. The author claimed that this policy was unfortunate, that parents did not do their jobs and the students were "at risk." As a result, the school had to transform itself from a "sacred" learning environment to one that dealt with uncouth matters such as sex and violence (he added).

Even the Port City High principal's opening line during most conversations with high school students was about the fear that students from neighboring cities had about coming to Port City High because of its violent reputation. Afterwards, he often provided a contradictory message to soften the blow, saying that he saw through the students he was speaking to, and that he was convinced that they had soft hearts and could get out of Port City if they wanted.

This conversation took place at work not long after I began my fieldwork:

ALIZE: Niggas made me fucking change my tights 'cause they think all the motherfuckers in there ghetto—'cause some of them real gangbangers. The principal told us how they fucking scared of us out there 'cause we like always fightin' and gettin' into shit.

LEXUS: Yeah, that's why we can't even have nothin' nice here. It's mad fucking boring 'cause every time we have a party some nigga takes out a knife!

ALIZE: Someone took out a fucking machete during break in school again, you heard that? [everyone nods in agreement]

CASSY: Yeah, 'cause I lived here all my life but like in my school they're like, oh damn, I don't wanna go to Port City High! I'm not scared though, like, what're they gonna do to you?

ALIZE: [jokingly] They gonna cut you up! Ranita, that's what you should write about, how these niggas be cuttin' each other up and being all ghetto and whatnot. Hell, I'm nottin' different, I'll prolly have a baby daddy in jail soon [laughing hysterically]. I better get off my pedestal.

By and large, all Port City youth were perceived as dangers to the community and to themselves; their actions were constructed as unpredictable, haphazard, and harmful to their own well-being. The youth were viewed as if they lacked thought or agency, and were rather dictated by some unknown, uncontrollable, and inherently destructive force. Alize even thought that she might become violent one day because violence was an epidemic. None of the young women in my study became pregnant; none of the youth encountered the law for serious charges. The vast majority of the youth had nothing to do with drugs, gangs, or violence. Still, their communities, families, school, and even the youth themselves viewed all the Port City youth as dangerous and "at risk" of becoming derailed from a path to educational and occupational mobility and falling back into a life of poverty. As we will see in the next section, the internalization of this narrative often distracted youth from their higher educational pathways.

Moral Panic Distraction

Toward the end of 2010, after I had been at my field site for several months, five young men of color murdered a young man of color who had been leaving work for home one evening. Panic engulfed the city. Following the murder, other youth of color were being picked up from their homes every evening for questioning. It was rumored to be a drug-related murder. Curtis and his brothers were among those who were taken to the station. Curtis and Franklin Junior speculated with two other boys from their school: "He [police officer] asked where I was the day before and whatnot. My man tells me that he on the phone, the guy who dead, 'cause he was involved with this big gang and whatnot and those other niggas gang-banging too, I don't know." Local newspapers reported on the Puerto Rican and Dominican drug gangs in Port City.

The school barred every liquid but water because one student allegedly brought alcohol to school in a water bottle. However, others speculated that the new policy was related to the murder and drug feud.

As the investigation proceeded, it was revealed (in the media) that the five young men who went to Port City High were watching a show on television after school one day. During the show they became "riled," and one of them challenged the others to "jump someone." They took a knife and went to the streets. After passing on a few pedestrians, they picked another young man in his twenties leaving his workplace and stabbed him. Although they did not intend to kill the man, they left him injured on the streets and he succumbed to the stab wounds. This new development left everyone in shock. While the drug narrative had seemed to offer an "acceptable" explanation for the violence, this alternate explanation contributed to the violent youth narrative like pouring gasoline on a fire.

Numerous organizations and institutions with a diverse, and often conflicting, range of missions—churches, local nonprofits, and after-school care centers—all became involved in what they called the "community rebuilding" project after the murder. Organizations and institutions that usually functioned in isolation, focusing primarily on their individual programs, came together. While some had rather abstract aims, like the "Art for Youth" nonprofit that claimed to provide youth with a creative space, others, such as the after-school care center and the youth employment center, fulfilled concrete and specific day-to-day functions. But all became heavily invested in collaborating to control "the dangerous youth of Port City." After 2010, several nonviolence trainings were organized each year, violence among youth was a regular topic at community meetings, and the school increased its policing efforts. One poster at a local coffee shop read "Stop Youth Violence," and nonprofits distributed fliers listing violence and drug abuse statistics in the school, at places where youth were employed and where they spent time regularly.

In one classroom, the principal spoke about the murder in relation to education:

> When kids have nothing to look forward to, no goals or ambitions, they don't value their own life or others'. Here in Port City High, we are trying to get all of you to college so that you can make something of yourself. You don't have to end up in jail because your brothers, sisters, or friends have.

Community meetings took on a similar tone. During one meeting I attended, an elderly white woman associated with a nonprofit organization that organized "nonviolence" camps for youth said, "Violence among youth has been prevalent in Port City for a while and the murder is just a major call for attention to the issue. We can't let our kids go down this path. We need to tell them about the importance of education and keep them away from prison."

Superintendent Dr. Snider told me he believed he was doing his part in supporting his students in following their dreams:

Five percent of students in the school are homeless, many don't have safe home and neighborhood environments, most come to school hungry, so I am trying to collaborate with local organizations to find emergency homes for students to stay, successful shadow alumni to motivate students, and at least one dinner at school per semester to satisfy the hunger of the students and thus help them concentrate on their dreams. You know, when students get sports scholarships or join the military, it makes us feel good when they're successful and, not to mention, it brings discipline and keeps them from ending up in jail.

A few days after the murder, as the young men and women tried to make sense of the event, the nonprofit for which we worked hired a young man with a criminal record. We knew nothing about the young man except the fact that he had a record. One of the employers had mentioned this to Evelyn the night before. Evelyn came to work with a frown on her face that day; she had texted me and Ashley, saying she had something important to discuss with us and asking us to come in approximately fifteen minutes early. As Ashley, Evelyn, Alize, Lexus, and I gathered at work, Evelyn started a conversation about the young man who had been hired:

EVELYN: Yo, I don't know. This nigga may be dangerous.

ASHLEY: I get what you sayin' all right, and more than that, though, Siete been out with this guy who is into drugs and whatnot and he almost bitch-slapped her. Like boys and men in Port City and like all over, but here, they are violent men like that. So you can hire them though, but then you gotta teach them discipline.

LEXUS: Yo, I'm tellin' you and I said to Evelyn when she called me last time, he [the boy who was just hired] is a good guy, he knows my brother but we just need to teach him. Maybe he can attend one of those nonviolence things. Like we just need to learn that stuff.

EVELYN: But you seen how they are? Those niggas kill someone just like that 'cause they bored. And the teachers at my school they, like, I don't know what to tell you. Like they just lost their shit.

ALIZE: I feel some of them were just there. Their mother said they were just there. They are all seventeen and one is eighteen. Most of them are in my class, I knew them before high school. The other one, who is getting charged for murder, he graduated last year.

LEXUS: He is nice. I met him and his younger brother and he was nice, they were just there.

ALIZE: Jordan [one of the five young men] got the Napoleon affect, like he small and he wants to feel like he is big and I think he started it. He is violent.

ASHLEY: This kid just got out of jail so he is just going out, he is in and out. Michael [another one of the five boys] just disappointed me, 'cause they were the sweetest, they were just in the wrong place wrong time. This guy, he would do anything for street credit, he got this tattoo and everything.

ALIZE: I dated him one time and I know his mom. He was very good and like he got A's sometimes and he did carpentry and all, and when the school heard they were like, what?

ASHLEY: This one kid, don't his brother work at the after-care center?

ALIZE: I am not gonna vouch for them, but you don't know what happened. Like, how did this happen? Like, are they dangerous, like now in school everyone is afraid. Like, when they gonna lose it, you know what I'm sayin'?

ASHLEY: But, like, for me, the whole thing of doing it for no reason, like, that scared me.

ALIZE: Yesterday when I was walking and there was a cop just chilling there, and there will be lot of fights and some of them was in a gang, and one of them, his brother who got shot was part of the goonies in Port City. That's mad tragedy for one family. If his brother was still alive he wouldn't want it, he just became different and didn't care about stuff.

EVELYN: Like that's what I'm sayin' though, we need to be careful and like learn to be nonviolent though, 'cause most of these niggas be rottin' in jail. You don't want that, better teach them not to be violent—we need to learn some lessons.

Many of the young men and women in this study sought to comprehend the contradictions in their peers' actions: those they had known to be sweet boys resorting to violence. Their communities stressed the importance of dealing with the criminality of young men and women, often stressing that Port City youth were inherently violent, participating in violence out of boredom. These kinds of explanations implied that any youth could fall prey to their inherent violent side. Ashley reasoned with Curtis one day: "Jordan, he doing angel dust all time before this happened. His whole family a mess. They got a curse of something I think, otherwise this is nuts." She went home that evening and asked her mother to do a tarot card reading to ensure that their family was not about to suffer the wrath of bad luck as Jordan's family had.

The Port City community collectively manufactured what Stanley Cohen, in his 1972 book *Folk Devils and Moral Panics*, conceptualizes as a "crisis" of youth violence. They responded with a variety of programs. The youth reacted by creating in-group/out-group distinctions to distance themselves from this crisis. Distinguishing themselves from their violent peers both enabled these young people to see themselves as successful and blinded them to the realities of the shared oppressions, which ultimately held back both college-bound and jail-bound youth. However, it was not enough to distance themselves from their peers; the youth learned that they must police themselves and learn discipline.

Evelyn is an example of how the youth internalized the necessity for discipline. She had been notorious, in her own words, as "a trouble child":

> In the teachers' lounge, they would talk about me and how I was a terror. No one was happy when I was in their class 'cause I was doing all kinds of things, bad things. And I was at the vice principal's office like all the time. And then it was two years gone and then one time the superintendent was telling us how like there are homeless people in Port City, I still remember, and like how some of them were in college and engineers and whatnot and I was like I don't wanna be stuck here! And I turned my life around. I did all the work. The vice principal now loves to see me. He is gonna write letters for me for college and all the teachers they talk about me and how I turned my life around.[14] I don't want this no more.

Messages articulating the "bootstrap" ideology, which asserts anyone can make it (including those who have struggled with homelessness), combined with the idea that higher education is one of the only ways to overcome poverty, instilled confidence in Evelyn. She did eventually gain admission to a four-year university not far from Port City for the fall of 2012. However, Evelyn opted instead to join the military. Sometime that year, a recruiter had come to the school and convinced Evelyn to take the Armed Services Vocational Aptitude Battery (ASVAB), and she received a fairly good score. Evelyn wrestled with the choice between college and the military for months:

I don't want [a] minimum-wage job and clean floors, you know, I mean at my work they be asking me to do that shit even though I serve...I won't clean no one's shit. With the military I can pay for school, housing, and will get veteran's pay in four years. Like, the marine base is in Virginia, it is within the required radius to University of New Hampton where I really wanna go and so I can live off campus and have my housing paid. Like, all the dumb ones get sent to war and the smart ones get all the advantages and they need smart people like me. He [the recruiter] asked me why I wanted to join the military. I like just sat there for a while and asked myself, I didn't go and ask anyone for the answer. But the thing is, I wanna travel the world and keep my options open, and you know what I believe most, though? That military will give me discipline, that's what you need to progress in life. That's what I wanna do, I don't wanna end up like my mother on the streets, that's for sure.

Toward the end of our conversation, Evelyn said: "I'm just thankful my ass ain't sitting in jail and I'm gonna make sure it never happens." Evelyn left Port City for basic training toward the end of my fieldwork, and she is the only person I never heard from again. According to Evelyn, she made this decision to enter the military so that she could cultivate discipline and not end up like her peers and family members who went to jail or lost their way. Her educational aspirations, at least partly, fell prey to the internalized idea that marginalized youth need to be disciplined. On the other hand, she also perhaps simultaneously used the discipline rhetoric to justify her decision to join the military instead of pursuing higher education.

In Port City, the goal of policing potentially violent youth contradicted the goal of providing these youth with educational opportunities. Victor Rios, in his 2011 book *Punished: Policing the Lives of Black and Latino Boys,* offers the concept of a "youth control complex" to understand how young men of color are criminalized by various institutions from a very young age—even before they commit any crime. In Port City, too, institutions and organizations such as the school and nonprofits, and youth and their families were caught in a moral panic revolving around violent youth. The outright criminalization of youth, in large part, shifted the aims of these organizations and institutions from creating educational opportunities to preventing violence among youth. The youth and their families also prioritized policing or self-policing over pursuing educational opportunities. Nonprofits fell victim to the moral panic around violent youth, and it affected their funding messages and goals. It also became easier to acquire funding from both individuals and foundations by spotlighting youth violence as a dire and pressing issue, in contrast to the promise and positive outcomes of educational programs.

One morning toward the end of my fieldwork, at approximately 4 a. m., a dozen police cars swooped into Port City and arrested over a hundred men. They came all at once so that none of the men allegedly involved with a Puerto Rican and Dominican drug gang could escape. The policemen went into homes and pulled the men out, sometimes several men from each household, and placed them in the back of their cars. For the young people in my study whose friends, brothers, fathers, and uncles were taken away, this was a particularly memorable day. It became a topic of conversation at school, at work, at home, and on the street for days to come. People talked about how many police cars were involved, when they came, who got arrested and their backgrounds, and how their families were reacting, among other matters.

Several days after the incident, I ran into Camilla Moreno, Curtis's aunt, a short Puerto Rican woman in her fifties, at a Port City convenience store. We exchanged pleasantries, and as I filled a paper cup with coffee, Camilla said to me, jokingly, "That coffee is no good if you need energy." An attractive woman who loved to dress up, Camilla looked exhausted that day. We made general conversation for ten minutes or so before Camilla revealed, with embarrassment, something I already knew: "You heard they took two of my boys?" I had, I told her. "I can't lose no one else right now, I am not going to see this happen to me," Camilla added. A few days later, I learned from Curtis that Camilla sent her remaining daughter and son, who were both in high school, to live with her sister in Florida— so that they would not risk being arrested in Port City. Curtis did not seem supportive of his aunt's decision and deemed it an extreme reaction. Yet he added: "Better them niggas get some work down there than sit their asses in jail like their brothers, though. They need to calm down for a bit." A.J., who decided to postpone college to join the military, agreed with Curtis:

I see it every day, people going in the wrong path. I just think I need to learn to be disciplined. That's why the military is good for me for now. Later when I'm an adult and learn to be disciplined, I will go back to college. Your cousins, they need to learn how to be, first, and then they can finish school and whatnot.

I often saw Camilla at Curtis's place—she was visibly devastated about losing her children, but felt it was necessary. "It hurts me but it better than them sittin' in jail . . . my youngins [the two she sent to Florida] are good children, but you don't know when they become something like their brothers," Camilla reasoned one day as we sat on the stairs in front of Curtis's house.

Organizations that provided youth with computers and assisted them in college applications, SAT preparation, and job searches slowly shifted their focus to assisting youth who were in trouble with the law. For example, in 2012, one of the youth who had been coming to such an organization for two years to look for jobs and learn about college was arrested. One of the three employees at the organization spent all of her time contacting the local youth center to seek support, making contact with the legal clinic at Yale University, and talking to the young man's family members. The young man was eventually sent to the juvenile detention center and had been in and out of the center since then.

I witnessed more and more youth coming in to seek help as they had gotten into trouble at school or outside. In an interview, one of the employees stated: "More and more youth are in trouble, and their needs seem just more dire to us." Slowly, the organization's assistance with educational matters dwindled, and it started to focus on matters such as fighting the school board about grade loss as a sanction for truancy. Another organization that paid the youth to attend a collaborative peer reading and writing camp mentored by the organization personnel slowly shifted their focus to "teaching nonviolence," claiming that violence was a more pressing issue than education in Port City. At the institutional as well as the individual level, policing and education often acted as conflicting goals.

While the nonprofits shifted their focus from education to policing, the school personnel linked the use of policing in schools to higher education goals. For example, policies such as the "three-minute corridor sweep" (every one must be inside their classrooms within three minutes) or "grades lost for truancy" were represented as necessary punitive measures for the students to become better prepared for college. Wearing a hat or Spandex to class, looking out the window, looking back in class—any of these relatively inconsequential actions could call for disciplinary action. An interview with a teacher revealed that the school's administration instructed teachers to remain vigilant and take immediate action at all times when an incident seemed probable:

> You never know what gets out of hand: one time a fight broke out in the hallway and some kid took out a machete! I mean, you just never know. So we have to always be on our guard, and who suffers if they get in trouble? It's their future that is ruined. If you want a future, a job, college, then you must be disciplined and that's our job—to discipline them for their own good.

The superintendent of schools told me in an interview that lack of discipline was the most significant obstacle to success among the youth of Port City High:

> Everywhere I go, I hear how undisciplined my kids [public high school students] are. Once the seniors went to a neighboring school and everyone there was anxious about our students' behavior. We have a lot of work to do here, they are infamous, our students. One will never be academically successful without discipline.

While the schools believed that policing was a route to education, research indicates that this is far from the truth. Scholars have linked increased policing of marginalized youth to phenomena such as the prison boom and racial and class politics, rather than academic success.[15] Policing begins early. In *Bad Boys: Public Schools in the Making of Black Masculinity*, Ann Arnett Ferguson (2000) draws on participant observation in an elementary school to highlight how black children are constructed as jail-bound by teachers. This view shapes the boys' critical evaluation of schooling and daily resistance, which is then identified as troublemaking by teachers who disproportionately label black boys as potential criminals.

Not only did the policing of youth in Port City impact those who came in direct contact with the law, but it also touched many others who feared that they would meet the fate of their peers. It shaped the lives of the entire community of Port City including the youth, their families and relatives and peers, taking away resources marked for educational programs, shaping their everyday lives and how they planned their future.[16] One can infer that the fear of the law deterred young people from freely pursuing academic goals and realizing their potential.

Like the majority of youth in Port City, the sixteen teenagers I followed managed to avoid jail and aspired to go to college and acquire middle-class jobs. They struggled to mobilize resources, taking small steps toward their goals, only to be set back to square one because of the slightest cracks in their plans. However, the youth held on to their aspirations.[17] This college-goer identity allowed them to differentiate themselves from their peers who were in prison or gangs, as well as from dominant discourses and stereotypes that construct economically marginalized black and brown youth as unambitious and lazy.

A TASTE OF HARVARD

As we saw earlier in the chapter, the young men and women of Port City were able to tap into a variety of resources that facilitated their access to community colleges and even certain four-year universities. However, the absence of a nuanced knowledge of colleges and universities created unexpected, and often invisible, barriers. The unspoken rules of successfully navigating the terrain of higher education best suited for an individual student's success were lost on the youth, who were otherwise deemed adequately prepared by school and nonprofit personnel and their own families.[18]

Sandra lived with her mother and their dog in a small two-bedroom apartment, located on a street adjacent to a park that looked like an abandoned lot. Sandra's mother kept the apartment clean and furnished with a living room set, two bookcases, a dining table, and a queen-size bed. Sandra had two half siblings, but saw them infrequently. Her maternal grandmother lived close by and Sandra visited her often. Their favorite activity was getting ice cream at Dairy Queen. Sandra's mother and grandmother were both deeply invested in Sandra's well-being, including her education. They did everything they could to acquaint themselves with the college admission system, from attending community meetings to dropping by at the youth center regularly to inquire about programs and resources that could aid in college admission. Sandra was adamant about not "ending up [poor] like them [her mother and grandmother]": "I done being poor, I don't wanna have children and be poor like my mother, she has it hard, I know." Both Sandra and her mother worked two jobs. Sandra's grandmother was very proud of Sandra. "My girl gonna make it to the top, she gonna go to college. I remember we didn't have no water to shower when we lived in South Carolina, but I told my girls the value of an education and now my granddaughter, she make it big," she said one evening as she, Sandra, and I walked along the pier.

Even though she weighed approximately a hundred pounds and was less than five feet tall, Sandra's personality loomed larger than most seventeen-year-olds. She claimed she had a "laughing problem," that is, she laughed a lot of the time and sometimes at inopportune moments and settings, such as in the local church where the family went every Sunday. Sandra always dressed in skinny jeans, neatly ironed shirts, and ankle-high boots. What was most striking about Sandra were her large brown piercing eyes that shone brightly. Looking at her, I always had the feeling that she was up to some well-meaning mischief: for example, one time she told her supervisor that her friend Cassy had a secret crush on him.

Sandra was fiercely loyal to her friends. When her friend Jovani's romantic partner cheated on her, Sandra went up to him at school and delivered a well-rehearsed speech about the objectification of women; she ran it by me the day before, and it was perceptive, heartfelt, and eloquent. Sandra always made a point of asking for help when she felt there was a source she could tap into in order to improve on whatever it was she had set her mind to do—from improving a comeback speech for her friend's ex-boyfriend to assistance in applying for college. For instance, Sandra had been introduced to a member of Port City's city council during an occasion at the church. After she narrowed down the list of colleges where she was going to apply for the fall of 2012, she emailed the council member and asked for a letter of recommendation. He never wrote her back.

Sandra had always earned A's and B's in her classes. She went to work after school and was home by seven to complete her homework. She regularly visited the local community college and all organizations in Port City that provided assistance with college applications. Sandra's final project, in which she formed a group of middle-school students and taught them a set of lessons about healthy eating habits, was one of the most talked-about senior year projects. She worked at a local organization that gave its employees money toward college funds. She also participated in a debutante competition hosted by the local church, for which she won $2,000 toward her college funds. When Sandra scored only 1524 (out of 2400) on her SAT, she went to the local community college to talk to an admissions office employee whom she knew through her church to find out where she had gone wrong. However, Sandra remained hopeful, since she would have more shots at the SAT. Sandra was planning to begin college in the fall of 2012, so she applied to five four-year universities with fragments of support she had collected over the years.

My phone rang loudly as I sat in a movie theater one cold night in January 2012. I left my seat to answer the phone call from Sandra. She had strict rules about not calling after dinnertime, so I feared it was an emergency. Turned out, Sandra had an interview with a Harvard alumna: "They wanna interview me . . . Can you believe it? I can't. Sorry, I woke you? I was so excited," she said.

I congratulated Sandra as I hung up. That Sandra had applied to Harvard and was in the process of being interviewed by an alumna had made quite a ripple in Port City. Sandra was not the only student who had ever applied to study at an Ivy League institution (some even attend Ivy Leagues), but it was quite rare. Everybody talked about it—people thought this was a major accomplishment. One evening, while I was driving Alize back home, she told me proudly: "Cha Cha [Sandra] is my best friend. We been close since long time back. She is real smart, not like girls who don't care about their career. We both been real, like we both had real ambitions, and that's why we close." Alize took great pride in her friend's interview with Harvard. Sometimes Sandra's overambitiousness came off as "snooty" and "stuck up." Ashley, for example, said: "It's like, we get it. You mad ambitious but do you have to be like that? Like people make mistakes, you don't gotta judge them all the time." Even so, after the interview with the Harvard alumna, other Port City youth also celebrated and basked in Sandra's success: "Yo she damn smart. Make us proud, Sandra. You gonna go places and take Port City's name with you," said Curtis.[19]

I was not in Port City when Sandra received the rejection news from Harvard, and she did not call me to relay the news. Usually, Sandra and I met almost every other day and talked regularly. When I did not hear from her in almost two weeks I assumed something was not okay, but her friends told me she seemed fine, "maybe a bit depressed or something." When Sandra and I finally met to spend time at her mother's house, Sandra downplayed any impact the rejection from Harvard may have had on her. "I worked mad hard, but getting into Harvard is real hard. I am not sad or nothin'. I just wanna get out of here, though. I wanna go to college somewhere else like Boston or something." Sandra tried to avoid the topic and I did not insist on talking about it. Soon, our conversations became more about Sandra's intense desire to "leave home" for college.

In the fall of 2012, Sandra began her first semester of college at the regional campus of a four-year public university near Port City, her heart somber because she would not be leaving home to live on campus and lead the "college life" of her dreams: "I don't wanna go here, but I didn't get through nowhere else." When we went out to dinner to celebrate the occasion, she told me she was "excited, but not really":

> To be honest, I really wanted to get out. I love my mom, she would be sad and I would be sad too. But like all these niggas here, they stay at home, or, like, go to Port City Rivers. I'm happy, though, I know it's big. I graduated [from high school] and I'm in fucking college, but it's not what I wanted.

Even after she enrolled in college, Sandra kept her minimum-wage job at a clothing store, and she continued to plan and semi-execute a clothing fashion line with another friend, Lauren, in the hopes of "makin' it big." They named their line after a friend who had died of a terminal illness a few years earlier. They designed and stitched simplistic outfits and sold them to their friends and acquaintances at cheap prices; they spent a great deal of time updating their Facebook pages and Instagram accounts for the business. Sandra aspired to finish college, but also wanted to keep her doors open to the "fashion industry"—"they [the clothing store where she worked] really liked me there and gave me mad hours during the holidays, and I love to dress up and tell people what to wear." She said:

I don't know what I wanna do. I wanna make money and do something, maybe fashion, 'cause, like, I work in the mall now and I'm learning about the fashion industry and I don't know what I wanna do with whatever classes I'm taking now, and like I gotta work two jobs, I don't even know when I'll finish college.

Although her minimum-wage work and the clothing line cut into the time she had for school, Sandra was uncertain about a future based on a college degree. No matter how her life would turn out, she could not afford to give up her job: she needed it to support herself through college and save money—she had to pay for transportation, her phone, clothing, and food: "I gotta work, so might as well try to do something. 'Cause I don't wanna work just for money. If I'm stuck here I wanna try to get out of here as soon as I can."

Sandra continued to attend college and was determined to finish, although she was unhappy that she was going to do so at a regional campus: "It's depressing that after all the fucking applications, I end up here." She and her family had various explanations about why she did not get into the colleges she had wanted to, ranging from "the bad reputation of Port City High," "Sandra being black," "simply not good enough," and "it's for the good because those places [elite universities] are too much." While their accounts focused on the weaknesses of specific individuals and institutions, social and education systems marginalize economically and racially marginalized youth in a variety of interlocking ways, from family and neighborhood resources to the hidden curriculum of schools and standardized testing practices.

Sandra had applied to five four-year universities—four selective ones, where she was rejected, and the one where she eventually enrolled. Her eventual college placement was not for a lack of trying, Sandra told me— "You know how much I done for college," she complained to me. "I did everything I thought I had to do, and I can't even leave this horrible place."

Ashley expressed her disappointment and bewilderment about Sandra's sole acceptance and ultimate enrollment at a regional campus: "Like, I don't know much about Port City Point [the regional campus Sandra was attending], but it ain't no Harvard or even UConn. I don't understand, though, 'cause Sandra is real smart. The best, and she done everything for college. Like, I didn't do nothin' until now." At the time, Ashley was in a pattern of reentering community college after having graduated from high school and then failing her classes at the community college, and Sandra's situation did not do much good for her own confidence:

> If I can pass my classes this time at Port City Rivers, Ima be mad happy. 'Cause I ain't no dumb nigga. I know I'm smart, but if Sandra is at Port City Point, which I know isn't that good even, Ima just take what I get. And this teacher, I still meet her sometimes, she told me Port City Rivers is good. People making it big there, 'cause all you gotta do is learn. You just gotta keep learning and doing well. No one ain't gettin' out of this ghetto-ass place, I guess.

In Ashley's case, being readmitted to a community college seemed like a considerable accomplishment. In the fall of 2011, the twenty-one-year-old Ashley was prepared to return to community college after failing both of her classes the previous semester. Before she began, she needed to fill out forms, choose and register for classes, and buy textbooks. Ashley owned a broken laptop she had bought with some of her financial aid for the previous semester, and she had no internet access at home. Ashley and I therefore decided to meet at the home of her older sister and the sister's boyfriend in the neighboring town to complete the required procedures for fall semester registration.

The network of community colleges in the state shares a center for information technology (IT) that provides assistance for setting up the school ID. Ashley was nervous and did not want to make the phone call (she could not recall how the process had worked the last time), as she was afraid of talking to "college people" and was embarrassed that she had failed her classes the previous semester. I told Ashley that the IT people had nothing to do with her classes, but she did not understand the difference. The whole system seemed a labyrinth to her. Indeed, after a series of complicated phone calls consisting of information exchanges and instructions, we were told that an email would be sent to us with Ashley's ID. After three phone calls, and attempting to understand the process, it turned out that a different internet browser was required. "I can't do this no more, it's too complicated," Ashley said over and over. I suggested that we go to the college itself and take care of it there.

We decided to meet at the college on a Thursday when Ashley was done with work. A young man at the registrar's office gave us the required information and we decided to use the computers outside the office to set up Ashley's student account. I pulled up a chair and sat next to Ashley while she tried to navigate the internet with minimal typing skills. As I typed on my smartphone and read the directions for setting up the account, Ashley struggled to find the letters of the alphabet on the computer keyboard and glanced alternately at the screen and the keyboard as she typed them.

An Asian woman passed by us as we returned to the registrar's office after completing the procedure, and Ashley whispered to me, "Think that was the Chinese lady that was supposed to be my advisor last sem, guess she just left now." When we inquired about Ashley's situation, the person at the desk told us that students can register for first-year classes without their own advisor, but they should meet with an advisor afterward. Then he looked Ashley up and gave us her transcript from the previous semester, Ashley's face turned bright red from embarrassment as she immediately shoved it into her bag. We were then told to go to the next room to register for classes. As we waited, the lady there pulled up Ashley's transcript on the computer once again and gave her a form to fill out. Ashley whispered to me, "Oh, she be thinking, wow, this one failed, and I am taking the professor's class again, he gonna say, oh, you disappeared on me, where did you go?" Ashley then started to fill out the form, looking up at me after writing each letter, in apprehension that she was spelling the words incorrectly.

A few minutes later a small-built white lady with short curly hair, presumably an advisor, came out of another room to talk to us. I asked her whether I could come in with them and she agreed. The advisor asked with a big smile, "So you want to register; what semester are you in?" "Second," Ashley responded. The woman then pulled out her transcript and said, "Oh, didn't do so well, hmm, okay." She began going over the classes, trying to find something that would suit Ashley's work schedule so class times did not conflict with work hours. After about twenty minutes of deliberation, Ashley was finally registered for the same two classes that she had failed.

We were also advised to email the professors since Ashley had already missed one week of classes. We went out to the hallway and began searching for their email addresses. Again, Ashley looked at me nervously as she opened the browser to compose the emails: "I'm mad tired, yo, can you just write it?" I eventually wrote the email and inquired about missed assignments and apologized for missing classes. "It's the same professor, I think I remember their names, but like last time I had to do a homework online and I couldn't 'cause I didn't even set up nothing, and I sat like a fool in the computer room not knowing anything 'cause I didn't know how to log in and I didn't have no laptop then. They [other students] were all so serious [in the computer room] and they mean, no joke, they came with laptops and shit and I didn't have nothing, now Ima do everything with this laptop!"

After we were done with everything, Ashley seemed relieved and screamed, "Yes!" with her hands up in the air for a high five as we walked out of the room. She said to me, "I knew I was gonna come back and everything, Ma was like, nah, you not gonna make it to college. . . But I made it. I know I got it, you know, well who she gonna bitch at now!" Later that day, we went out to celebrate what Ashley perceived to be a considerable achievement.

As the youth struggled to put together resources they acquired for college admission, every small success seemed like moving a mountain. Each modest academic achievement led them to believe they had achieved something worthwhile. Their deep unfamiliarity with middle-class cultural capital made tasks that middle-class students are very familiar with excruciating for the Port City youth. Accomplishing them thus became celebratory. Seen from another perspective, then, they indeed achieved something worth celebrating, given the odds against them. But seeing small things as big achievements gave them a false sense of how far in the process they had actually gone and tended to impede their progress. The youth felt that they had both the opportunity and the ability to attend institutions of higher education and obtain social mobility without fully realizing the profound implications of attending particular institutions of higher education.[20] I often felt doubtful that Ashley would be able to graduate. The struggles were too many, and rather deep: academic unpreparedness, the lack of access to computers or the internet combined with computer illiteracy, and unreliable transportation. All of this was compounded with the constant emotional turmoil in reaction to falling behind in classes.

RESOURCE GAPS

The resources Port City youth received from local institutions and organizations can be effectively conceptualized as pieces of a very complex puzzle. Their resources included encouragement, knowledge about the importance of college, information regarding colleges, scholarships, and the SAT, financial aid, and temporary access to computers and the internet as well as assistance in filling out applications. All of this gave them a taste of—and partial access to—college. However, while these resources collectively facilitated their college goals in some ways, such as admission and homework completion, they fell short of preparing the youth for the myriad daily struggles involved in navigating institutions of higher education and for on-time graduation. They were unable to put the pieces together.

As I will discuss in chapter 8, the youth's lack of success in attaining their college dreams further constrained their chances by facilitating a wrong path. This was the case when youth considered "getting out of Port City" to be an achievement and therefore left the city without concrete plans.

When I told a local nonprofit worker about Ashley's inability to use the computer, a crucial resource of information about education and opportunities, she informed me about assistance that was available at the local public library. Yet, although the public library had free internet and computer assistance, the library's hours of operation did not align with the hours when youth did their schoolwork and other activities that required the internet, since they completed their assignments late at night after work. When the youth were able to access the internet at nonprofit organizations, there were not enough personnel to assist all of them in navigating the internet or typing efficiently. When a worker at one of the nonprofits used the organization's resources to provide rides to and from the community college, the organization ran into personnel and resource shortages and faced questions from the community regarding the risks involved in driving the youth.

The insufficiency of resources was also evident in the case of scholarships and loans. Although all the youth who began at four-year universities were able to obtain some form of funding during their first semester with the help of the resources available through their school, nonprofit organizations, and other local institutions, they found themselves struggling to remain in college. Brianna arranged for loans and scholarships for her first semester at a private four-year institution. A young woman who was two years Brianna's senior in high school had been admitted to the same university, but quit in order to begin working at a local nonprofit. She assisted Brianna in the application process, and Brianna was able to pay for her first semester entirely through scholarships. During the second semester, Brianna was told that the scholarships would no longer cover her costs entirely and that she needed to access a Parent Plus Loan for the remaining semesters. However, this required having her mother co-sign, which was not possible due to her mother's adverse credit history.

Devastated by her inability to pay for her education or get financial support, Brianna returned to Port City. She decided to enroll at the local community college the following year. During this period, she struggled to find a job. For almost six months, Brianna "shadowed" at a local bakery. Brianna claimed that she was "too broke to go to college" before finding work because her mother had also lost her job. Eventually, she found a job at a local nonprofit organization and was excited about starting at the community college. However, her time to complete homework or attend classes began to compete with work hours.

After her first semester at the community college, Brianna was offered a job at minimum wage at the bakery where she had shadowed because one of the employees had quit without notice. This would be her second job, in addition to the work at the nonprofit. Although she had received B's in all three of her classes during her first semester, Brianna was not confident. She had internalized the responsibility for her lack of academic preparedness: "I'm not smart like that, like, I had to study mad hours and stay back with the professor and finish stuff, so I can't do it like that if I have another job." Brianna's mother warned her that she should focus on getting good grades so "she can get a real job after college." Still, Brianna found it very hard to turn down the second job, "'cause last time I went to college my ass ended up broke with no job for like six months. Ima play it safe this time, I am taking the hours I get. I done being broke."

It came as no surprise to Brianna or her mother when her grades suffered the next semester. Yet, college was a far-fetched goal. Having witnessed its unreliability firsthand, Brianna was not prepared to give up work, and monetary security, for a future college degree.

The youth understood the major elements of the college application process to some extent. They knew they needed to apply for loans, write winning statements of purpose, and get good recommendation letters. Nonetheless, their "know-how" was quite vague. The youth received mere snippets of information and guidance from school personnel, volunteers, youth-serving organizations, and their workplaces.

The sum total of resources available for educational success almost always fell short of meeting the needs of Port City youth, who lacked comprehensive familiarity with the landscape of higher education and its many intricacies. At the same time that uplifting speeches and partial access made college seem more like an attainable option, both major and minor complications regularly created real obstacles to obtaining a college degree, contradicting these uplifting messages. The institutions that had failed the youth were far too many: their lack of college preparedness was deeper than the dearth of computers or transportation. Youth, who had high aspirations of obtaining a college degree and white-collar work, continued to hold on to their aspirations as they struggled to navigate college, work toward a degree, and balance it with work.[21] But even as the young men and women stood by their dreams and persevered through many challenges, they transitioned into the low-wage service economy.

6 The Making of a Teenage Service Class

> I know we are still young, but what you do today will matter later on! I think it's time we as a generation step it up! We literally are the future. Everyone we looked up to is either getting old or fading away, and it's time we prepare ourselves to take charge! So get into school, start up a business plan, start grinding towards your dream. Start building your life now so you can live it up.
>
> —Lena

Lena was preparing to go to a four-year university in New Jersey during her final year of high school. The university had a high proportion of first-generation college students and one of her cousins had been admitted there three years back. During the last few months of high school, Lena was tapped to work for Team Dream Big (pseudonym), a marketing scheme. One evening, she called me:

LENA: Ranita, I have a question. Like, this friend of mine, he works for this company and they pay him mad money and he is gonna buy a Mercedes soon! And all they have to do is like promote their product and he gets to travel all over the country.

RANITA: Wait, what's the name? I can Google it.

LENA: Team Dream Big. They make all kinds of things and we have to sell them and we need to put [in a] little bit of money but then you can win a car and travel all over and get your money's worth.

RANITA: You have to pay? Wait, don't agree to that, don't pay money. It sounds like a pyramid scheme.

LENA: Yeah, that's what my mom was sayin', like it don't mean nothin'. For real, though.

I searched for Team Dream Big, and it did appear to be a pyramid scheme. This is what their website said:

> You dream when you sleep, but do you even need to sleep if you're actually living your dream? Loved from New York to France to Mexico, Team Dream Big is a global revolution. We signify the finest in music, events, media and fashion.
>
> Who are we?
>
> We are musicians, artists, promoters and average people living their dream by simply achieving what they love. We are the best in our individual fields and we are at the top because we had faith in our dreams, and because we worked hard.[1]

I found out from Lena's mother that, far from getting paid, the "job" involved putting in some money that would buy a "traveling lifestyle"—the promoters would travel on vacation together, go to concerts, and meet people from around the country who were also participating in Team Dream Big. Lena would also have to take part in other recruiting events and personally recruit her own friends. In the end, depending on how much one invested, one could win the ultimate bonus, which was a BMW (according to Lena's mother). Lena's mother told me that Lena used her own savings and borrowed some money from her relative to start.

After Lena put in the money and bought her "#teamdreambig" sweat-shirt, she was very excited. However, her family did not approve of her investing the money. Lena called me to complain: "They just don't under-stand what is about to happen this year! Quote me on it, my life is not gonna be the same. Thank God I saw the Bigger Picture!"

Two weeks later, Lena was even more thrilled—for the first time in her life, she was going to be on a plane, all thanks to Team Dream Big. She was going to Texas for a recruitment event and the crew of youth from various cities on the East Coast would go to a concert (all of which they had paid for themselves). When I tried to persuade Lena not to get involved, she was visibly irritated and said to me: "People claim to want to be successful so bad, but aren't willing to put the effort to get them there! Respect to those who do as they say. It's like falling in my lap and how am I not gonna take it?"

As I picked Lena up to drop her off at a friend's house, she said to her family: "About to be in the clouds some, like, real talk. It just hit me—I'm actually traveling. This is crazy. Who would have known, Lena Diaz is going to see the world. Texas can be crossed off my bucket list!"

After Lena returned from Texas, she was finished with Team Dream Big. She said she was required to put in more money, more work into recruitment, and the payback did not, even remotely, match what her "mentor" in the program had promised. Other than that, she did not speak very much about the event. On the contrary, Lena told me that she wanted to meet to discuss her college scholarship options. It turned out she would not be able to afford to attend university in New Jersey: her scholarships would not cover the entire cost. Lena decided to complete a certificate in cosmetology. After she worked at a makeup store as a makeup artist for a few months, her hours were drastically reduced and she decided to enroll in the local community college. When she enrolled, her mother said: "Finally, you using your genius for something good."

Soon, Lena was working at a women's undergarment store in a shopping mall, while attending classes at the community college. She was exceptionally proud of her achievements and told me that she was working her way up in the "fashion industry." She claimed she was "becoming an expert" in the brassiere business and this did not contradict her higher educational aspirations as she would be taking classes related to the "fashion industry" and later transfer to a fashion school:

> Like, I'm real good at telling women what size [bra] they are. I measure them and stuff sometime when the other lady [worker] isn't there, and it's cool, you know, like I know something and it's a skill, for real. My boss told me how many of them [women] wear, like, wrong sizes. I love this job, it's not like serving idiots from the window [referring to a drive-through at a fast-food restaurant], like, I could go to fashion school, which is what I wanna do with my life, and I wanna design like swimwear and this is a good start.

In her day-to-day life, however, Lena struggled to balance the demands of schoolwork and her job. Eventually, Lena decided to apply to another clothing store in an attempt to gather "as much experience for my resume." In order to take on the second job, Lena had to drop one of her two classes at the community college. She came home exhausted from her two jobs late every night after the mall closed. In the past, Lena devoted evenings to finishing her schoolwork, but when she began her second job, she had no energy left at the end of the day. However, rather than climbing up the ladder, she was soon fired from the job at the undergarment store for arriving late for work on a regular basis. She was unable to land another job that had anything to do with brassiere fitting. Lena continued to struggle with a few classes at the community college, hoping to attend a fashion institute in New York City, and continuing to work at the clothing store for a minimum wage.

Lena's transition to life after high school and her fairly arbitrary, complex, and vacillating trajectory between school and work reflect the uncertainty that defines the coming-of-age experiences of marginalized youth in contemporary U.S. society.[2] Among Port City youth, open access to certain institutions of higher education reinforced the belief that social mobility through a meritocratic system of higher education was feasible. At the same time, youth confronted dominant ideologies connecting economic independence to dignity and personal responsibility.[3] Youth strategically navigated these conflicting expectations by keeping footholds in both school and work—constructing a continuity between the two. Yet, the continuity they constructed impeded their educational progress. Youth postponed college degrees indefinitely while claiming to be invested in higher education through isolated community college classes. Simultaneously, like Lena, youth imagined that their jobs, combined with their haphazard classes, would eventually allow them to build careers by developing related skills so as to foster a skillset.

Participation in institutions of higher education effectively strengthened youth's commitment to low-wage work, as it allowed them to hold on to their expectations of better jobs through college education while investing more in low-wage service jobs at the cost of higher education, thus, gradually becoming part of the contingent labor force. The structures and systems of low-wage employment also bolstered their educational and professional aspirations, even as it kept them from getting ahead. The youth workers creatively deployed a wide array of knowledge and skills to satisfy their customers and perform tasks, which they imagined were linked to a larger skillset they were developing through their higher education.[4] The big companies they worked for conveyed the idea that workers at the bottom are part of the industry and can easily climb up the ladder to more white-collar jobs through hard work, degrees, and training.[5] Youth like Lena felt that they had multiple options after high school—more hours, more jobs, better jobs, college, or all of them.

However, during the three years I spent in Port City, not a single youth found a job that directly drew on skills he or she had acquired in a previous job. Port City youth were seldom able to transfer their skills from one job to another, and were forced to take on multiple jobs as the low-wages and few hours they acquired made it difficult to earn enough from any single job.[6]

THE BEGINNING OF THE END OF DREAMS

It was the summer after Angie had returned from Florida. It rained earlier that afternoon, and the earth had the distinct smell of rain after a warm day. Summers usually made Angie very happy because she liked to wear shorts and tank tops and also because she did not have many warm clothes. I parked my car right outside Angie's grandparents' apartment in the housing project. We were planning to eat Chinese food, but Angie had told me over the phone that we needed to do something "important" at her home before we went to eat. I walked into Angie's house, where she was playing with a black Dell laptop.

ANGIE: "Look at this shit, Ranita! A-diz ['A' for Angie, and the youth often used 'diz' as a suffix] moving up in the world!"

RANITA: What you up to?

ANGIE: Making resume! That's why I wanted you to come home 'cause you gotta help me, then we go get Chinese, okay?

I sat down next to Angie and opened a new Word document on her laptop—which, I found out, she had borrowed from a neighbor for the day.

ANGIE: How you make this [resume] stuff? Like write about the jobs I have?

RANITA: Yeah, the jobs you had and, like, your school degree and volunteer services and whatnot. Let's start with name and address and high school diploma, and then tell me all your work and volunteering.

ANGIE: Aight! My high school diploma and then I did this volunteering thing, like, in this CPR job, kind of. I don't remember what it was called, though. I think it was with Public Allies [thinking deeply] . . . no, no, I didn't apply for that. It was like at the healthcare center, they taught us stuff. It was like years back. Forget that, just write I volunteered to paint the school.

RANITA: Okay, forget it for now. Work, tell me what you do now, then go back, like, give me the descriptions.

ANGIE: Dang! Aight, now I got Bed Bath & Beyond, and, like, I am floor crew and sometimes I get hours for stocking, sometimes I clean, and sometimes I do other stuff. And the other job is like taking care of old people, like just babysitting them, and whatnot. Like rich people! Ooh, that's gotta be good for the resume, no? Before, I also done this thing at Planned Parenthood, I went to D.C., too, and then I also did this liquor store and 99 cent store. Damn! I have lots of experience if you think about it! Angie, moving up the world!

We created Angie's resume that afternoon because she wanted to quit her care-taking job and find something "better." She had her mind set on working at the local Hollister clothing store, where responsibilities, she said, were in stark contrast to her present job, but she claimed "they hired only white people." Angie's job search was futile and, to make matters worse, a few months later Bed Bath & Beyond started cutting their payroll and giving Angie haphazard hours depending on when they needed her, mostly on Sundays. She began applying for jobs once again. Angie did not have a car at the time, and this restricted the area where she could work:

> When my [financial] aid check comes in . . . Ima go get license. It's like I'm happy to be outta this ghetto-ass Port City High, and I feel all grown up, but I miss school 'cause I had something to do all day. Like I was at school or like dancing and shit and then work. Now I need to work.

It took a while, but Angie found, and unhappily started, a job at a coffee franchise. It was the end of the school year in Port City, and I was parked outside her house to give her a ride to work because she was sick with menstrual cramps. As she got into my car with a pensive look on her face, she said:

> While everyone gets ready for prom and shit, I'm going to work. Didn't notice I had it good when I was younger so these youngies need to take advantage of these last free days of your life 'cause once you get that diploma it's every man for himself, nigga. Nothin' ain't free. You gotta take what you get in this world. I don't know, nothin' ain't working out the way I want, I hate my job, Ranita.

After Angie had returned from Florida, sometimes she planned to enter a culinary school in Minnesota to "make it" as a chef. At other times she planned to move to Miami again to attend Miami Dade College to become a dancer. Still other times, she adopted a dimmer view of what adulthood looks like: low-wage coffee shop jobs.

Angie had extensive work experience. However, Angie's jobs across her work trajectory did not logically line up to resemble a career. She had moved from job to job because employers did not give her enough hours or gave her inconvenient hours, a manager insulted her, or a coworker did not respect her. Her next job almost never resembled the preceding one, and there was never an increment in pay—they were all minimum-wage jobs. The only factor that could lead to more pay for Angie was more hours.[7]

FINDING MEANINGFUL WORK

The Port City youth looked for work through three primary means (in no particular order of importance): first, the internet, where they applied through websites such as snagajob.com, or in response to flyers that employers used to advertise; second, families, lovers, friends, and acquaintances who informed them of vacancies and/or put in a good word for them; and, third, employment services. A few of the jobs held by the youth during my time in Port City were at coffee shops, restaurant franchises (where one youth found work as a server but most found jobs as bussers), fast-food franchises as servers and custodians, and in retail stores that offered clothing, footwear, electronics, pet specialty and domestic merchandise, mainly as floor crew or loading crew. Local institutions such as several nonprofits, the after-school care center, the library, and the school itself were also options for the youth. There were also entrepreneurs like Sandra, who held jobs but also tried to start their own businesses, albeit with little success or expansion. As in many other cities and towns, some of the local employers in Port City were T.J. Maxx and stores at the local mall: Bed, Bath & Beyond, Target, Radio Shack, McDonald's, and Dunkin' Donuts. Other employers were relatively unique, including two local casinos.[8]

Illusions

One summer I was volunteering for a nonprofit that was collaborating with Youth Services to host general "assistance sessions" for youth who were contemplating higher education. Many Port City High students dropped by since the program was advertised on social media and at school. They would come and look, ask questions about college, sit around and check out the youth center's four computers, then leave. Most of the time, the youth's very low level of preparedness meant that the personnel were unable to give them any functional assistance in one sitting. All they could do was to help the students create resumes, tell them about Port City Rivers Community College, and walk them through its website, hand them a pamphlet that listed all available scholarships (which the school already did), and show them how to navigate the College Board website. Occasionally, when a youth was well prepared, the nonprofit helped them revise their personal statements. Yet, as I indicated in the previous chapter, these resources never cohered to facilitate a clear and successful trajectory for youth.

The college application process intimidated even the teenagers who had the basic requirements for applying to colleges, including high GPAs, strong relationships with teachers who would write recommendation letters, and the potential to score admissible SAT scores. While sometimes youth came with the resolve to begin their college application, they also desired to take a "quick peek" at available jobs in the neighborhood. Seeing that they could so easily access the internet and apply for a few jobs, they found it hard to pass up the opportunity. After all, jobs were not the easiest to find in Port City (as we will see later in this chapter). However, the probability of hearing back from jobs was much higher, and the turnaround time was a matter of weeks. By contrast, college seemed far-fetched. The vast majority of the youth who came to work on their college applications ended up asking the personnel to help them with job applications or assist them in finding work.

I asked Franklin Junior, who had been looking for a second job for a very long time, to come to the program in order to seek guidance about college and/or work. He was working at the nonprofit, but he wanted more hours. He gave some money to his parents, paid for his phone, and often treated his dance group at the Chinese buffet; sometimes the group had to chip in to pay for travel to dance competitions or even enter them. Franklin had been looking for work for months—he had visited the employment center, asked his friends to be on the lookout, and begged for more hours at the nonprofit organization—but, to his dismay, nothing was working. His uncle sometimes hired him at his car repair shop, but Franklin quit. The hours often conflicted with his dance practice, and standing for long hours, because his uncle did not like him resting on the job, hurt his back.

Franklin showed up at the program around five one evening. Wearing his hat backwards, he hummed a tune and danced gently as he entered the room. He always had a large presence, and his willingness to B-boy whenever requested was entertaining. Some of the other boys high-fived him and asked about his dance crew:

JOSEPH: How's your dance, man? You guys doin' good stuff?

FRANKLIN: Yeah, we are. We just entered this dance competition and had to pay. I need money, man, I need money. That's what I'm here for. Ima work my ass off. I owe Curtis some money too.

I sat next to Franklin at a computer, where we opened the website Snagajob.com and entered his zip code. The Snagajob page listed multiple (mainly service) jobs that were available in the area. As we scrolled down, looking through the jobs, one advertisement appeared for a "Sales Associate" at a pet store.

RANITA: This one looks good, right?

FRANKLIN: It's too fancy-looking, sales associate and whatnot [loud characteristic laughter as he turns around on his heels to show off his dance move].

RANITA: The requirement says high school or GED. And you gotta be able to lift like fifty pounds or whatever, and like basic math and talking.

FRANKLIN: [talking loudly to Joseph] For real? Dang! This boy movin' up in the world! I guess school still pays off. You heard this? Ima be a sales associate and whatnot! What do you think I need to do [looking back at me]?

RANITA: We can read here [pointing to the description on the screen].

The job advertisement used convoluted sentences and abstract descriptions such as "you'll work with others who share your values and commitment," "people skills," "professional development," and "personal enrichment." The responsibilities for the job were also phrased obliquely and confused Franklin further: they included phrases such as, "sharing product knowledge," "suggest the appropriate merchandise," and "effectively employ suggestive selling techniques to increase sales."

FRANKLIN: Ooooh, enrichment! What does that mean? How am I gonna get product knowledge though? I don't know. This is making me nervous.

RANITA: Dude, trust me. You'll learn, it's nothing.

NONPROFIT WORKER: [looking over our shoulders] Yeah, that's bullshit, doesn't mean anything. Just apply.

We began the application process by registering for the website, which required an email ID. Franklin didn't have one, so we created an email for him. The website also asked for his Social Security number. Franklin said: "I don't know if I got one." We had to call his mother to ask, because Franklin didn't know if his mother had an email address either. Then the application asked whether the applicant received AFDC (Aid to Families with Dependent Children). Franklin didn't know what that meant; he said that his mother received food stamps but he didn't know anything about AFDC. When one of the nonprofit workers mentioned the word "welfare," Franklin immediately denied it and said: "Oh that, welfare, no no, not that."

After filling in other basic information, we began answering what would turn out to be some sixty questions to complete the application. The wide range of questions was somewhat vague and could be interpreted in different ways, and many were curiously unrelated to the job description. For example, one asked: "How would you resolve a conflict with your co-worker?" Franklin raised his eyebrows and said: "I don't know these things. Resolve [loud voice] a conflict [loud voice]? I can't do all the shit, man!"

We went on to answer all the tedious questions, mulling over some of the vague ones that asked, for example, whether one should complain to management if a coworker steals something or try to resolve it with the coworker. "Yo, this one asks if Ima be a rat or like fight some bitch who stealing from the store?" Franklin and his friend joked. After a few hours, the application was completed and submitted. However, Franklin never got a call from the employer. This did not surprise me. I had assisted a number of youth in filling out online job applications, and no one was ever called. It was as if the employers did not bother to go through those applications. Yet youth often resorted to this method when they were unable to find jobs through their networks.

After Franklin completed another round of online applications the following week, one of the youth center workers, Jessica, suggested to me that he should drop off his application / resume in person at the gift shop he had applied to online. So I told Franklin that I would give him a ride there.

FRANKLIN: You gotta teach me how to do this, 'cause I really need this.

JESSICA: Okay, so some of the main things are: look them in the eye, say full sentences, and don't use cuss words.

FRANKLIN: Hello sir, I want an interview for the job. I really need this job.

JESSICA: No, tell them you're good at this job.

FRANKLIN: Hello sir, I am here for the interview and I am gonna be good at selling things 'cause I love people.

JESSICA: Good! There you go! Here it is, here it is—this is what you say: Hi. I am Franklin, and I wanted to drop off my resume. I applied online. What is your manager's name so I can call and follow up?

FRANKLIN: Like, he gonna ask me if I sold shit or how do I know I'm good at it? I never sold nothin' and like the shit we did at Port City Youth Center was no good for this! And I worked at the school computer lab and then I worked at the food truck one time when my uncle had odd jobs and whatnot.

Franklin repeated the line: "Hi, I am Franklin, and I wanted to drop off my resume. I applied online. What is your manager's name so I can call and follow up?" again and again until he got it "right." Then he asked: "Do you think I should take off my hat, though?" We said yes.

However, Franklin did not get that job. Instead, he started work at a small local restaurant washing dishes. They paid him above minimum wage, under the table. Franklin found this job because one of his cousins had quit the same job because of crippling back pain after working there for two years. None of the jobs that Franklin had worked had anything to do with one another. However, his aspirations were firm:

> You can't do nothin' these days if you got no education. I have a plan. I am gonna work mad hours and do my dance thing 'cause we good. I'm gonna save my money now, and once we like a little known Ima go to college for dancing, and then we hit it big. 'Cause ain't no one giving niggas no job without the paper [degree].

Advertisements for low-wage, entry-level jobs such as the one above often used language the youth did not know. These job descriptions made the work seem more complex, presenting it as if it required a skillset that a high school diploma would not provide. Companies portrayed entry-level jobs in ways that youth interpreted as white-collar jobs. Youth imagined that the tasks they were required to accomplish were more complicated than they actually were. Companies used language such as "work with others who share your values and commitment" to portray ideals of belonging. Job advertisements claimed that workers needed to determine customers' needs, provide product details, and resolve conflict.

As Robin Leidner (1993) illustrates in *Fast Food, Fast Talk: Service Work and the Routinization of Everyday Life*, tasks necessitated by these types of jobs are highly routinized, even when it may seem that customers receive custom-tailored service. While applying for jobs, during the interview process, and when starting new jobs, youth imagined that they were acquiring and employing white-collar skills. But they were paid minimum wage and employed skills that were not transferable to higher-paying jobs that would allow them to build a career. Sometimes, the process of applying for and acquiring these jobs online seemed to the youth as complicated as applying for community college.[9] The constrained low-wage service job market of Port City (as discussed in chapter 2), combined with the language used by employers, created barriers for youth, but also supported their sense that these jobs were a positive step forward.

Opportunities

While online applications were an overwhelmingly ineffective way to find work, jobs frequently came through parents, siblings, friends, neighbors, and acquaintances from the church. The youth were most successful in finding jobs through word of mouth. As soon as an employee quit somewhere, the other employees quickly spread the news to their friends and families. Employers who liked the references were happy to hire their friends and family—no resume required.[10]

As I discussed in chapter 3, siblings were often very effective in finding jobs for one another because they navigated the same job market and work for their siblings would mean additional income for the family. For example, at a local after-school care center, four of the ten employees were siblings. Seven out of the sixteen youth in my study found at least one job through their siblings.

The nonprofit where I met the youth employed about twenty youth throughout the year. When one of its employees quit, the organization started the hiring process immediately. The two leaders wrote a job description, created an application, and distributed them at the high school, the youth center, coffee shops, and other public places. They received quite a few applications from youth. However, because Ashley wanted her boss to hire her sister, she made a plan (after her initial plea to not begin an application process but to hire her sister did not work out) and asked Evelyn (coworker and friend) to play a part in it. One afternoon John, Ashley's employer in the organization where I met the youth, was on his way out after a grueling workday of writing grants. Ashley approached him timidly:

ASHLEY: Hey, I saw you guys makin' applications and whatnot. Guess lot of them applied?

JOHN: Yeah, yeah, we got a lot of applications this time. Good stuff.

ASHLEY: I know, 'cause like Kiana applied and whatnot. But she crazy though, like she gets in trouble all the time.

JOHN: That's okay—we like to give at risk youth a chance.

EVELYN: I understand you, it's about giving opportunity to everybody, but if you're fifteen and been arrested two times you don't deserve it and you'll bring the others down who work with you. I'm talking from the point of view of someone who was like that [talking about an ex-employee, Tyrone] and he thought everyone thought less of him. So what did he do? He didn't work and he made us look bad and he acted like a gangbanger everywhere we went, and he did all these things and made us look bad and so he'll spoil everyone and if he is rapping and everyone next to him will do what? Start rapping and then you got eight shitheads rapping. I got stuck with all the gangbangers and everybody thought my job was like shit. That's why I felt like quitting 'cause like it's like ghetto job they give out to gangbangers who get shot afterward anyway. There is no value in that, what you gonna learn from these shit niggas?

JOHN: I hear you.

However, John did not seem to pay much attention to their argument.

Siete filled out the application like the other youth, but Ashley directed her very carefully, often having her note skills that were needed in the organization even when the application did not ask for them. However, it was not her better-prepared application alone that eventually got her the job: John's wife, who led the organization with John, said that she had gotten very close to Ashley and was incapable of turning down her sister: "It's like they're all kids. How does it matter who we take? We're giving someone an opportunity, why can't it be someone we know closely?"

Romantic partners were also crucial in finding work. Evelyn got fired from her only job for being late to work on a regular basis, and as part of downsizing. We were all a little taken aback, and Evelyn was desperate to find a job. Everyone brainstormed that evening to come up with possibilities, which were constrained because of her lack of transportation. Her boyfriend Danny sent instant text messages to his siblings and some of his friends, saying: "My girl needs work, hit me up if you know anything out there." His brother had a friend who was about to quit his job at a local liquor store, and another friend told him about a local organization that helps youth with job opportunities. Evelyn landed a job at the liquor store in a week and a half.

While one of the ways youth could reliably find jobs was through their networks, their networks were usually plugged into exactly the kinds of low-level jobs they wanted to escape. Although the types of jobs the youth searched for and found at the bottom of the service economy were not perceived by the employers as requiring training or skills, the companies nonetheless advertised these jobs as requiring specific training and skill-sets. Because employers thought that anyone could serve coffee, wash dishes, or clean tables, they were more likely to hire someone they knew through personal connections. This approach, perhaps, also saved them time and energy. When I went to a franchise restaurant for children for a Port City friend's nephew's birthday, I casually asked the manager about his procedure for hiring, claiming that I had a young friend looking for a job. He replied:

> You can ask her or him to fill out an application. But to be honest, I am more into hiring people I know. Port City youth, a lot of them are . . . not to be rude, but they're not always good kids. In the sense of doing drugs and gangs and not studies. I mean I just want someone not in trouble because I don't want to deal with that.

The manager's honest statement made me aware of the impact that the perception of youth as "dangerous" and the moral panic around youth violence (see chapter 5) had on the youth labor market. Supervisors wanted to hire youth only when someone they knew would vouch for their "characters." This attitude is probably typical of other socioeconomically marginalized neighborhoods, and it limits youth's opportunities to find jobs with resumes that reflect the skills they have acquired.

Nevertheless, in some instances, such as public sector jobs, employers seriously considered applications from the youth. When Shivana went to apply for a job at the local library in Port City, she listed me as one of her references. I received a call from a lady who inquired about Shivana in great detail. She asked questions about her disposition, work ethics, and whether she was good at her job at the nonprofit where we worked together. The woman seemed very pleased to learn that I was a volunteer at the nonprofit. I immediately called Shivana about the phone call and she said: "Oh, that's good because someone is retiring tomorrow and they are understaffed so they need someone right away; I don't know if I'll get it." She did get the job. However, although there were numerous instances where the youth put me down as their reference, this was the only call I received over the course of three years.

Keeping Jobs

Once a job was found, it was hard work to keep it. As I noted in chapter 5, the lack of public transportation meant that the youth traveled long hours to get to the local community college. Like going to school, going to work also meant that they were often exhausted and hungry. Lexus found a job at a mall right outside Port City, and her mother promised to give her rides every day. But this turned out to be an unreliable source of transportation, as her mother had many other responsibilities including her new romantic relationship.

One cold winter afternoon when I was at work at the nonprofit, Brianna's name was on the work schedule but she had not shown up and it was almost an hour into work. John seemed to be angry: "We needed her today, I told her. This is unacceptable." We went about our work while some of the youth talked about responsibility and work ethics. Sandra said, "I would never do something like this. Like, nigga, let us know." An hour or so later, Brianna walked in cold and shivering. She could barely talk. We asked her what happened: "Well, I had to go home 'cause I was sick and hungry and forgot medicine. Then my mom was in [the] shower and she had to give me bus money. I was late [for the bus] and walked." It took her forty-five minutes to get to work that day, and she made roughly sixteen dollars.

Most of the young men and women came to work right after school, many of them hungry, having last eaten during lunchtime or even before school, and exhausted after a day of classes. While some had family members who occasionally brought them food, others waited until work was over, around six or seven in the evening, to have their next meal. Many gave up attending birthday parties, social gatherings, and family events in order to go to work. They did not mind working on weekends. They woke up at five in the morning and went to bed at two whenever they were needed. Many of the young men and women found it hard to sustain romantic relationships as they juggled the often-competing demands of school and work (as we saw in chapter 4).

MEANINGS OF WORK AND MONEY

While work was hard to find, it was also coveted. Dominant stereotypes in the media and among policy makers portray economic marginalization as a consequence of the lack of personal responsibility and individual desire to work. On the contrary, or perhaps in response to these narratives, Port City youth, like the majority of U.S. Americans, learned that work was about acquiring money, as well as indicating dignity and personal responsibility.[11] The young men and women started to absorb these lessons from a very young age.

Every one of the sixteen Port City youth started working legally at the age of fourteen. Most of them entered the informal labor market much earlier than that. For example, Ashley was eleven years old when she got her first job as a hot dog vendor one summer. Her father's half sister had a hot-dog truck, and her only employee quit due to irregular pay. Ashley woke up at seven in the morning and walked downtown to the railway station where her aunt did most of her business. Then her aunt found another job, at the dollar store, and she asked Ashley to run the truck by herself. Ashley started to dress like a much older person and wore clothes that accentuated her breasts so that men would give her more tips. She ran the truck efficiently.

Franklin Junior started working with his uncle at the car repair shop when he was ten years old. His uncle began by paying him money for odd jobs here and there and then started to pay him five dollars an hour when Franklin became very devoted to his work. Sandra started helping her mother's friend at a threading salon for six dollars an hour at the age of twelve, "'cause my mom was, like, whatchu gonna do sitting at home, might as well bring some money and it was fun, too, like I swept the floor and helped her and everything. If I didn't, some illegals would do it for less anyway."

The $8.75 Day

Employers in Port City often gave youth hours just short of full-time work in order to avoid responsibility for their health insurance or the possibility of paid days off. This led the youth to take up multiple jobs. They then claimed that having multiple jobs helped them log more hours and make more money—giving them the opportunity to work a potentially unlimited number of hours. The young people conceived of their days in terms of hours, each hour worth the minimum wage.

Ashley, who was an employee at the nonprofit organization where I met her, was not given full-time hours, although she supervised the other youth [according to her] and had a job description similar to the two full-time employees at the organization. It is worth noting that Ashley did not fulfill most of her responsibilities, sometimes because of issues such as transportation, the homework due in her college classes, or simply from being overworked. She and her supervisor, John, were stuck in a vicious cycle:

JOHN (SUPERVISOR): Ashley, I would give you more hours, but you're late to work. You don't come in when you put your name in the roster. You haven't submitted the spring plan yet.

ASHLEY: I get it.

John later told me he thought Ashley was not yet competent to supervise the youth and that he wanted to train her first. He identified with the youth workers and wanted to "do good work in the community." Yet, he claimed, good work did not mean "enabling bad work ethics." One day he told me: "Even if she just tried and was earnest and came to work on time, I would trust her." Ashley laid out her version of the events as follows:

I'm fucking mad I didn't tell him nothin' [after he declined her request for full-time hours], but I am gonna go back and tell him, "Ima do all these things, John. But I'm not gonna do it for free. Like you don't give me health insurance or nothin' 'cause, like, I wanna go get checked up and stuff, and I am not gonna do it for free.

However, the confrontation between Ashley and John went down very differently than she anticipated. One morning Ashley texted me: "Come down now, shit about to go down." I was already on my way to Port City when I received the text and so I drove straight to her house. Ashley was pacing outside, and when she saw me, she immediately got in my car.

ASHLEY: Let's go . . . [to her workplace]. That fuckin' nigga [John]. I went to work as usual and changed my schedule and like put in the roster that I can't do what the other youth were doing yesterday 'cause I was working a lot for the art show that the center is fucking putting on. And the bitch, Anna [a full-time worker], I think she called John, and he texted me and asked why I didn't go. And he asked me to come to the office.

RANITA: What happened? Did you go? This was yesterday, right?

ASHLEY: Hell yeah, I did. I just put on a dress on top of my PJs and came running and there was nothing to do at the office anyway, but I came and found this letter.

When we reached the nonprofit, I saw Ashley's car parked there. She got out of my car and walked over to hers. There was a bottle of water on the street next to the car. She picked it up and said: "It's definitely mine and I was looking for it." Then she took out the letter and asked me to read it out loud. It was a very stern letter, which Ashley found to be rude, saying that John thought that he and she had had a good conversation about why he could not give her full-time hours. However, late in the letter he claimed that she did not come and show any responsibility, and she would "need to be professional" and know "how to be guided" and "come to work." John explained that Ashley should look at this as a "learning opportunity" and asked her to get a driver's license. He mentioned that they had discussed this for eighteen months, but she still had not gotten her license. At the end he wrote: "You cannot work more than 20 hours if you don't get your license, and if you don't get it by [the] end of June you cannot work at all," and then he quoted her job description.

Ashley was fuming with anger: "That fucking nigga, he has some balls. He ain't tellin' me shit and treat me like I'm nothing and show me no respect." She asked me to assist her in writing a letter saying she was giving him two weeks' notice. Afterwards, she took on two new jobs while she was struggling to pass her community college classes. Ashley justified her situation:

I think it's good, though. 'Cause Ma read my tarot cards and she said, Ima make lots of money now. Money is gonna come in. I think that's why the shit with John happened. Ranita, you know I'm smart and smartest in my family. He liked what I do and I do it well. I don't know what's up with that nigga, but it happened for a reason, now I can work mad hours at three jobs!

Because full-time work was rare, youth understood the labor market potential of workers in terms of the hours worked. I had noticed regular discussions concerning hours at the youth's homes. Cassy's mother was a first-generation immigrant from Honduras. She spoke Spanish and some English, did not have a high school degree, and was a homemaker. There was not a single day that I spent at their home when I did not overhear a conversation about her inability to find a job and its effect on their household finances. Cassy's little sisters, aged six and eight when I first met them, knew and often spoke about how they were "broke" and how their father needed more "hours" at work or another job. The phrase "more hours" held a strong positive connotation in their home. One day when Cassy managed to get more hours at the local coffee franchise and announced the news when I dropped her off at home, her sisters sang with happiness, "Cassy got them hours."

The youth began to understand the value of jobs through the value of hours at a very early age. This became clear while I was volunteering at an after-school care center where I came to know two fifth-graders, Jovan and Rick. The two boys were the center's favorites. The director of the center, whom they called Miss Debbie, told me that they were among the best ten students she had seen at the center over the two decades she had been there. Jovan and Rick were both at the top of their class, and math and science were their favorite subjects. They asked me questions about India and UConn and were tough competitors in the board games I played with them. One afternoon when I was just getting to know them, I casually asked: "So what do you wanna be when you grow up?" Contrary to my expectations, Jevon told me that he would start working at Sears in a few years: "I can't wait to start working 'cause I'm passionate about money!" Rick responded to this by saying that his father would find him a job at a local repair store even before he turned fourteen, because his older brother had also started working there when he was twelve years old: "I don't wanna be broke like my parents, I wanna work like all the time, like mad hours." As we saw, as children transitioned to adolescents, however, they began to also learn the value of college degrees.

Although youth, as they transitioned to adulthood, often required their jobs to meet basic needs such as housing, food, and transportation, minimum-wage jobs continue to be perceived as jobs young people take on for pocket money. Consequently, the teenagers and young adults who focused on the hours a particular job would offer, instead of the nature of the work, were judged by employers to be "too greedy" and "not committed enough." A summer program through Youth Services in Port City allowed certain workplaces to hire youth, and Youth Services would pay part of their wages. Youth Services conducted multiple rounds of interviews for several employers, starting with the first round after applicants filled out a general form. Following this, the different organizations, institutions, and businesses that hired youth conducted their own interviews. When I drove Letisha to the youth center in summer 2012, an acquaintance invited me to sit in on the interviews.

A nonprofit organization working toward youth development was hiring youth. Work at this organization included trips to various neighboring cities, flexible hours, dialogue about youth issues, and learning public speaking skills. Every young person who came in for an interview showed a keen interest in the nonprofit organization, highlighted issues at their school, and discussed their passion for change. However, the organization was unable to offer work until three days into the summer program, which meant that the youth would lose three days' pay. No one took on the jobs at the organization, mainly because they would lose the three days' pay. During an interview with me, two employers at the nonprofit organization explained that there were opportunities for training that might increase chances of promotion within the organization or other future benefits but that no payment was involved. Therefore, they usually did not ask their employees about these opportunities:

> No one will work without pay, why should they? They don't have the time because time means money and money is not plenty in most families of the people who work here. For example, there was this leadership training provided by a funding agency for two days and we asked and no one was willing to go but they would've done good for them in the long run. They may have had an increase some time later or something, but no one wanted to go because it's like losing twenty hours of pay, you know.

Young people gave up potentially fruitful opportunities for a few more hours because the hourly wage job system placed the onus of making money on the youth. Striving for what the youth needed at the moment undermined their future plans. According to the young people, if one could potentially work an unlimited number of hours in a variety of jobs, not making enough money was one's own fault. As Ashley put it while speaking to her eighteen-year-old sister:

> No, you can't miss work, no matter how bad you feeling, like you're not dying, you feel sick, but that's okay. Are you gonna miss work every time the hot weather makes you sick? Do you wanna be like those ghetto niggas who don't have no work? And who don't care about this shit but only their baby-daddy dramas? You gotta work and you don't seem like you like it, you need to like to work? You know what I'm saying? Like responsibility and shit like that, you need it. Unless you wanna be in this shit ghetto in Port City all your life and have Ma's life with a fucking bitch-ass boyfriend at the age of fifty with no real income. And her Walmart card for food even be running out.

Money

Money held emotional and material rewards for the youth. While some youth needed money to help support their families and others to take care of themselves, spending money also often brought status and helped draw boundaries between the Port City youth who had money and those who lacked money and were therefore "lazy."[12]

Ashley and I decided to go to a bar on her twenty-first birthday, and stopped at a gas station so that she could withdraw some cash. While we were waiting to use the ATM, a middle-aged woman ahead of us vehemently pushed buttons on the machine but was unable to withdraw anything, due to what seemed like insufficient cash in her account. Ashley looked at me and chuckled as the woman tried repeatedly. As we walked out after withdrawing our cash, Ashley said, "I been there and it's not nice. That lady was in for a bad surprise. I been there, like no money in bank and I keep trying, maybe something will come out, but na ah." Ashley laughed hysterically. "Port City is full of poor people, so you can see them trying hard to take money out of machine." She continued to laugh while putting the money she withdrew into her purse: "When I didn't have this job, my ass was broke. You need money, no matter what, see that's what I don't like with so much time at college, I only get to work like twenty-five hours a week now." At the bar, despite my repeated insistence on paying for Ashley's drinks, she refused to let me pay. As I kept saying, "It's your birthday, I should really be buying," she would respond, "Nah girl, I'm an adult now and I just got paid."

Shortly after Ashley started retaking classes at the local community college in fall 2011, she told me that the most difficult part of rejoining college would be "getting used to few hours [of work per week], like twenty-five maybe." After Ashley had attended college for a few weeks while holding on to her two part-time jobs, her mother told her about a position at the retirement home where she worked—a position that would pay $12.50 per hour, which was quite a few dollars above minimum wage. Ashley found it very hard to resist this offer, too. She struggled with making a decision, but ultimately justified taking on a third job:

> Now I'm like taking care of people at the [retirement] home, working at the liquor store, and selling phones. Like, you can do all this, it's proof that you can have, like, as many jobs and make money if you're not lazy. And I can finish college and make money. And why finish college? To make money, right? So then why give up money in the first place 'cause I don't even know what job I will get [after graduating from college]. But I wanna finish college but not at the cost of money. You feel me? It's like sayin' I don't need money if now I don't take up a job paying like thirteen dollars. Like, I done being poor.

Even though Ashley's instructors asked her to meet with them and continuously urged her to devote more time to her assignments (as per Ashley), she thought that money was important. Initially, she took her assignments to work, but when her employers chided her for doing so, she stopped.

Sometimes I tried to discuss Ashley's decisions regarding school, hoping to influence her to devote more time to her courses. One day, as I was delivering one of my enthusiastic "take college seriously" speeches to Ashley, the deep-rooted meanings of work and money as status, dignity, and security became clearer to me. Ashley refused to buy her nephew the video game she had originally promised, and he threw a tantrum, screaming: "But Titi, you promised!" I whispered uncertainly to Ashley, "Can I buy it and then you pay me later?" Ashley responded loudly, stretching every word in an attempt to impart a very important lesson to her nephew:

> But are you going to buy whatever he needs, though? It's time he learn that shit don't come from nowhere. People gotta earn their own damn money. You be working mad hours in Port City, why you buy his video game? I be

working mad fucking hours. He needs to value money and work, and know that your ass have to work for your own shit.

After staring at us awkwardly for a few minutes, her nephew started to cry again. Ashley noted that she had started working when she was eleven:

> I understood, like, as soon as I was lil' mature that if I don't work I get nothin' from thin air. My aunt had a [food] truck and I looked older than eleven. Mommy didn't even have to tell me, but as soon as my aunt asked, I was like, hell yeah. So Ima teach my nephew [looking at her nephew] the same thing.

Then she turned to him again and said, "You heard me, nothin' ain't free like that."

Sometimes lessons about the value of money did not come from kind aunts—they arrived in the form of soul-crushingly embarrassing moments of helplessness. I was traveling back on a bus with Franklin Junior after one of his dance practices. It was a hot summer day; my car was in the shop and I had hitched a ride with a friend who had family in Port City. I was supposed to stay over at Ashley's place that night and leave with my friend the next day. My friend dropped me off at the high school. As we came out of the school, we realized how hot and humid it was. Franklin was especially exhausted after his practice and drenched in sweat: "Can we take the bus? I can't walk," he said. Most seats on the bus were taken and I headed toward the back. The bus fare had gone up from a dollar to a dollar fifty, and as Franklin came in after me he handed a dollar to the driver—who began saying: "You think you can get all the free rides, am I right? Next time Ima kick you out, I'm not even kidding." I turned around to offer the fifty cents, but the embarrassing moment had already taken place. Franklin turned red, his head hanging low as he sat down on the bus seat. After walking in silence for a few minutes after we got off the bus, Franklin spoke, his face grim with worry: "They don't give me no hours! I fucking hate not having money. I even gotta pay back like forty to Curtis. Don't know what the fuck I'm gonna do. Gotta get a job, gotta get a job" (Franklin later told me that a white boy who got on after us also did not know about the fare raise and was fifty cents short—he was not threatened. Youth of color are stigmatized more heavily and constructed as lazy while their white counterparts are more likely to be absolved, illustrating the racialized nature of how economic marginalization is experienced in everyday life.)

Once money was earned, after considerable effort, it was used not just for basic necessities but also for tattoos, piercings, brand-name clothing, hair color, a vacation to Florida, and even plane tickets for a friend to visit. It was obligatory that the youth took care of all such desires before they "went broke again." There appeared to be endless ways the youth could spend money to establish status, but each of them had to be visible, because the ability to spend money meant social mobility. Sometimes, for the youth, money was not a path to social mobility; rather, it *was* social mobility.[13]

Moreover, because income was unpredictable, a desire often felt like it had to be met when resources were available—or it could remain unmet forever. The moment twenty-two-year-old Shivana was paid, she went to the best tattoo artist in town and got an elaborate tattoo: "I've been wanting to finish this up, but the fucking place just don't give me hours, so I was broke as hell." Lena bought tickets for herself and her sister, and Angie bought tickets for herself and a friend to travel to Florida for a vacation. Angie commented: "I just gotta get outta here, I can't take it no more, my dad's driving me crazy, that nigga bring ugly-ass bitches back home every night, like I can't deal with this right now, Ima just go soak in the sun, 'cause I'm working like mad hours, you know it. I don't deserve this shit no more." A few weeks later she had to borrow money from me to pay her phone bill. Cassy's favorite activity on the day she got paid was to get highlights for her hair.[14]

THE SERVICE CLASS

The youth's learned appreciation of the value of work and hours, combined with the type of labor that characterizes the contemporary service industry, helped shape a hierarchical structure that organized various jobs available to the Port City youth. The more "white collar" a job was imagined to be, the more desirable it was. Jobs that required employees to wear nice clothes, sit at a desk, interact with people, or utilize expertise in any area were valued. Drawing on the malleable nature of emotional labor mediated through haphazard participation in higher education, the youth imagined that knowledge acquired in isolated college classes immediately boosted their skills in low-wage jobs. They also believe that such knowledge prepared them for a better career in the industries where they worked for low wages. Concomitantly, the low-wage jobs at the top of the hierarchy, or the jobs that resembled white-collar work, were viewed as providing youth with "work experience" that would boost their career opportunities. These young men and women viewed the labor market payoff from their isolated college classes, as well as the educational and career opportunities emanating from their low-wage work, in an exaggerated manner.

While I served as a volunteer at the Port City Youth Center, the youth who came to apply for jobs seemed to be in agreement regarding what constituted the best types of jobs. Alize told me about her job search experience:

> They didn't call me back from Forever 21, I went there but this lady, she doesn't seem to like me. Victoria's Secret is hiring but there you have to wear black slacks and nice top and like talk to people. Like, you know, buy this and all, I can't even talk, like, proper like that. You know how bad my English is? I don't know. . . .

When she was offered a job at a clothing store at the mall that previously hired only white employees, Alize decided to take that job over another job at a discount clothing store, even though the new job paid her the same wages and the hours were less convenient: "Yo, but I gotta take it up, Alize movin' up in life! I done been ghetto, I got a white people work now." Youth found meanings in their work through racialized understandings of labor.

Adam had washed dishes for $300 a week at a local restaurant, but he was not happy with the job: "Like my cuz [cousin] gets to serve and talk to people and that way, you know, you learn and all how to talk to people, but I'm just washing dishes, I wanna apply to Petco, I think they're hiring." A.J. was very proud that she got a job at the local T.J. Maxx. She boasted about the people who shopped there, about how she handled interactions with them and guided them regarding what they should buy. Those who worked in restaurants also valued the customer service element of the job and imagined that their talent and self-presentation skills had landed them the job. The youth often felt embarrassed about work that required them to clean bathrooms or tables, which they frequently had to do when asked by managers. Evelyn often told me, "I mean, at my work they be asking me to do that shit even though I serve and I'm like, yeah, you can ask the Mexicans 'cause they gonna do it for that money, but I won't clean no one's shit." A. J. commented: "Yeah, I know whatchu mean, girl. I ain't doing any of that shit, that's why I like my job, it's all nice and fancy." Working in fast-food chains was the least valued of the legal jobs but was often preferred over illegal and semilegal jobs.

Regular pay was also important to the young men and women. Curtis left his job at a local nonprofit organization "'cause they don't pay much and mess up my checks and all, like, we count our hours and put it in and like they're not professional or something. I want real job and all." Semilegal and illegal jobs were not ranked highly, not only because of the risks they entailed, but also because they did not guarantee a regular paycheck. One summer, Curtis worked for his brother, selling drugs. During this time, he bought numerous pairs of shoes and a car and took a trip to Florida. However, soon the market began to run dry and he and his brother found themselves low on funds. Curtis took on a job at the local public school, in the computer lab, where he had to look into simple issues that students encountered while using the computers, such as software updates. Curtis was "bored outta my skull" and his brother was unhappy about the missing manpower, but Curtis told me he valued the regular pay: "Like, I go to my bank and I can get twenty dollars, that's what I want, I don't want crazy cash one time and then it's all like, nigga, give me a dollar."

As the youth moved horizontally from one job to the next, for the same pay, within this hierarchy of jobs, they imagined that they were moving up the ladder. Even as they continued to work in minimum-wage jobs, they framed their skills as related to their college classes and their hopes for white-collar work.

During her first semester, Cassy enrolled in three classes, but dropped one class mid-semester, unable to juggle the two-hour commute to college, her classes, and her job. The next semester, she enrolled in two classes but dropped one because her employer liked her work and offered to give her more hours. She told me: "The owner of Coffee and Doughnuts commended how clean the store was and suggested I get extra hours by going to her other stores just to clean. That's a big compliment, coming from her." I stayed over at Cassy's house one cold November night. Cassy had returned from her work at the coffee shop very late the night before. But in the morning she woke up tired, her body ached, she had a class at the community college in two hours, and her bus ride to the college would take an hour and forty-five minutes (I did not have my car). Cassy jumped out of bed, pulling up her pants as she sprinted to the bathroom, and was in and out in two minutes. Then she threw on a jacket and rushed out of her home to the bus stop. It was a chilly fall morning, "Oh, dude, wish I was in bed," Cassy said. Some days Cassy said she was proud of what she was doing—going to college for her sisters, for her dream of becoming a psychologist, and because she knew she did not deserve to worry about money all her life but instead deserved a prestigious job because "[she is] smart and good at school." On this chilly November morning, these visions provided her with the warmth of a brilliant future.

By two in the afternoon, Cassy was hungry but had no money to buy food. She had another class at four. She tried to steal a bag of chips from the student union: some days when it was crowded this was possible. "I know how to do this shit," Cassy said. "I have my system but I'm not gonna do it when I am not completely sure that it will work—I am not a dumbass." When I offered to buy, Cassy said that she would rather have me take her to the Chinese buffet afterwards. At 2:30, Cassy's boss called her to ask whether she wanted extra hours to clean, and Cassy said "yes" without a thought:

> Well, I can't give up hours, you know—I'm good at my job and that's why they asked me and it's not just about serving coffee, it's not just some talentless job, you know, you can actually be good at serving coffee and move up the chain and my classes here will help as I do, but for now I also need the money and think of pleasing my boss, you know.

Cassy decided to take the four o'clock bus home so that she could then get to work—she was hungry and sleepy, but she wanted the money.

Cassy was torn between work and school. As she continued to work, her enthusiasm for work escalated and she tried to find continuity between the career she aspired to and the coffee-shop service job. "It's more than serving coffee," Cassy replied when I inquired about her schoolwork and her aspirations of becoming a psychologist:

> A woman ordered a large hot decaf with twelve fucking Splendas. Not many people order decaf, so it's easy to forget. I ended up having to remake her coffee 'cause, of course, I forgot it was decaf. I took care of it as quickly as I could. The lady behind her was the mean one. She told me she wanted a medium iced hazelnut regular and she paused, so I thought that was it. So I hold out my hand slowly for her card and she adds an onion bagel with cream cheese, with an attitude. I put it was toasted, and she said it wasn't. She just wanted it "as is." Okay, I get her bagel and I get ready to wrap it but I ask if she wanted it sliced. Then she snapped at me and told me to just put it in a bag, loudly. So I did. And when I gave her the bag, she snatched it out of my hands roughly. I remained polite the entire time. The lady after her noticed it and she tipped me two dollars 'cause she felt bad, so that uplifted my hatred for humans a bit. I don't think I've ever met anyone so intolerable. Needless to say, I'm glad I know how to deal with people and calm them down. It really is not just coffee, like you gotta be calm and have these skills to read people and understand their state [of mind].

Serving coffee "the real way," Cassy explained, involved quick wit:

> I asked these two girls that came up to the counter what I could get them, and one of them said a tall, dark, and handsome military man who isn't a lying, cheating piece of shit. Without missing a beat, I replied by saying, "The item you are looking for is currently unavailable. I'm sorry to say we are all out of stock, ma'am." Both of them busted out laughing. Like, I enjoy healing people in whatever small way.

As Cassy performed emotional labor and assigned meaning to it in relation to her aspirations of becoming a psychologist, she managed the conflict between her aspirations of a white-collar job and the reality of minimum-wage work. Cassy's emotional labor highlights the autonomy that workers have in how they experience emotional labor beyond the control of the organization, creatively molding labor to resemble a certain skillset.[15] A few months later, when the coffee shop was downsizing, the manager fired Cassy without batting an eye.[16] In some ways then, the organization benefited from the ways in which workers like Cassy experienced labor. The workers may have experienced some emotional benefits, but no stable and concrete material benefit came from devoting oneself to work.

Like Cassy, the youth who worked at clothing stores for minimum wages claimed that they were becoming part of the fashion industry, and the youth who worked at the electronics store boasted about their place in the technology industry. Alize was very excited when an opportunity arose to work at an electronics store. We were at a store, looking for a cheap phone for her, when one of the workers wearing a shirt with the store logo came up to us and inquired whether we spoke Spanish. Alize spoke Spanish fluently, and the worker requested that she assist a customer who was not comfortable speaking in English. Afterwards, the same man handed Alize an application for a job at the store. He told her that she would have to attend a training session, after which she would be an expert in "selling electronics." Alize was very excited at the prospect of becoming an "expert":

> He called me later and was like, you're one training away from the store shirt and then you're an expert. I feel like I am into those things and technology, and I can help, like, those who speak Spanish. Like it's no joke, you gotta learn real things, like if you were in business school, whatchu think they be teachin' you anyway.

Alize became even more certain of her aspirations to become part of the "tech industry": "Yo, they make like mad money with startups, that's what like one of my teachers' son is doin'. She be tellin' us all about it. I been thinkin' that's what I wanna do 'cause now I'm sellin' phones and I'm into this kinda things." She wanted to enroll in a computer applications class at the community college after passing her placement test. She had a difficult time passing the test. She spent two semesters in basic English and mathematics classes at the community college. But she remained enthusiastic. The only things between her and the tech industry, according to Alize, were the remedial classes: "Why they not let me take the shit I want to, I'm not into English, and you don't need that even to learn technology."

When Brianna was unable to find scholarship money for her second semester at the four-year university she was attending, she enrolled in an introductory course on nutrition at Port City Rivers. Brianna imagined that her work for minimum wage at the bakery fit well with the course:

The teacher told us about Aspartame and sugar and how our body, like, dissolves it and whatnot, and what it does to us. And now I use it on people, customers who come to the store. The other day I just educated an older gentleman about Aspartame in soda and how diet isn't good, and I tell them, like, which cake is less sugar and gluten-free and all. We have to know that stuff and you really have to know this if you want to be a good employee, even at a bakery. Nothing better than getting paid for teaching someone something new, college comes in handy.

In the service industry, the line between experts and amateurs is fuzzy, at best: more and more services are being organized in numerous and unpredictable ways.[17] This enabled the youth to imagine their work as skillful and to link these jobs to other white-collar work.

ENTREPRENEURIAL YOUTH

A few of the Port City youth were more enterprising and intrepid in their attempts to build careers. These young people took drastically different routes from their friends and family, routes that did not resemble the school and work pathways available to them. I include this section to give readers a glimpse into the wide range of strategies that the youth adopted when trying to climb up the socioeconomic ladder. Indeed, we often hear stories about young people who come from very modest beginnings and have built an enterprise. As I write, not enough time has passed for me to know whether or not the innovative young men and women I met in Port City would enter the white-collar job marketplace. Instead, I document their lives as they attempted to make it through their innovative pathways, under the dire conditions of poverty.

Sandra's close friend Tywan had died of a brain tumor during their last year of high school. One day during her first semester in college, Sandra, Lauren, and Siete sat on her bed mourning his death and talking about the old days. They began by discussing the "college life" and how happy Tywan would have been in college because people were more open-minded than in high school. They said that before he passed away, the three of them had contributed money to buy him chocolates and flowers. Tywan was a very well-dressed black young man with blonde hair. Sandra lamented with tears in her eyes, "I remember when back in the day like everyone was making fun of him 'cause of how he was. 'Cause he was not, like, you know, like, the men and whatnot. He liked to dress up and he like wore dresses and whatnot. But he was so fashionable." Lauren added: "I never made fun of him. I was always nice and that's why we became best friends."

Sandra took out a pair of black silk, sleeveless, bareback overalls, went to the bathroom, and changed into them. As she came out, Lauren and Siete marveled at how great they looked on her.

LAUREN: We gotta do something about it. We need to, like, continue his dreams, you know what I'm sayin'? Like he was crazy smart and he had all these ideas and we was gonna start this fashion clothing line. I am good at designing too.

SANDRA: Yeah, yeah. I've been thinking the same thing. 'Cause we [Tywan and Sandra] talked about this a lot too. After high school, we planned to do this and take classes to like learn about it.

SIETE: I don't know nothin' about fashion. But you need to do what you gotta do. 'Cause business is where the money is at. 'Cause all these niggas be working and serving fries but the thing is, they pay taxes and they don't make no money. You gotta dream big to make it big.

SANDRA: I'm never gonna do that shit. I'd rather have a job at Old Navy. But thing is, if you want [a] job in the fashion industry, you gotta be all well-dressed and speak nice and stuff. 'Cause you gotta talk to people and, like, guide them about the store. These niggas here don't know that shit. But I'm also learning with my job at Old Navy.

LAUREN: Aight, we gonna do this or not? I'm in. No one else for now, though. . . . 'Cause I don't trust no other niggas out there. And, I'm not playin', I am serious about this.

SANDRA: Me too. We need to do something different, though. 'Cause like people be wearing the same shit from same store. Like everyone's buying Target. We gotta make some new stuff.

I stayed until dinnertime that evening while the three girls discussed their plans of founding a clothing line. Sandra was a decent artist. She could look at a piece of clothing and sketch it out. The trio sketched out some dresses and discussed where and how they could buy material and paraphernalia to make their dresses. First, they started with their web presence. Sandra was quite familiar with computers and the internet. Her grandmother had been seeing a man, and he gave Sandra a laptop to use. He had also suggested that she read at least one book a month and take her college applications seriously. I never got to meet him, but Sandra spoke of him very fondly.

Lauren and Sandra set up their Facebook pages and Instagram accounts. They also wanted a website but did not know anyone who could help. When I offered to have one of my friends assist them, they declined because they did not want to pay for the domain name or learn how to navigate the website to post pictures and the like: "We can't be asking you every time we need something!" Sandra said. They posted information about their new business and enthusiastically designed a few shirts and dresses, including a leopard-print racerback and a silver cowl-neck shirt.

They and two more girls from Port City brought the plan to life. Sandra and another friend stitched clothes with sewing machines they bought with money borrowed from Sandra's mother. They bought material online. They frequently looked up how-tos on YouTube. A few months later, they had some of their friends pose in their dresses, and they posted the pictures online. They also actively marketed the clothes they designed to their friends, neighbors, and family.

A few months later, Lauren quit. When I ran into her, she said, "Sandra ain't doing what we started. She is doing the same shit that looks like all the clothes in stores. It's nothing new and that's not what I wanna do. She can do what she wants." But when I met Sandra that same day she contradicted Lauren's story:

> No, it ain't that. She just lazy, that nigga. Like, always fooling around and whatnot. And she has this ghetto-ass nigga [boyfriend], she up to no good. Like here I am going to college and doing this shit 'cause I wanna make it big and ain't no one getting in my way.

I never found out for sure why Lauren quit, although she continued to pose for some of their pictures. The remaining girls continued their endeavor. I asked Sandra's mother what she thought about Sandra's time investment in the clothing line instead of schoolwork. Ms. Robinson told me:

She is smart, my girl. She would've been good in Harvard but she gonna do good here too. But she had big dreams and I am not standing in between her and her dreams. My mother lived without water and my daughter is in college. It's big, how far we came. She is talented. I don't know but college is hard, but she is doing okay. It's only been starting now.

The clothing line has not received national or statewide acclaim since it was launched, but the young women did receive orders from friends, family, and acquaintances. The highlight of the enterprise was when Sandra's mother's sister asked them to make her a gown for her daughter's wedding. It was a red gown with an embellished neckline. Sandra also tried to do a lot of marketing for the Port City High prom, but no one ordered any items.

The general uncertainty of the youth's work history reflects the uncertainty ingrained in people growing up poor or working class in the contemporary United States. Despite higher ambitions among marginalized youth, opportunities to attain social mobility and economic stability are at a historic low among them. Not only have the conditions of marginalized communities worsened due to mass incarceration, evictions, unemployment and underemployment, as well as shrinking public assistance, but the service industry does not offer stable and secure jobs to those without a postsecondary education.

I, like many other scholars, do not wish to romanticize the industrial era. But in contrast to the past, unpredictability has become the most predictable characteristic of coming of age in poor America. A complex set of factors interacted in the Port City youth's everyday decisions about school and work such as whether to go to school, complete schoolwork, take schoolwork to work, go to work instead of school, and take hours that conflicted with school. The youth did not conceptualize the importance of college through lifelong socialization, as middle-class children do—as an almost compulsory step toward adulthood. Rather, the Port City youth slowly learned the importance of higher education through their schools, local nonprofits, the middle-class actors they encountered in various settings such as their workplace, and their own struggles to find the kinds of jobs they desired. Their ambivalent desires for work and education, and newly acquired, often confused, knowledge about the long-term payoff of college interacted with everyday obstacles to continuing both college and work, such as transportation, health, hunger, and personal struggles at school and work. Sometimes, the youth felt more comfortable, successful, and worthwhile in the world of work than they did at school where tasks were harder to complete and short-term praise or gain was less present. At all times, work hours brought money, and money represented agency. The young people found ways to manage their uncertain lives.

7 Internalizing Uncertainty

BAD GENES, HUNGER, AND HOMELESSNESS

I don't know. I don't know what I'll do, but at least nigga ain't with a big-ass belly [pregnant] right now. All I wanna do is move out of my mom's house, 'cause I don't like how her new boyfriend looks at me. So I told her Ima move out and gave her notice 'cause I pay rent and she gonna get someone to rent it. So, I gotta move out but I haven't figured out where. But I will. Real talk. It's Thanksgiving and I just heard a gunshot outside . . . am I surprised? No! But, I'm gonna go ahead and say I'm lucky I ain't in jail or with a baby daddy even if I don't know where I'm gonna be living next month, at least it's not jail.

—Lena

Perhaps because of her quiet disposition, the other youth of Port City often found Brianna irritating. Alize explained to me, "She like one of those people who is very quiet but like evil." Brianna herself once told me that she avoided talking too much because once she got into trouble and got hurt for "opening my mouth too much in school." She usually dressed in jerseys and jeans, her hair tidily done and never any makeup on her face—a stark contrast to her mother, a stylish, talkative, and warm woman in her mid- to late thirties. Brianna was a self-taught piano player, and in her free time she liked to practice songs by Rihanna and Nicki Minaj on her electronic keyboard. Although she was generally a timid person, Brianna was quite willing to play the keyboard in front of me, especially when she was hurting inside.

Whenever Brianna missed work or was not scheduled to work, the other youth talked about how "irritating and weird" she was. Perhaps the habit of keeping to herself and not opening up made other people feel uncomfortable around Brianna. However, Sandra sometimes stood up for Brianna: "Don't be rude to her just 'cause she doesn't talk back. She is gonna go a long way, more successful than most of you."

Brianna's father lived with his girlfriend in Virginia and they had two children together. The household also included her father's two sons from a different relationship—one of them was a teenager named Reno. Brianna lived with her mother. Brianna used to go to see her father and family in Virginia when she was younger, and her father occasionally visited them. When Reno, whom Brianna rarely saw, committed suicide in 2011, Sandra told Brianna that "family is family and you gotta be there for them." Although Brianna had last seen Reno in 2004 (she had not been to Virginia in a while because her father had been coming to visit her family in Port City), when he died, she stayed in her room for almost three days. Brianna's mother called Sandra, who called me to arrange a visit to Brianna's house.

Brianna's sadness wasn't very visible because she always looked tired, and she already talked only when necessary and for the most part responded in monosyllables. The day of her brother's death, Brianna talked more than usual. She recalled happy times with Reno: "Oh I remember last time I was there, Reno be asking me every two minute[s], 'Yo, you want some ice cream?' and I was like 'No' and then he asked again. I miss him." We stayed for about five hours while Brianna occasionally reminisced about whatever she could recall from the old days with Reno. Her main source of anger and frustration was that she didn't have the money to travel to Virginia for his funeral. She lamented, "I got no money and mom doesn't have a job no more so I don't even know what to do. But it's my lil' brother, how can I not go, you know what I mean? But I feel bad asking my mom."

A large number of marginalized youth in poor America are left to regularly manage threats to basic human dignity and everyday struggles of poverty—sudden death or regular untreated illness among family and friends, evictions from their homes,[1] imprisonment of their loved ones, empty bank accounts and refrigerators,[2] and families breaking up due to a guardian's drug problem. Social scientists have statistically documented the impact of growing inequalities on the lives and futures of urban American youth. In 2013, one in eight poor families renting homes in America could not afford the rent and feared eviction.[3] In 2014, more than 41 million Americans lived in households that were food insecure.[4] That same year, 32 million nonelderly Americans did not have access to healthcare.[5] How do young Americans manage these uncertainties in their everyday life as they transition to adulthood and attempt to become socially mobile?

Some scholars argue that communities that regularly confront dire conditions of poverty often "normalize" such violence in order to manage the day-to-day reality of continuing struggles and uncertainties that might otherwise paralyze their existence. For example, In *Death without Weeping: The Violence of Everyday Life in Brazil* (1993: 272), a twenty-five-year-long ethnography among three generations of women in a Brazilian shantytown, anthropologist Nancy Scheper-Hughes theorizes mothers' love as a bourgeois luxury—women confronting the severe realities of absolute poverty in the town of Bom Jesus de Mata cannot grieve their infants who die regularly. Scheper-Hughes shows us how infant mortality is "normalized" in the public as well as the private realm; she draws on the concept of the "social production of indifference"[6] to demonstrate the mechanisms through which the death of children—which should, it seems, garner immediate attention from the state as well as families—instead becomes routine.

Growing up under the constraints of poverty requires that children learn to live in highly uncertain and precarious conditions and to readily deal with various types of crises and disruptions, often unforeseen, that occur on a regular basis. While those with access to certain basic necessities can make tentative plans, or at least have a sense of what their overall life will look like in the immediate future, the Port City youth had internalized a valuable lesson: life is uncertain. Predictability and certainty, it seems, is a bourgeois luxury.[7] The Port City youth internalized unpredictability to manage the continual disruptions in their lives, constructing home as transient, mortality as imminent, and health as precarious. They developed the ability to make short- and long-term plans against the constant background of instability, to adjust when plans fell apart, and to hatch brand-new plans with relative ease, all without becoming too flustered or emotionally distraught by the disruptions. They learned to manage their uncertain lives and everyday violence through systems that were equally unpredictable. For example, Ashley quit her job, and validated her decision by her mother's recent tarot card readings.

These young men and women manage the everyday violence of poverty, caused by persistent threats to basic necessities. They "normalize" these uncertainties by drawing on highly individualistic and often uncontrollable and otherworldly accounts such as "bad genes," "fate," and "unknown conspiracies"—accounts that helped them deal with the unpredictability of life. In a similar way, they developed and enacted a guarded perception of what home meant—often imagining home through a symbolic connection to the place they were born or the country from which their parents or even grandparents immigrated to America—which left them always prepared and eager to move. Strategies like these enabled them to find meanings amidst their struggles and uncertainties.

DEALING WITH DEATH

In the summer of 2012, I was deeply affected by my existential crisis resulting from the death of a seventeen-year-old boy, Tywan, in Port City. I had gotten to know Tywan because he was a close friend and classmate of Sandra's. He was diagnosed with a terminal illness, and died within a few weeks of being admitted to a university hospital. While death always brings sadness and loss, and we hear every day about tragedies that occur far away from home, it was the first time I had personally experienced the death of a much younger person. I was struck hard by the very obvious, yet often ignored, reality of the impermanence of life, and I came to the (re) realization that death could come at any age and that I and other loved ones could also die young. Managing this uncertainty was taxing. I wondered how young people growing up in dire circumstances deal with the constant reminder of death.[8]

When I left India to pursue a higher education in the United States, the last thing I had in mind was the possibility of my death in a land far away from my family. So I initially passed it off as a joke when Evelyn, who was insightful and mature, said that she did not plan on applying to universities on the West Coast due to a fear—which I assumed was unfounded—of sudden death. I pondered about an otherwise driven woman's seemingly irrational fear.[9]

Of average height and weight, Evelyn was particularly concerned by her acne but claimed she didn't care about her looks. She always dressed with simple jeans and T-shirts, and she spoke with a loud stern voice. She was perhaps the only person louder than me in Port City. If there is one thing Evelyn knew herself to be, it was resourceful. About two months after I met her, she told me about her childhood as we chatted in the well-maintained apartment near the highway where she lived with her foster mother and siblings. We sat on plastic chairs around the living-room coffee table. With a stern look on her face that was already stretched by her tightly bound ponytail, which she played with constantly, she told me:

> I've been in foster care since the age of nine. Like, I'm lucky that I don't live with my mother though, she be homeless most of the time, and to be honest there are girls out there who mad touchy about it. I'm not, so I can talk about it and you can write about it!

We talked for hours about her biological mother and her foster mother, with most of our conversation centering around Evelyn's gratitude for what her foster mother had given her: a home.

One day, as we wrote her statement of purpose for college applications, Evelyn said to me:

> My sister [by her foster mother] is just born and by the time she is six I'll be done with college, and I come for vacation, I wanna take her out for ice cream and buy her stuff. Kids that age are the deal, they want everything and I wanna give her those. It would be great to come for vacation and be like you want this? Ya sure! I wanna do that, you know.

Evelyn graduated from high school in the summer of 2012. She diligently applied to colleges while she worked two jobs:

> I ask whatever I need, like I didn't know nothin' about nothin' and then, like, I went to the youth center and I'm like you gotta help me! I came this far, you know, I coulda been on the streets so Ima make this happen and people wanna help you.

Evelyn knew what to find where: she knew where to get free printouts for things she needed, how to take practice SATs, how to write a statement of purpose in ways that made it stand out. Evelyn did not attract much judgment. Although she could often come on strong with her sarcastic humor, she was also the type who did not like to talk about other girls or boys and who mostly kept her judgments to herself. This meant that other than her occasional humorous comments and loud voice, she often disappeared into the background.

On a sunny, but relatively cold day in Port City, Evelyn and I met at our regular spot in a local coffee shop. Ever since we had become friends, Evelyn—who was initially fearful of entering what she thought of as a fancy place—preferred to meet at the coffee shop. It "made [her] feel all college-y," she claimed. We were looking at her College Board scores and her letter when Evelyn said, "I ain't going to California or nothin'. 'Cause what happens if I die? What happens if I can't pay for phone? They don't have pay phones these days. My foster mother or my mama can't really find tickets and everything to go get my body. You know what I'm sayin' though? I don't wanna be rotting, what's gonna happen to my body until they find me?" Evelyn did not apply to colleges in California, and I never insisted. However, it was not until much later, when I began to realize the higher frequency with which untimely deaths occurred in Port City, that I was able to fully comprehend the complexity of her fear, which was grounded in her understanding of her mother's lack of resources, but also in the constant reminder of sudden death and uncertainty of life through the deaths of her peers. Of course, not every individual struggling with the violence of poverty considers sudden death as an imminent possibility. Yet, like Evelyn, far too many of the young men and women I spent time with in Port City did not think of early death as an aberration; they had seen enough of it.

By the time I left Port City, I had seen enough of it as well: not only did Sandra's best friend, Tywan, die of a brain tumor at the age of seventeen, as I mentioned at the beginning of this section, but Cassy's close friend died at the age of twenty due to a drug overdose when he was alone at home while his mother worked the night shift; Shivana's best friend committed suicide right after high school, after her depression went untreated for years; and Brianna's half brother, who lived with their father in a different state, also committed suicide at the tender age of seventeen due to untreated mental illness. Shortly before my time in Port City, Ashley's mother's sister had a tumor and died when she was in her early thirties, leaving two young children behind.

When I say that the youth accepted untimely death as routine, I do not by any means intend to suggest that they did not mourn these deaths or that death did not affect them emotionally; in fact, it was quite the contrary. The Port City youth grieved immensely when their loved ones died, but they also had to manage the reality of death's regularity. When Tywan was admitted to a university hospital, Sandra planned her days around visits to her friend. Sandra's other friends, who did not themselves know Tywan well, all visited him too, in order to support Sandra. They brought him stuffed toys and flowers every day. He was not able to tolerate the chemo treatment and did not stay in the hospital for very long. The day of his death was, as we had expected, a dark one. Sandra cried until she lost her voice, at the same time trying to remain strong for Tywan's mother, who considered Sandra to be nothing short of her own daughter. Tywan's mother attended the graduation at Port City High even though her son would not be there, and she cheered for Sandra and others in the graduating class: "I wish he could've done this. It was his dream. But he is resting in peace and watching out for us. He is always with us," she said of Tywan. Sandra talked about Tywan for months after his death—often endearingly—about his fashion sense, the bright future he had ahead of him, and his vivacious disposition. She said, "He was something. Always laughing and he had the best sense of clothes, though. Like he was real fashionable and not like ghetto style, though. He was real classy. But he was smart too, he woulda gone to college for sure."

Along with sadness, there was also anger around the untimely death of loved ones. Predictably, given her nature, Cassy was more enraged than sad about the passing of her young friend:

It sucks when young people with so much potential and life ahead of them die, you know? And I bet it doesn't happen with rich people, because they are taken care of? In some way or another. It's lives of other people that are wasted. And like, so many old bums in here. Not to be mean, but I'm like, why my friend though. But that's how it is here though, drugs, gangs, guns.

Like Cassy, many of the other young people were perceptive and often articulated the structural oppressions that caused the untimely deaths of young people in their community. On one occasion, we discussed the death of one young man in a gun shooting.

RANITA: Did you know him, Ashley?

ASHLEY: Nah ah, I didn't know him. But I knew one of his stepbrothers. Everyone in his family, they real crazy, I think.

LEXUS: It makes me crazy. 'Cause I have so many brothers.

ASHLEY: They don't care about us. 'Cause we don't do well in school. We not good for nothin' but ball games. My friend got this sore throat, alright. And she asked me like I wanna go to the doctor. But she got no money and she got no insurance so she was like, yo you got any medicine like antibiotic? And I read somewhere, alright, that you don't give your medicine, like antibiotic and all, to no one. But that's why so many youngins dying in here. 'Cause they don't care about us. We need to take care of ourselves 'cause the government won't, and we shouldn't do drugs, alcohol, or violence, and respect education.

ALIZE: I agree with you though. I think they just want us to die. 'Cause some of us poor in here and all these girls gettin' pregnant and then their babies are no good. And they not going to college or anything.

The youth often spoke of their jobs that did not provide them with health insurance, how some of them did not have access to healthy food, and how drug addiction went untreated among young people in their community—indicating their sophisticated understandings of inequalities among them. Yet I noted conflicting explanations when it came to understanding the random deaths among their own family members, with the youth often drawing on unearthly factors such as fate, deeply internal causes such as genes, or larger conspiracies by hospitals or other unknown organizations. Uncertain life called for random explanations. Perhaps, acknowledging how the system impedes them was harder to manage, while shifting their analysis to random events made it easier to digest the randomness of their lives and the inevitable fate of poverty that awaited them.

Lexus heard the news of her father's death a few months after he died in New York City. One of her stepbrothers came to Port City when his girlfriend needed to visit her home there in order to get her parents' Social Security number (they had refused to give this to her over the phone because they did not think that she could actually go to college and they deemed FAFSA applications useless). Since her stepbrother was passing through Port City, he decided to drop by Lexus's house and deliver the news. He told Lexus and her mother and siblings: "Nigga dropped dead in his apartment or almost died or something and then police came to take him to hospital and then he died there, oh yeah, that's what they said. That he died in the hospital 'cause something was wrong with him." Lexus repeated her stepbrother's words the next day at work. "And he be tellin' this to you now? Why he didn't call you guys though?" asked Ashley, who was always sentimental about family bonds. Lexus replied that neither her stepbrother nor any of her siblings were living with him at the time. Two of them had moved in with their romantic partners, and one of them had moved out with their mother. What unsettled Lexus most, however, was that "Nigga was mad healthy though, as far I knew. How he just dead?"

ASHLEY: Oh yeah, that's how it happens, though. Was your father an organ donor?

LEXUS: I think so.

ASHLEY: [with conviction] Yeah, they prolly didn't give him all the treatment and medicine and whatnot. 'Cause if they are organ donors then the hospital wants the organs 'cause they have a line and gets lots of money for organs so they didn't give nothin' to your father to save him. They prolly did some stuff but not everything, alright, 'cause my aunt, and we think that's what happened and my cousin too, she dead mad young, like people don't die like that so young.

LEXUS: [with enlarged eyes and mouth gaping open, apparently appalled, shocked, and relieved at the same time] Yeah, that makes sense, cause I been thinkin' like how he be dead like that so young and everything.

ASHLEY: And your dad, he died with dignity at least, it ain't that bad 'cause I read somewhere that poor men are paid money to run like animals while the rich pretend to hunt.

Other explanations for the uncertainty of life and sudden death included internal flaws such as bad genes. When one of Curtis's distant cousins suddenly died at work, the family attributed it to bad genes. Curtis and his brothers discussed the death the day they got the news. It was cloudy and the sun was just setting. We sat on their porch as cars drove into and out of the housing project.

CURTIS: Ranita, my mother got cancer, and one of her brothers also got cancer. And we got some family in Puerto Rico and they got cancer and lupus too, I think.

ONE OF CURTIS'S BROTHERS: [cutting him off, while sipping on a beer can] Nah, no one got no lupus! I don't think so.

CURTIS: How do you know? You don't know nothin'! I'm talking to mami all day and she tells me these things about our family. Her other sister died of cancer, and she has cancer and it might've spread, the whole family got bad genes and nothing can be done. You mad thin [pointing to his brother]. 'Cause we all got bad genes. Our father be dead too, so he prolly got bad genes too. What them doctors gonna do anyway? You can go to them all the time but no one done nothin' for you an' they won't.

Random deaths make us all uncomfortable. When a healthy person dies a sudden and premature death, it reminds us of our own mortality, which is rather fragile. But, such random and premature deaths were more frequent in Port City than among my wealthier graduate student friends, and therefore, it shaped local explanations among the youth that were random, and yet routinized so as to not paralyze their existence. Random explanations, including genes and conspiracies, allowed youth to continue in the face of helplessness as their friends and family died randomly, or suffered through illnesses without treatment; at the least they provided momentary order to unfathomable questions. Yet, random explanations also created further obstacles by allowing random actions on the part of the youth.

EXPLAINING AND MANAGING ILLNESS

Regular preventative doctor's visits are a relatively modern Western phenomenon shaped by capitalistic profit goals, a culture of fear, and growing value added to human life.[10] Earlier generations probably did not have every mole, lump, or aberration from what is perceived as a "normal" body examined by professionals, and this is not inherently dangerous. However, while preventative care has now become routinized (at least among those with relative socioeconomic privileges) in U. S. American society, the youth of Port City and their families not only lacked preventative care, but also often lived with bodily discomfort caused by illnesses arising from that lack of care. Ashley's mother had constant excruciating stomach pains that rendered her bedridden. Ashley's mother had visited the doctor twice to find some relief, but the doctor's treatment of gastrointestinal reflux disease did not work, leading him to recommend more tests as he was uncertain of the cause. However, the family was exhausted from navigating medical institutions, which usually led to a lot of anxiety, cut into hours at work, and required them to deal with transportation hassles, as the family had one car (Such anxiety is not unusual; Lareau [2003] documents how marginalized families feel constrained when interacting with unfamiliar middle-class institutions such as hospitals.) So Ashley's mother decided to ignore the recommended tests. The family planned their daily lives around the possibility of the sudden onset of her pain, and Ashley and her sisters believed their mother could die like her sister at any time.

It was a harsh winter for the Northeast, and Port City was hit by numerous snowstorms and one week-long loss of electricity. Ashley did not have any work that winter, and she claimed this did not bother her because she was taking a break: "I been working my ass off, alright? I been working all year, all summer. Ima just sit here and enjoy the winter 'cause it's mad cold out. The wind hurts my face," Ashley said, laughing loudly, as we huddled on her couch eating some leftover vegetable soup she had made the night before. Although I was afraid of driving in the snow, I had gone to Ashley's house because she wanted to have a movie marathon: "Come here, 'cause I'm mad bored, alright? We gonna watch movies on your Netflix," she said on the phone. Her mother was supposed to leave for her work in the afternoon, but she had not come out of her room all morning. Ashley and I wondered why.

When she finally came out, her hair was disheveled, she was still in her pajamas, and she could hardly stand up straight: "I came out to take some cold water and get me some soup. It's back again. I'm gonna call them [her workplace]. It's the devil. It ain't gonna get better today." Then she went back into her room. "Good we watching movies, we gotta put it loud 'cause bitch gonna scream from pain all day," Ashley joked. I was aware of the pain by then and knew the routine—Ashley would check on her mother all day, her mother would sometimes scream out, Ashley would give her water and food throughout the day, and all would hope that their mother woke up well the next day—if she could sleep though the pain that night with the help of cough medicine. We watched movies, only to stop while Ashley went out and bought some cough medicine. Throughout, Ashley said things like, "I don't know what to do, it's just bad. They [her family members] all not healthy." She would often try to comfort herself: "I don't think it's serious though, 'cause bitch be dead by now. She gets them all the time." The family had gotten used to her mother's way of managing pain and the accompanying screams.

Just like Ashley's mother, Ashley's sisters were also thought to suffer from "bad genes." They had olive skin, full bodies, long dark hair, and brown eyes, and Sandra was certain that the two girls took after their mother's side of the family in terms of their superior beauty. However, they were both often ill. They missed classes, work, and social events. Sandra told me:

> The girls are pretty but frail. They got bad genes. They look that beautiful and they just got bad genes. They always getting sick, feeling sick and what-not .... Siete missed a lot of classes last year, she was also unhealthy and passed out all the time and she got MRI and they said it was not [a] tumor 'cause most of the time that's what it is when you pass out like that, but it's not, but they don't have good genes. Her mother made beautiful daughters but they don't have good genes, they are not healthy.

Ashley and her family certainly tried to be proactive. In the absence of medical care, her mother regularly read their tarot card to evaluate their present and future health. Sometime in December 2010, Ashley's mother declared that she was going to get something done about her weight—she was going to the Dominican Republic for weight reduction surgery, as advised by the tarot card readings.[11] Ashley told me that it was much cheaper there and the doctors spoke Spanish:

> She gonna get lipo and whatnot 'cause like she put on all the weight. And I told her: Ma, if you got the money just do it. 'Cause she put on weight after

her stomach pain all the time and maybe it's cancer 'cause, you know, her sister died of cancer mad young. And I was like I don't give a shit, I'll even give you some money 'cause if she dead then I'm stuck with her sister's kids too. And like I don't even know how long she'll live, so she should do what she wants, you know, 'cause life is short.

While regular bodily discomfort was often attributed to bad genes, sometimes people in Port City made an effort to string together explanations from memories of visits to doctors. Constructing explanations with vague memories and incomplete information often led the youth to misunderstand their bodies. Alize had severe pain at a spot between her chest and abdomen. When I searched her symptoms on Google, it looked like gastrointestinal problems that were probably exacerbated by the gaps between her meals once she started attending community college while working, sometimes at multiple jobs. Things got so bad that she dropped out of her classes, primarily so that she wouldn't have to travel back and forth to school and sit through classes while her abdomen hurt. There were days when she would call and plead with me to pick her up from college because the bus was not scheduled to come until much later and her pain was unbearable. Alize chalked up the pain to a cyst she had been diagnosed with months earlier, although the site of the pain clearly indicated that it could not be a cyst. When I told her that the pain could be related to gastrointestinal issues, she responded that "gas" could not be a serious issue: "It can't be this bad 'cause I got gas! Trust me, it's bad." When I explained that it could be more serious than just flatulence and that even regular gas could probably lead to other health issues such as gastroesophageal reflux disease, Alize refused to consider this. "Yo, I know what it is. It's those cysts, nothing can be done. It's just cyst[s], the doctor told me when I went last time, long time back."

Explanations aside, many youth were, like their parents, left to manage regular bodily discomfort and their uncertain causes as if it were just another part of life. One hot summer day, we are all walking to the office after lunch at the local pizzeria. We had been asked to leave work after lunch because the employer's daughter was sick. The young men and women had to return to the office to enter their hours and then we could leave. I was supposed to drive Cassy and Gigi back to their homes. Cassy was her usual jovial self, galloping and telling me stories about her culinary class and the very handsome Spanish-speaking teacher: "Oh, I'd marry him any day, although I told you, right, I am bisexual?" With beads of sweat on her forehead, Cassy was enjoying the day. I was deeply engaged in Cassy's story; she had a particular way of narrating it, with dramatic pauses and suspense and an even better ending. Some time had passed when we stopped to wait for the others. When we looked back, we saw the other youth had gathered around something or someone. We screamed their names to grab their attention and waved to them to come. However, they seemed engrossed and didn't pay much attention to us. We reluctantly walked back to where they were, because when I tried to call Ashley to ask what was happening, she had disconnected my phone call a couple of times.

As we approached the other youth, Ashley told us that Gigi had "passed out" again and that they were debating what to do. Gigi passed out somewhat regularly—she would feel weak in her knees, nauseous, and dizzy. She had been to the doctor once, with her stepmother, according to Gigi. The doctor recommended more tests for Gigi, including some blood work. However, Gigi did not have any of these tests; rather, her father told her that "passing out" ran in the family. Gigi explained this to me once with certainty: "We got this thing in our family . . . . We're just weak and pass out. And you just gotta drink water all the time and water cleans the system, and we up and running." I asked, "Is it 'cause you're dehydrated that you pass out?" "No, no," she said, "I don't think that's it, but it could be. I just think it's some genetic thing." That day, when Gigi passed out again, Ashley remarked:

> It's 'cause she only drink soda. She gotta drink water and ginger ale. Ginger ale solves everything. Like my aunt, too, she used to pass out and she would just drink water all the time and then it stopped. Gigi is fine though. My aunt got [a] brain tumor and died, so we gotta be worried 'cause it's in our genes, 'cause my mother might have it too. But Gigi's mom, she good. Her own mother, she's a crack addict, but otherwise she's healthy.

After Gigi rested on the pavement for about fifteen minutes and Curtis went to the nearby convenience store and bought a bottle of water and splashed some on her face and gave her some to drink, she seemed to be feeling better. "How you feeling, girl?" Cassy asked, gently rubbing her hair. Gigi was generally very perky and didn't like to look sick. "I'm fine, though, let's go, it's the same thing, I'm just gonna go drink some water." She gagged for a bit, sat for a bit, and then was ready to walk. I offered to get my car or call a cab because we were still a little ways away from the office, but Gigi refused. Perhaps I should have run to get my car right away when I saw Gigi had passed out, but I too was nervous.

After we returned to the office, Gigi sat down directly in front of a fan and Ashley brought her a cold bottle of water from the refrigerator. Alize looked worried. "Hey, Gigi," she said, "you need to get something checked though, 'cause I don't know that you supposed to pass out like that all the time." "I'm good," Gigi said as she went to the bathroom to freshen up before we left the office.

ASHLEY: [talking about Gigi] That girl, she mad immature.

ALIZE: [interrupting Ashley] Yeah, I got this stomach pain all the time. And then I can't put on weight. You can ask my mami, I eat all the time but I can't put on any weight. I don't care about these niggas about a big booty, but I just can't put on weight. And I got these stomach pains. So mami took me to see the doctor and he said something about cysts in my ovaries. I don't remember, but I think it means I can't have no children easy or like I should have them soon or something. I ain't doin' none of that. But I think it was like a cyst. It hurts, that's why sometimes, and I feel nauseous and whatnot all the time. Can't put on weight.

RANITA: Are you gonna go back to the doctor and figure out why you still got the pain?

ALIZE: Yeah, I gotta do that, like I don't feel too good right now, these days, and I can't eat all that much and even when I do I don't put on no weight.

ASHLEY: But you went to the doctor and you been eating and whatnot, but Gigi she only drink Coke and no water, how do you think she not gonna pass out?

The Port City youth dealt not only with bodily discomfort and their uncertain causes, but also with depression, anxiety, and stress. The lack of mental healthcare among marginalized youth remains largely underexplored by social scientists, even though research shows that constant worry about food, paychecks, and stable homes often leads to stress and other issues.[12] Among the youth of Port City, this was a glaring problem. Shivana, for example, suffered from depression, anxiety, and a range of other mood disorders. Sometimes these were almost debilitating.[13] Weeks at a time would go by when she would disappear into her own room, not see anyone, and barely eat or shower. Her mother usually brushed this off as: "Her lazy ass don't wanna get outta bed and go to work, what else you think." Shivana was aware of her debilitating mood disorders:

I went to therapy twice in my whole life. I was in school and I couldn't do anything. I have like this anxiety all my life, and I even had a breakdown. I couldn't do anything for weeks. The first time I went, I was not happy about being here in Port City 'cause it's just messed up in here and I had no friends 'cause I was quiet in school. The therapist, she never really encouraged [me] and she didn't even explain to me what was wrong with me, and she just agreed with me and said it was a bad neighborhood. And it's best to leave. The other time, I wouldn't get out of bed, and at the school they sent me to [a] doctor and the doctor gave me medicine, but I didn't go anymore after what they had recommended.

Cassy also had no access to mental healthcare after she graduated. She said, "I loved to go to therapy, I told you. That's how I also knew I wanted to study psychology. And I'm kind of depressed now but I don't know what do to. It's mad expensive for therapy, I think. I don't wanna go to emergency." While Shivana and Cassy were somewhat open about their mood disorders, many youth felt that mental healthcare was a stigma. Alize once mentioned to me that she probably needed to see a therapist for bulimia, but immediately added, "not doctors for psychos, just [a] regular one."[14]

The expense and unavailability of proper healthcare, combined with partial information, had definite negative effects on physical and mental health of the Port City youth. While they developed ways of managing early deaths and illnesses in their everyday life, these obstacles, and the ways in which youth managed them, often impeded opportunities of upward mobility by interfering with school.

RACE, GENDER, BODIES, AND POVERTY

The ways in which the youth explained and managed regular bodily discomfort and internalized uncertainty was naturally related to their understandings, albeit racialized and gendered, of a "healthy" body. For example, the young women accepted Western white middle-class ideals of "thin" as not just desirable, but also emblematic of fitness, and they often constructed weight as a cause of their illnesses.[15] The youth often attempted to treat their bodily discomforts, which were often unrelated to weight, by trying to lose weight. The "perfect" body weight was, however, much more complicated than just an issue of thinness. The process of constructing the ideal body was dialectical for the young women of Port City as they simultaneously experienced hegemonic beauty standards influenced by dominant discourses that construct obesity as an epidemic in poor communities and ideals of beauty that construct "full-bodied" women of color as beautiful, especially in contrast with thin white bodies.[16]

Much like youth elsewhere, the young people were constantly bombarded with images of "size zero" models. One day after work, Ashley, Alize, and I decided to go shopping at a discount store that sells name-brand clothes. Ashley's father had given her some money when she briefly visited him in New York City, and she said she would pay for a dress for Alize and also buy some clothes for her sisters. I didn't shop for anything myself, but walked around browsing while Ashley talked on the phone, asking her sisters what colors and which cuts they liked, and Alize looked at lingerie.

Alize, who was a proud Latina, seemed unhappy with the lingerie sizes that fit her. She phoned me and asked me to meet her outside the fitting rooms. I walked over and saw Alize standing there with a few pairs of lingerie: "I'm just sick 'cause Latina women have real big booty and they're beautiful. I ain't like that 'cause of my cyst. I don't wanna be like skinny white girls looking all nasty with the skinny jeans. I want big booty—they don't fit me right 'cause I'm mad thin right now. I called you 'cause can you get me [a] smaller size and look for the color 'cause Ashley didn't answer her phone?"

Afterwards we decided to go over to Ashley's house so that Alize and Ashley's sisters could try on their new clothes. Alize came out wearing the new bra she had bought over her jeans, asking in jest, "Do I look like a Victoria's Secret model?!" Siete barked, "You size zero! Oh, man!" Ashley said, "You fucking size minus zero, you sick, man, you look bad." Siete added, "Yeah, you look like [a] Heinz commercial model who ain't been eating nothing but ketchup." The girls all laughed out loud at this joke. Alize spoke with nostalgia:

> I'm mad Latino. I am Puerto Rican, we even got family in Puerto Rico. I grew up eating rice and beans. Mami always made me rice and beans and like, I'd eat a lot of food 'cause our people, they like to eat good food. Not like nasty MacDonald's. They like to cook healthy food like rice and beans and vegetables. Not them white people good with hummus and veggies but like real food. But I got these bad stomach pains and I can't eat nothin' no more. I think it's the cyst and I gotta have babies soon and they can take my ovaries and I can eat again.

These same girls who wanted to become full-bodied women also remained vigilant about how much they weighed. Ashley weighed around 210 pounds and was 5'6" when I first met her in 2010. She was perpetually on a diet. Every day, we discussed the things she should not have eaten and the terrible things they must have done to her body. When I would say, somewhat awkwardly, "You look good, though, stop worrying," she would respond to me with humor and scorn: "You a skinny bitch, so shut up" (I am not particularly skinny). Most days Ashley was angry with herself: "I did it, I ate fucking McDonald's again, like those fucking thugs. Ima tell you this much: Siete's ghetto-ass man friend is no good for me. Whenever I hang out with them they be eating mad ghetto and disgusting shit. I feel like mad fat right now." Gigi also thought herself overweight, but she claimed that she was definitely not as heavy as Ashley and did not mind being big, and everyone agreed. One day Lexus said to Gigi, jokingly, "You a fat ass but most of it is in yo' booty though. Ashley is all fat ass."

Ashley's weight frequently fluctuated. One November, she declared that she was "mad ugly": "You seen all those white girls, they look good in skinny jeans, not me. I look like a fat fucking ass." Thus began months of intense concern about her weight. By Thanksgiving, Ashley had had enough and was ready to take action. She decided to survive on liquids alone for two weeks in order to lose some weight and become healthier and then to continue to lose weight at a slower pace: "Right now Ima go crazy and like not be fat-fat, you know? And then when it's reasonable then Ima go on like a diet. 'Cause you know, I'm sick of being sick." "Are you sick?" I asked. "No, I mean like fat 'cause every time you go the doctor that's what they'll tell you when you get sick, like go lose weight, 'cause my aunt was sick and everything and like they asked her, told her that she was simply fat." Ashley told me she lost five pounds during her first week of the liquid diet: "I haven't pooped, but I can tell my pants are not tight! I read somewhere that's what happens, you won't poop, but that's it." A few weeks later she had to stop because she wasn't feeling well. Then, a few months after that, when her boyfriend wanted to take things more slowly with her, Ashley was back on a diet. She claimed that he didn't want unhealthy genes for his children and therefore did not perceive her as a suitable partner. So she went on a liquid diet yet again, and stopped only when she felt tired, weak, and constantly sleep deprived for days at a stretch.

Even though Ashley feared that she was unhealthy because she was not thin, Gigi had other explanations for her own "fat ass." When Ashley and I went to visit Gigi after she missed work owing to the passing-out incident, Gigi said:

> I don't think I was sick 'cause of my weight, though. I think it's just in Port City you got bad water, like it's got some stuff in it that gives you dehydration. 'Cause when I was in New Jersey I was fine. And I became fat after I came here. My stepmom was like it's 'cause I'm having sex. 'Cause you put on weight if you having sex. But [looking at Ashley] why don't you just run or stop eating junk?

Ashley replied with certainty:

> Yo nigga, I'm fat and I ain't even gotten laid in months, but if nothing works Ima just go get lipo in DR. I know someone got it for like two thousand or something, I just gotta work mad hours. I love working out, I was paying ten bucks at Planet Fitness. I didn't weigh myself or nothin', I let the clothes speak for themselves, but I ain't losing anymore.

We speculated about the relationship between sex and weight gain for the next hour or so before Gigi's mother returned home and asked us to leave, as she had to make dinner and needed Gigi's help.

Enacting the perfect body, which is classed, gendered, and racialized, within constrained resources, irregular healthcare, and partial knowledge, created added physical and emotional health stresses for the youth and was experienced as invisible violence in their everyday lives. The women took pride in their bodies at the same time that they wanted to lose weight.

Such paradoxical ideals reflect the rampant gendered and racialized body-phobia that characterizes modern society.

THE VIOLENCE OF HUNGER

It's hard to go about one's day on an empty stomach, and it is even harder to pay attention in class when hungry. Hunger is probably one of the most common experiences of people living in poverty and one of its most violent experiences. Yet we hardly talk about how young people deal with the constant discomfort of going about their days on empty stomachs and the uncertainty of not knowing when they will eat next. Do they simply get used to it? Of course, the youth in my study were not living in a time of famine, and they didn't live in a country that produces insufficient food for its population; however, as Nobel Laureate Amartya Sen wants us to understand, food insecurity should be measured at the individual and family levels.[17] Hunger was a very common experience among the Port City youth. Often, parents could not go food shopping because they didn't have the money or time, and accessing food through the food pantry could not be done with dignity. Even the use of food stamps was frowned upon, and Port City did not have many affordable grocery stores.

Long hours spent at college also meant that some of the youth went hungry when they were unable to prepare lunch at home, since food at college was expensive. Like Cassy, Ashley would sometimes steal a bag of potato chips from the cashier's counter if she felt positive that no one was looking. Siete already had gastrointestinal issues, and a semester of eating in the morning and then not again until dinner exacerbated her ulcer.[18] When Cassy went to school early, without having eaten at home and without bringing any food to school, she did not eat for the entire day because she was unable to buy food at school. She said, "We never have too much food at home. And I got no money to buy food at school, it's mad expensive. I could make my dad buy those ramen-in-cup noodles, but I feel bad though, 'cause he doesn't have too much money."

It didn't take long after I started my fieldwork to witness the torture of regular hunger. On the day noted below (an abstract from my fieldnotes), the youth had come to work straight from school:

Cassy walked in, her hair all disheveled; she looked tired today. She was wearing her colorful printed tights and a sweatshirt. The first thing she said when she entered was "I'm hungry, I am so hungry, don't know how I'll work rest of the afternoon. But I need the hours." Gigi was chirpy today, she was singing out loud as she entered work. She was wearing black tights and a hoodie. Her hair was tied tightly into a bun, her nails were nicely done with designs and she was wearing gold-colored jewelry. She walked straight to the refrigerator in the pantry at work. The pantry sometimes had food because another non-profit organization would store some food for their gatherings with us. Anyway, to Gigi's dismay there was no food today. There was a carton of milk, however. Cassy screamed from the other room, "Gigi, if you want food, there ain't any 'cause I'm starving in here." Gigi stomped out annoyed: "Oh my god, I am soooo hungry today, I don't know why." I didn't know what to do, I thought of offering to go buy some Subway sandwiches for the kids but wasn't sure if John would mind because I was looking at some grants for him today. It is also raining heavily outside. I wondered whether I could tell Alize to pick some up if she had any cash and I would give the money back to her. But it is raining and I feel bad asking her to wait. Cassy and Gigi were both working on the same computer; they both looked up food yelp. They searched for neighboring restaurants and looked up their food pictures. It made me hungry too. Then I remembered that I had a protein bar in my bag. I asked them if they wanted it. I felt kind of bad asking because I know that Gigi is very reluctant to accept things like money and food. Anyway she did take it and they had half each. Cassy contemplated eating the half-eaten, stale donut that she found on one of the desks with a computer but decided against it. Curtis and Alize came in together an hour later. We were all sitting in the room quietly, I was writing while looking at several printouts of grants and all four of them sat on one computer. The day seemed to drag longer than usual. After it was five I asked them if they wanted to go to the Chinese buffet [in a neighboring town]. Cassy and Gigi agreed. We went in my car. Cassy screamed, "Shotgun!" Both of them were quiet but they seemed excited about the buffet: "Oh my god, I can't wait. Drive fast, do you see all the saliva in my mouth, I'm mad hungry I hate being hungry I can't do nothin'. I'm such a fatass you're thinking!" Gigi exclaimed. Once there, Cassy filled her plate to the brim, she came back to the table and screamed, "I don't know when I'll eat next!"

For many of the young men and women of Port City, whether and what they would eat on a given day was uncertain and random. While Sandra's mother always tried to have some food ready for her daughter—or at least to have packets of Ramen or canned pasta at home—most of the other youth had no such guarantee. Angie's father, for example, would often eat whatever Angie had made and stored in the refrigerator, leaving her hungry. For most of the youth, work after school or community college meant that they did not eat for long hours. Most of them had a running tab at a local Jamaican place called "Jamaican Restaurant." Run by a family of four, Jamaican Restaurant had been there for at least two generations. Inside, the restaurant resembled a small corridor. The front end had three plastic chairs and one small table with a bottle of Tabasco sauce and salt and pepper. In the back end was a kitchen with a stove, spices and ingredients on a table, and a cupboard with utensils. Jamaican patty was their most popular item and there was always a small line outside the restaurant—on the days they were open, that is. The family was not thrilled about the running credit that most of the youth had with them, but the word on the street was that they never turned anyone away. However, there was one problem: their hours were rather uncertain and no one knew what day and time they would be open. The young men and women came to work after school and college, hoping that Jamaican Restaurant would be open, but if it was not, then most would have to wait until they went back home to eat. Lena did try to get credit from the convenience store right next to Jamaican Restaurant, but the "Asian lady" was not willing to give away "food for free."

The everyday experiences of hunger presented invisible obstacles as youth struggled to study and work, thus progressively and cumulatively further impeding their well-being and chances of upward mobility.

UNCERTAIN HOMES

Lena was in her fifth year of high school when her mother lost her job at an elderly care center and was evicted from their home in Port City. The first few nights they lived with Lena's mother's sister, who lived with her three sons in a housing project in Port City. Then Lena's mother decided to move to a town about sixty miles away to live with her new boyfriend. Her mother had been warning Lena about this for a while. The day her mother left, Lena came to work thinking that she would still return to her mother's sister's home at the end of the day.

I gave Lena a ride to her new home that evening. She took out a cigarette from her backpack and lit it with a lighter that was on the passenger's side door of my car, where she had left it weeks back: "Oh, you still got it! I been looking for it!" I said, "So how's your aunt, by the way? Like, she is nice to you?" "Oh she aight. She okay. I don't know her that much though," Lena replied as she puffed away, blowing smoke out the window. She looked more pensive than usual, so I did not continue the conversation. When I parked in front of the main gate outside the housing project, Lena asked, "Can you wait here a minute? 'Cause I gotta make sure she will take me." I was a little taken aback and could not suppress my surprise: "What the fuck, you don't know that she will let you stay? What're you gonna do? All right, go ask her, or you can come with me—though I don't know if I can drop you off tomorrow, I have to teach." I said this in a high-pitched voice. Lena ran in, and I waited in the car for about twenty minutes. She walked out with a charming-looking man who was in his forties or maybe fifties, well built and tall. He said, "Hello, miss. I am her uncle and I was out of town but now I am home and we have a room shortage. So if you don't mind, would you kindly drop her at Martin Street. She has room there." Then he left abruptly. Lena got into the car and asked me to drive and then spoke in a hushed voice, "He a fucking drunken asshole, he be beatin' her up and he can't if I'm there. He was not out of town, he was just fucking gettin' it on!" "Where do you want to go?" I asked, somewhat panic stricken, contemplating dropping her off as well as teaching the next day. Lena said calmly, "Let's go to Martin Street, 'cause I got my boo there, my best friend, she got a kid and I can babysit, then she'll let me stay. Don't worry." "Are you sure you don't wanna come with me?" I asked a few times. "Nah I'm good, 'cause I wanna be here. I gotta go to school and then I got work. And I can make some money this way too. I can stay with her for a bit." I dropped her off and waited until she went in. Lena would stay with her friend and her friend's baby for a few months.

The regular threat of an uncertain home along with the need to regularly move and live with whoever would have them often led the Port City youth to imagine and define their homes in more symbolic terms. "Home is where the heart is" literally described the youth's situation, and they internalized this lesson at an early age and passed it on to those who were younger. One late afternoon in the fall of 2012, I was volunteering at the local after-school care center when Lena was working. A little boy named Oliver who had light skin and big brown eyes and thick brown hair sat in one corner of the room for most of the afternoon (Lena identified the boy as white). His eyes were constantly teary, but I never noticed him cry. I wanted to go over and ask how he was, but we had strict instructions to let him sit there: Earlier that afternoon, Miss Debbie had ordered, "Nobody talk to him." I didn't work up the guts to ask Miss Debbie what had happened, but Lena asked her when she came into the room to tell one girl that her parents were there to pick her up. Miss Debbie told us that Oliver had hit another boy and that he was upset because Miss Debbie forced an apology out of him. Miss Debbie told us that we could try and talk to him and explain why he had to apologize: "If you can make him stop sulking like that, just do it. I don't like seeing them like this. But Oliver is tough to please."

I asked Oliver why he was upset.

OLIVER: [responding candidly and without much prompting] I don't like it here, I don't like after-school programs. I have a life and I don't wanna be here.

LENA: Well, it's like school, you can just hang out with friends, like school.

OLIVER: I don't like school. This school sucks. People are not nice here and some them boys there threw something out of the window. A branch fell and almost killed a janitor.

LENA: [jokingly] Well, if you don't like the after-school center, it doesn't like you either!

Lena then asked when his parents were coming to pick him up.

OLIVER: My mom is coming 'cause I live with her now. I don't like my mom and sisters. I don't like it here. I wanna move back with my dad and my sister is supposed to move too. I used to live with my mom but then I moved with my dad and it's nice there, his girlfriend is nice.

LENA: [trying to make conversation] Do they got room for you?

OLIVER: She has three sons and when I move I'm gonna share my room with Robin and then Jessup will share with us too 'cause my sister will move too but we don't know where she will sleep 'cause before she lived with my mom when I moved with my dad. I don't like my mom's boyfriend anymore. He has a wife and I don't know why he doesn't leave my mom.

LENA: [attempting to console him] Well, then, if you're moving soon, try to enjoy it here for now.

OLIVER: But I have a life at home. I nap and then play baseball, like real games
and we gonna play on Sunday in a field next to the Yankees. My dad
drives trucks and he got a new job, so he will buy video games for me
for four thousand dollars 'cause he got money from somewhere. But I
don't know when he gonna come take me though. But before I liked it
here, now I don't.

Sensing the boy's restlessness with the recent frequent changes of his home,
Lena tried to comfort him and equip him to deal with uncertainty:

> Look, you got food in both places? You got [a] bed? What else you want? It
> doesn't matter where you live, you gotta be ready to live anywhere. It's just
> life, you don't know what's there for you. Like people livin' now and now
> they dead. How you know what's gonna happen to you? You just take it as it
> comes and don't be angry at it. That's just how life is, alright. You can make
> home wherever.

Another incident that revealed the extent to which the children of Port
City grew up internalizing the uncertain nature of home was especially
sobering for me. When Ashley's mother's sister moved to Ashley's home
from Puerto Rico, it was her first time there since she had never "had
enough money to buy airfare" (according to Maria). By the time I met
Ashley, her aunt had already died and was survived by her son and daughter, who were between eight and ten years old. They knew very little
English and kept quiet, always occupying the corner seats or standing half
hidden by the door, quietly and uncertainly observing everyone and never
asking for anything. Ashley and their sisters mostly treated their new
cousins like members of their own family, and they also thought that it
was incumbent upon them to train their new family members in the ways
of their household—the eating rules, sleeping rules, showering rules, and
even bathroom rules. When one of them put mustard on their bread,
Ashley screamed from the other end of the table: "You supposed to put
mustard and ketchup! How you gonna eat with just mustard! I gotta lot to
teach y'all."

Along with endearment and care certainly came anger and frustration
with the two new family members in their small house. Once, when Ashley
and her sisters showered one after another, their little cousin sat in the bedroom waiting for her turn to use the bathroom—she said something in her

quiet voice but no one heard, and she had to run into the bathroom [presumably to use it due to an emergency] while Siete was taking a shower. The sisters held a meeting that evening to discuss what could be done about the overcrowding and the fact that the two new family members were "culturally" very different. Ashley said, "I know they gotta be here, like what they gonna do otherwise? But it's pissing me off." Siete chimed in, "Don't they got nobody from their father's side?" The sisters discussed several possibilities but then decided to include the cousins in their family. Months later, the two cousins were more fluent in English and friendlier. I would often go over and spend time with them and Ashley's mother when the other sisters were not home. One such afternoon, Ashley's mother asked me to help the two siblings unpack their suitcase: "I emptied space for them. Can you do it." The two cousins and I went upstairs, "You been living out of your suitcase this long!" I exclaimed. One of them responded immediately, "We did not know when we was going to leave here."

While some young people of Port City were resigned to being constantly ready to move, others missed their family members when their living arrangements changed. When Cassy's father rented out their living room to some of his family members who had just arrived from Honduras without a place to stay, the house became very crowded. But Cassy's father did not have many options—he too needed the money. However, his family members were unhappy with the living situation because the living room was a very inconvenient place for three people to stay. Cassy's father asked his daughters to stay with their aunts and uncles, and Cassy went to live with her father's brother while the other two sisters went to live with one of their mother's sisters. They did not know exactly how permanent these living arrangements would be, but dire conditions call for dire solutions, and at least their father could make some rent while his children lived with other family members. Cassy missed her sisters, who didn't have a cellphone. She would sometimes call her aunt, who was very nice to them, and Cassy would then be able to talk to them:

> She [Cassy's aunt] loves my sisters, she seen them since they were a kid. She seen me too 'cause one time my mom like went back to Honduras or California or something... And I lived with her for a bit. She always been nice to our family.

The aunt and uncle that Cassy moved in with, however, had stricter house rules. Cassy had to return home before dark because they were responsible for her, she was not allowed to talk on the phone, and she sometimes had to cook. But Cassy hardly ever complained; it was less crowded than her own home, although she was often tired of living out of her bag and not having all of her precious beauty products.

Internalizing uncertainty as a part of life allowed youth to manage the unstable conditions in which they lived.[19] More often than not, illogical explanations were tied to incomplete information youth gathered from institutional actors such as doctors. Institutions such as schools and healthcare are often daunting for youth growing up in economically marginalized households, and in the face of the mysteries of institutions youth formulated oftentimes illogical and heavily individualized explanations for what was structural and systemic. Amidst the persistent uncertainty including threat of homelessness, discomforts of illnesses, untimely deaths of loved ones, and the constant pain of hunger also resided the youth's tenacious hopes of overcoming these struggles, their belief in the American dream of "moving up in the world," and their unrelenting efforts to establish their worth and respectability as socially mobile Americans.

8 Uncertain Success

"I grew up thinking I was mad rich. Okay, maybe like middle class 'cause I always got birthday presents and everything. Then I was like, damn, we got no money."

—Lexus

As they transitioned to adulthood, the Port City youth were certain that
their birth families were not middle class. As Lena and I sat outside the
Jamaican Restaurant in Port City one day, I asked her casually about her
relationship with her mother. She replied:

> We came here from DR [the Dominican Republic], we were in Florida and
> then we came here. My mom was like, you get good grades. You have to get
> good grades. But she is poor and she is not educated, and when her husband
> was in jail we went back from Port City so we could visit him in Florida, and
> I loved it there but we moved back. I wanted to finish school and in Florida
> there was too much going on. So, my mom is not like me, but she taught me
> not to be like a ghetto-ass McDonald worker. Even though she has no educa-
> tion she wants me to . . . she helped me to get to college. . . . That's why I
> have to [continue to] go to college and get a good job. For her, 'cause she
> dreamt this for me.

It was a crisp afternoon, we were hungry, and the restaurant was closed.
Lena had hoped, albeit reluctantly, to buy some beef patty (the restaurant's best seller) on credit because it had been an unusually long day:
"You know, I don't like this type of things, I pay for my things. I don't take
things like food stamps or other free food." Lena was always eager to dis-

tinguish herself from her mother, or at least her own class position from her mother's—she was upwardly mobile. While she was uncertain about finishing college, she wanted to be able to "buy her food."

The Port City youth, who were well aware of their family's struggles, were also certain about their eventual pathway out of these struggles and their access to the American dream. In previous chapters I discussed how youth constructed milestones, such as avoiding early parenthood, graduating from high school, and attending college, as well as work and money, as indicators of social mobility. I think of these mobility markers also as "cosmopolitan" markers[1] insofar as they indicate and facilitate participation in the larger societal structure.[2]

In this chapter, I continue to explore how the Port City youth invest in displaying their socially mobile markers not only through school, work, and bourgeois heteronormative life, but also through their everyday styles and consumptions. Youth performed class in their daily lives by producing mobility symbols, rooted in larger race and class structures, in their leisure practices, clothing, music, vernacular, and food preferences.[3] To manage their haphazard educational and occupational trajectories, the youth redefined mobility into goals that were achievable. In theorizing the reproduction of class positions, Bourdieu argues that cultural class differences foster exclusionary middle-class practices, which then make it harder for marginalized youth, who are uncertain about the rules, to be successful in school and other middle-class institutions.[4] The Port City youth, however, attempted to partake in what they constructed as superior, middle-class taste in everyday life.

Several influential ethnographers writing about youth have shed light on individual agency and the independent role of the cultural by illustrating the processes of cultural production that youth engage in.[5] Bettie was one of the first to highlight *the gendered and racialized* performance of class through her school ethnography among white and Mexican girls in California.[6] My findings on the Port City youth's class and mobility performance dovetail with the existing work on youth cultural production. But the majority of our understanding of youth regarding race / ethnicity, gender, and class are based on school ethnographies, a context in which students often perform class through memberships in groups that are part of a hierarchical order. I frame my observations about the meanings of class by considering how youth perform social mobility in everyday life as they transition to adulthood.

I am most interested in how youth learn, enact, and experience middle-class symbols within the limits of available resources.[7] While achieving success in school and college was a bit uncertain for the Port City youth, everyday mobility markers were more easily achievable. They enacted mobility through symbols of middle-class membership they learned from popular media as well as their interactions with other middle-class individuals like their employers. They also gleaned insights from the college students who volunteered in various organizations and institutions in Port City that the teens participated in, as well as other nonprofit members. When highlighting how youth managed uncertain trajectories by redefining mobility in this chapter, I emphasize the points of *contact* between the marginalized Port City youth and middle-class people who facilitated the youth's access to middle-class cultural capital while also causing "hidden injuries" of class and race.[8]

WINE AT THE BEACH

Sequence Beach, Port City's most prized asset, is located at the end of Port City's affluent Sequence Street, where large, glamorous, old houses stood along a steep road. Various nonprofits often organized "beach-cleaning days," old-timers spoke nostalgically about their dates at the beach when the city didn't offer much else, and most residents were enraged about its possible privatization by one of the local casinos. "Beach day" was a common leisure activity for the Port City youth, especially those who couldn't get away from the small city.

Ashley invited me to beach day with her family one especially hot and humid afternoon in August: "It's gonna be mad hot tomorrow, so you better come down to the beach with us, and get your bathing suit, too." "I'm just gonna go in my sports bra," Siete jumped in, "'cause I'm gonna be at work till late so you gotta pick me up from there." "Then we gonna eat at Shabby Shack, they have crazy burgers alright," Ashley planned. We said our goodbyes at Ashley's house that evening while her mother wrapped a few chocolate-chip cookies for me to take home.

The next day, I met Ashley at Sequence Street's free street parking area. I had followed Ashley to a particularly convenient area that was close enough to the beach and always had some empty spots. After we parked, Ashley, Siete, Liana—one of their friends whom I had met for the first time that day (she was Siete's ex-boyfriend's half sister who was visiting from Florida but once lived in Port City)—and I walked to the beach with our duffle bags. "I never used to come to the beach that much when I lived here," Liana remarked. Ashley chimed in,

> Yeah, it's more expensive than other beaches nearby 'cause you got rich people coming down here all the time. Like we used to go to the rich people side all the time 'cause my mother got this season pass that all the rich people buy. I mean we're not as rich as them, but I'm mad proper about the beach though. Like I don't wanna go near ghetto niggers eating and throwing nasty shit, you know.

I remained quiet for the most part during our walk because I was thirsty and also tolerating a painful blister on my foot brought on by a new pair of shoes. "Yo, you been here before?" Siete asked, in an attempt to include me in the conversation. "Yeah, I've come a few times," I replied. Then, to my embarrassment, Siete began joking with Liana: "Yo, she a professor, did I tell you that, she's real smart, your dumb ass can learn something." Liana, also embarrassed, mumbled something under her breath.

Ashley had asked me to bring her a bottle of red wine of my choice. She had recently begun to take an interest in wine. As we continued walking, Ashley asked me about the wine. I took out the ten-dollar bottle of Pinot Noir, and when I gave it to Ashley she looked at it carefully, squinted her eyebrows, and said, with a knowing smile as if certain about her knowledge of wine, "Wow, this motherfucker is like 2008, it must be fancy. I know my wine, the older the better."

We sat in a row on the beach with our legs stretched out straight, and Siete took out her Aviator sunglasses that covered most of her face, her hair tapering upward into a tight topknot. The two sisters, Liana, and I wore two-piece swimsuits (Siete had gone home to pick hers up), and Ashley wore a white cover-up over her swimsuit to hide what she called "a winter body" not yet "beach-ready for the niggas." Ashley took this opportunity to articulate the relationship between her leisure activities and class position:

It's time like this that makes me feel that I'm moving up in the world. You sitting here, on the beach, drinking fancy wine, and you talking about stuff. Not baby daddy stuff. [Looking at Liana] You did good by moving outta here. But we doin' good too. [Looking at me] I'm trynna get degrees and we done with this place, we been chillin' with Ranita the whole time and I'm trynna get into college again, ask her.

I nodded to agree with Ashley.

The youth creatively enacted social mobility through available resources and symbols drawn from various middle-class and local actors and symbols. For Ashley, avoiding early parenthood to experience the finer things in life, such as (good) wine and afternoons at the beach, while also spending time with others who are, according to her, higher in status through participation in higher education, automatically meant that she was climbing the social ranks.

PRESSURE TO PARTY

The Port City youth embraced celebrations.[9] Whether it was a birthday, Valentine's Day, New Year's Eve, or the weekend, the question was the same: "What're you doin' [to celebrate]?" The underlying question wasn't whether or not one celebrated, but *how* one celebrated, because how one used their free time and structured their leisure activities was an important way to indicate class mobility. Whether one went to the casino or Applebee's to celebrate their twenty-first birthday said something about one's aspirations. Brianna's birthday serves as a good illustration. Brianna was merely celebrating her birthday with a home-cooked meal and then ice cream at Rita's, a local dessert shop, with her friends. She called me early one afternoon to say, "Mom's making me a birthday dinner, Ranita. You should come over. She's good." I dressed, picked up a present, and headed to Brianna's house. When I got there, three young black women were hovering around the dining table, which was neatly decorated with flowers in the centerpiece. Brianna's mother regularly cleaned the walls, put covers on a sofa set that had multiple holes, and had a big-screen TV on a small coffee table with two flower vases on either side. And, I learned that she liked nice sheets. The refrigerator had pictures of Brianna and her mother along with a few other people I did not recognize, and the walls had several posters of landscapes and birds. One of the three girls wore a fashionable outfit—ripped jeans and a white lace shirt—while the other two wore black tights and sweatshirts. They chatted about one of their recent decisions to "go natural."

I knew one of the young women, Keisha, and she approached me for a quick bear hug. I had not gotten to know Brianna's friends well because she tended to be more reserved than the other girls. Much later in my fieldwork, Brianna told me that she "enjoy[ed] hanging out and gettin' close, but I can't talk too much and people think I'm just boring. But I love to talk and chat if you give me a chance." Keisha said to me, agitated, "I didn't even know we're not goin' nowhere fancy or I would've just dressed casual! I thought it was a birthday party." Brianna responded defensively, looking at me,

> This is what I wanted, my mom's making me a birthday dinner. 'Cause I thought I would be away at college now, and I didn't plan on having a party or nothing this time because I didn't know! So I'm not really doing anything special. I'm definitely gonna plan something for next year though.

Keisha continued, almost cutting Brianna off:

> I mostly hang out with my brother and his friends. They're all rich and everything. They celebrate their birthdays like at the casino bar and like restaurants and stuff, or they'll just take a trip to Boston or something. They're from not around here, they're rich and fancy.

Brianna kept quiet for a few minutes, not certain what to say. Eventually she responded timidly, as if she were whispering, "I was supposed to party with college friends," to repair her punctured ego with the fact that she was attending college.

Even if Brianna had planned her party and had the money, navigating middle-class spaces like expensive bars and restaurants required classed and racialized etiquettes, which was a frequent cause of anxiety among the youth. For example, when Ashley was invited to a gathering at the local high-end pizza joint, located on the wealthy neighborhood of Sequence Street, by someone she had come to know through Public Allies, she fretted about it for days. "I'm nervous! I don't know what they have in there [on the restaurant menu] and I don't know who else is there. I don't even know what to wear. I don't want anyone laughing at me," she told me. I drove her to the restaurant, and she was gagging and wanted to use the bathroom twice between her home and the restaurant. "I'm nervous," she mumbled.

After Ashley found a new job, and turned twenty-one, she was very excited about going to a dance club at the local casino. Many days could go into planning a night out, as if planning was also part of the enjoyment. Two weeks before the casino trip, Ashley and Alize were already envisioning their night:

ASHLEY: You been to the club in the casino? It's fancy.

ALIZE: Of course! I was there like last to last week. The guy even knew my face and that nigga just plain let me in.

ASHLEY: Where you got ID from? They ID, I think.

ALIZE: No, uh, they didn't ID me. Prolly 'cause they know me.

ASHLEY: They know you that well? Like you spend money and all? But you didn't even work, I worked mad hours last month and my cuz [cousin] is like twenty-four and she got me in. Anyway, I got this mad cute dress to wear when we go out, have you tried their coconut martini? I have it all the time there. You also gotta take extra cash to tip 'cause you gotta tip well.

After Alize left that day, I drove Ashley home, and she said: "I know mad like rich people who don't even go there and she does? I don't even know if she has nice pants 'cause they won't let you go in, like you can't wear ghetto shit, you know, you can't wear shoes with big tongues." She laughed hysterically.

Ashley and Alize ended up celebrating at a local Mexican restaurant and bar instead of the casino club. However, she wanted to take her friend Alyssa, who had just given birth and was experiencing financial troubles, out for her twenty-first birthday or organize a party herself. Since Ashley didn't have the money for this, she decided to work extra hours at both her jobs and save some of the earnings. It was hard to get the extra hours at one of her jobs, since the employer was already cutting back. But she used her personal relationship with the manager to bring it about: "I didn't want to do it, 'cause I might need some time off later and someone to cover for me and might even need more hours for next semester. But I asked him anyway." Youth had to make frequent irreconcilable choices like these—between school or family, romance or work, school or work. Such choices also came at a high price.

The celebrations for Alyssa's birthday began one Friday with the purchase of a new dress. Then the girls dyed their hair blonde using a new pricey designer product. They tried on an assortment of eye makeup over the next two days. On Saturday night, it was time for the party at Ashley's friend Tamara's house. Ashley was excited and bought party trays from the Stop and Shop in a neighboring town along with rum, vodka, three bottles of red wine, and other ingredients to make mixed drinks for all her friends. She spent several hundred dollars, but Ashley wanted to show everyone a "good time": "I know what good parties be like. I been to this one girl, she went to college, I been to her parent's house. I knew her 'cause she went to college here . . . and then she came to volunteer where I worked at."

Tamara lived in a housing project that was a little ways from Ashley's home. I drove Ashley and Alyssa to Tamara's house, and although Ashley insisted that I join them, I could not due to a prior commitment. Ashley decided to go inside to check whether the house was still available for the party. She came back out to tell me that the party had already started. About three hours later, when I was back home, I got a call from Ashley, who was using another friend's phone, asking whether I was still in the area. When I asked her why, she reluctantly told me that Tamara's father had kicked them out of the house, and she didn't have a ride home. Her mother's phone was out of order, and she was not supposed to pick Ashley up for another three hours. Her sisters didn't drive. Ashley's boyfriend was at work and unable to answer his phone. I tried calling everyone I knew in the area to find a ride for Ashley and Alyssa. After waiting around for a while, they reluctantly walked home in the dark. The next day, Ashley, who was very irritable and embarrassed about the previous night's events, told me:

> I'm mad annoyed 'cause I wanted to do something nice, alright. Like I know how to have a party, so why spend all the money at the casino. I wasn't takin' her to downtown Port City, now that's real ghetto. I was gonna have like a fancy party at home. With like cocktails and cheese and everything. Tamara's father, that nigga doesn't know nothin'. You can't pick a nigga in the ghetto

for a fancy party! But I'm starting to get too old for this, like I don't just wanna party, I wanna get serious and do real stuff. College and work. You could spend all the money partying when you dumb as fuck.

How youth had a "good time" was an important indicator of the path they were on. If one went to a hotel party, it was "ghetto."[10] Having wine and cheese at home or going to the casino club, on the other hand, meant that they knew what they were doing. Picking up the right wine and cheese required knowledge of such things, and going to the casino club meant you had nice clothes and money to buy drinks and pay the cover charge. Then youth could use these experiences to talk about the fancy wines, cheese, and cocktails they had tried. Often, enacting class to indicate socially mobile status further constrained opportunities by diverting resources such as money and time, and caused anxieties.

WHAT SUSHI OR *MAURY* CAN SAY ABOUT YOU

As the youth transitioned to adulthood, they began to denounce certain class symbols, like partying, as immature. But they encountered other class symbols, and their inability to perform them often cut more deeply into their sense of self-worth. They began to realize that the food they ate and the neighborhoods they lived in indicated their class position.[11] Moreover, some of these were indicators that were harder to overcome or remove. Working a few extra hours could allow the youth to go to clubs or spend money on dresses, but they certainly couldn't easily leave their neighborhoods.

One cold afternoon, I suggested to Ashley that we pick up some fast food before heading over to A. J.'s place, but we decided to go to A. J.'s first and then order pizza from there. By the time we reached A. J.'s house, we were both hungry. A. J.'s friend Shiela was from a neighboring town. She began telling Ashley and me about her school, comparing it to Port City High:

Well, you know it ain't nothing like her [A. J.'s] school. You not gonna find no one beating others up or with booze and stuff, it's more whatchamacallit

. . . like, suburban. But you know, 'cause my mama was tellin' me the other day, like, they're poor here, some of them they live in the projects.

When we called to order Domino's, we found out that Domino's did not deliver in A. J.'s housing project after dark. A. J. reacted sternly with certainty, but also with anger and embarrassment.

A. J.: No, I mean, about what you said about Port City High School being bad and all, we live in the projects. Yeah, some of them are like that, but my family is not poor, we like eat steak and all, that's what rich people eat, we don't eat Domino's usually. We was gonna make steak, but we was busy.

SHIELA: Girl, there was the Domino's guy that got robbed right here, in this project, who you telling about not being poor?

A. J.'S MOTHER: [chiming in] We eat from Domino's all the time and those eating don't rob them—it's those ghetto-ass niggas, and now Domino's don't deliver after dark apparently.

ASHLEY: [who also had a stake in defending port city high] Well, you can ask Ranita, I don't even eat Domino's, to be honest. Before we came I was mad hungry but I won't eat fast food. I don't even eat Domino's and pizza. So I don't even care they don't deliver 'cause that's not what we eat anyway. I would rather eat sushi.

Ashley's ego had been brutally punctured by Shiela's comments about Port City and Domino's decision to not deliver food. In an attempt to overcome this injury, Ashley rolled her eyes and said Domino's was beneath her anyway. She told us about her resolution to not eat "junk" food such as Domino's:

I don't really like the idea of fast food because, like, the meat that they use, more female dairy cows, and most of them are filled with tons of sickness and antibiotics and they are omnivorous. But, they are fed like they are carnivorous, like with other dead cows, and some of them are dead before they go to slaughterhouse—they have been there for days and they mush it all together, all age and dead and living. And when you're buying this sandwich for one dollar you're like wow this tastes so good, but it is designed to taste good. The society that we live in now, we are at a place where we see—we don't really—we are not really seeing what we're seeing, we believe what's on

TV. It's some kind of magic, before we would have to use our sense of sight, smell, and taste and we knew what food was okay and what it smelled like and what was okay or not. And, you could choose, and now they make omega-3 fat that is found in fish and the pig has it, how can it have this thing that comes from another species? Because it's genetically modified. Life is completely changed, the way we see things or eat things or feel things.

Ashley looked at me and said, "You all educated, how do you not know?" Ashley assumed that educated people did not consume fast food. Ashley expressed aversion to fast food in order to indicate that despite where she lived and went to school, she was part of a more "cultured" group.[12] It wasn't enough to just tell us who she was—sophisticated and not poor— but in this moment, Ashley had decided to use her ultimate mobility card: sushi consumption. She had confided in me at an earlier time that she did not know how to use chopsticks very well, but she could learn, and she knew from her friends at Public Allies that eating sushi was something that rich and educated people did often. At that point, I decide to drive us all—Ashley, A.J., Shiela, and myself—to the Thai restaurant in downtown Port City that also served sushi.

We parked across the street, and Ashley took a picture of the entire group in front of the restaurant: "Ima post it on Facebook." We went in and were seated at a corner table near the window. Ashley and I sat on one side of the table as the waitress handed us a menu. Ashley looked through the appetizers carefully and said loudly: "I'm gonna get the edamame, it's good here, I heard." Everyone nodded. I asked whether everyone wanted sushi rolls. A.J. looked at Shiela and uncertainly said, "Whatchu gonna eat—I'll have the teriyaki, I think." Ashley snapped back, "There are so many you can order, get whatever sushi roll," and then she announced that she was going to get the spicy tuna roll. I ordered one as well, and the others ordered spicy salmon roll. We chitchatted about the UConn basketball team until the food came. Ashley and Shiela both took pictures of the food, and Shiela apologized, looking at me: "Sorry, I'm being annoying with all the pictures and everything. But you know, it's fancy. I'll bring my friend here next time, she gonna love it 'cause they eat at the Chinese buffet all the time. It's like so dirty and all of them go there." She added, "I love sushi." Ashley continued, "Yeah, my teacher at Port City Rivers, she loves sushi and she said there are good ones in New York . . . it's like cultural."

A. J. and Shiela picked up forks and quickly began to eat. Ashley took the chopsticks out of the paper bag and tried to uncertainly copy me. I was reluctant to provide direct guidance, as I was uncertain whether she wanted to let the others know her low comfort level with chopsticks. She struggled for a while, successfully consuming a few pieces while the other pieces fell apart. I made a general remark that I liked to use my hands since it was easier and had myself learned how to use chopsticks during an embarrassing moment when I first moved to the United States. Shiela said, "Eew, I don't think so." After dinner, A. J. asked for more chopsticks to take home, and Ashley appeared to be embarrassed by her request. We finished dinner off with fried ice cream. As we were leaving, Ashley said, "Now you can say you eaten sushi. I don't play around—you only eat good food when you with me."

While participating in certain activities could bring mobility status, participating in others could just as easily damage that status. For example, watching certain TV programs could indicate that one is not smart or "cultured" enough. Youth often distanced themselves from stereotypes of what people like "them" watch and like and what they don't appreciate. One afternoon while sitting outside the movie theatre, Lexus, two of her friends, and I engaged in general conversation:

LEXUS: *Maury* show is the best, but everybody on that show is stupid because all their business is on TV, like, really. It's like telling girls getting pregnant here, oh you gon' be on TV someday 'cause yo ass got knocked up?

CHANEL: Ahhh, but I miss our fifth period, I wanna go back so we could play *Maury* again [everyone laughs].

RACHEL: Jess got tickets for the *Maury* show for next Friday, crazy.

LEXUS: For real? The one in Stamford or whatever they said?

RACHEL: Yeah, yeah.

LEXUS: Oh nice, but I would not do that, though, it's stupid, like you got nothin' to do like nothin' better so you sit and watch stupid shit on TV, but why you gonna go out of your way to watch some ghetto niggas be on TV selling their business? I think that's stupid.

Everyone nodded their head in agreement.

CHANEL: I don't watch nothin' like that. You watch these shows and you act like that. I watch like History Channel or like Netflix.

The teens also detested forms of music to establish status. Expressing aversion to popular rap music with explicit sexual lyrics signaled a "non-ghetto" individual. One afternoon at work, Curtis put on a YouTube Eminem song. The song had explicitly sexual lyrics. Sandra commented, "Wow, you be listening to mad ghetto shit, I like it but I listen to other stuff, this is not my typa' music." The others nodded their heads in agreement. After work, while I was driving Alize home, she told me, "I don't like the boob-ass songs that lack any musical taste," thus aiming to establish her own status through her taste in music.

Similarly, African American Vernacular English was considered by many to be an inferior, or "ghetto," way of talking.[13] I observed youth often correcting one another's English, parents telling their children about the disadvantages of not speaking "proper English," and teachers in school reprimanding students for the same reason. In addition, the youth in Port City also held opinions about language use. When Cassy and I ate lunch at a local Chinese buffet we often ran into her friends and acquaintances. One day, Cassy and I were eating lunch when three young women walked in. Cassy pointed to them and told me that she went to middle school with them, and they came over to say hello to Cassy. When they left, Cassy said, "Wow, how much things change, you know, I feel bad for them 'cause we went to the same middle school. Did you see how they talk?" "What do you mean?" I asked. "Super ghetto! Most girls talk like that, you've heard Alize and all, don't you think I talk different? I watched a lot of shows and read books and learnt how to talk properly. In school I did that to fit in sometimes. They're still stuck there, they'll prolly have kids soon," she said.

Detesting symbols that were visible around them, and symbols that teachers, nonprofit workers, and family members constructed as being partially responsible for youth's marginalization, was one way to establish a socially mobile status. Yet in the process, the youth marginalized other community members by creating oppositional identities to those who, in actuality, shared similar historical and structural positions. The youth built this oppositional identity to establish themselves as socially mobile. However, that opposition was also the source of cleavages in their community and hostility among peers.

A CLEAN HOME IN PORT CITY HEIGHTS

For many of us, where and how we live reflects our class position. For the youth, living in the projects was a major class injury that they often tried to overcome by comparing their home against the rest of the neighborhood. Living in a clean house became an important indicator of class position. Like Brianna and her mother, most of the youth and their families took great pride in their clean homes and suggested that this set them apart from other "ghetto" dwellers.

After Hurricane Irene hit hard in the Northeast, housing projects in Port City lost power for an extended period of time. A week or so later, some men came around knocking on doors and asking residents to throw out everything from their refrigerators—and when the residents were not home, the men went through their refrigerators and threw out all the leftovers. There was much discussion and anger around this issue. Most parents talked about how their privacy was not respected because they were poor and needed government assistance. Most of the young men and women agreed that invasion of privacy was wrong, but they felt uncomfortable with the argument that they were poor. Brianna argued that her house was always extremely clean and did not look like "the ghetto" in any way: "Well, they can't just come in like that, I mean, you can't even tell we live in the ghetto if you come in here, right?" Brianna's mother was livid that evening when she got home from work. I had dropped by so that Brianna, her mother, and I could go to an Indian parlor to thread our eyebrows; it was going to be Brianna's first time. Brianna's mother opened the door with: "You think we live in the projects? You said you even like it here more than your house and you don't live in no ghetto up there [in Storrs]. These niggas come and throw away my fucking food like I didn't know, I was gonna throw it myself." For a generally together person, Brianna's mother was visibly shaken; her pride had taken a beating.[14]

Later that week, when Lena and I visited Ashley, Lena said:

Yeah, we're the same way [referring to a conversation about our preference for clean homes]. We don't let no roaches around and all them empty bottles and beer cans. I'm always cleaning all the time. Forreal. And that's what makes you ghetto though. It's not living in the projects, 'cause everyone facing a hard time. My aunt she used to have a job and be rich and every-thing and now she living here in Port City. So that's not the point, it's how you live.

Ashley nodded in agreement, privileging lifestyle over economics as class indicators.

I knew Ashley had strong feelings about the importance of clean, neat houses. When she first invited me to her house and was giving me direc-tions, she added, "It's where Deryn lives, so it's in the projects, but it's nothing like his house though. It's as if we live in different countries. My house is like fancy, it looks nice and all, we put nice sheets and pictures and everything, you'll see." Then Ashley moved to a working-class neigh-borhood through a Bank of America–Habitat for Humanity collaborative program. Ashley was beyond excited to invite me to her new home. The first time I visited, I parked in front of her house next to a black truck, which was Ashley's at the time. Her mother opened the door and was wearing a tank top and long skirt—she was cleaning the kitchen. The small house looked immaculate and clean. Small knickknacks were every-where. Ashley remarked, "See how many trees there are here? It's nice but there is a price 'cause when there is a thunder we get scared, 'cause the trees can literally fall on us," following this with a throaty laugh. Then Siete woke up from a nap and came downstairs to greet me.

SIETE: Yo, whatchu think of our new place? It's nice, right?

THEIR MOTHER: What you excited for, we heard a gunshot already.

SIETE: [ignoring her mother] It's mad nice! Not like the white house up there but we not ghetto anymore. Them ugly-ass niggers living in the projects.

ASHLEY: Don't be like that. We always had a clean home. But yeah, we definitely doing better now. Even in the projects it's all the black people that have dirty houses, but you can't judge every one, though, 'cause of some black people.

SIETE: I think it is the opposite, it's like we are the ambassadors of our race. 'Cause like I know I did, but mami told us we were not allowed to fight in school, you know, and many kids would say, oh fight that person and this, but we had to be friendly and good at our work and it's like, you know, if they see you fight they won't be like oh that's just them, they'll be like, Puerto

Rican people fight, so we weren't allowed to do any of those things. For example, if you see fifth graders here and you have never seen them before and they behave well, you go and say ohh, fifth graders are really well behaved, you know, 'cause you haven't seen any other fifth graders.

The youth found creative ways around a very sticky marker of class—the neighborhood—by reinforcing the importance of personal agency as indicated by cleanliness.

LEAVING PORT CITY

In Port City, you could try to overcome class stigma by consuming sushi, shunning *Maury*, and living in a clean and tidy home. An even more certain way was to leave Port City altogether to show that you have indeed made it. Youth often heard from their teachers, principal, family members, peers, and nonprofit workers how they could get out of Port City and make a better life for themselves. Youth imagined that leaving the city would mean leaving their poverty behind. When they met volunteers, who were students at the local liberal arts college, youth marveled at how far they had come from home and wondered what their hometowns and cities looked like.

When Gigi moved to the outskirts of Boston for college, she mentioned "Boston" in every sentence she uttered. "Thank you Jesus, I'm far away from this hell" summarized her sentiment. One weekend, when she was home to visit her little brother, we went to the pier.

GIGI: I need a job, so where to look?

DANNY: [a friend of gigi's who still lived in port city] I filled out about ten applications in Port City and called mad times and got nothing!

MARIA: [another friend of gigi's who still lived in port city] I filled out seventeen applications and called, not even one is hiring.

GIGI: Well, I'm in Boston, so, and it's mad places out there.

DANNY: That's right! This place is for the poor. Boston, well, you should be good then.

MARIA: Umm, where you live it's not really Boston! You trynna be all classy!

While Gigi had gone to the outskirts of Boston for college and took pride in where she lived, trying to pass it off as Boston, many other youth left Port City simply for the sake of leaving, even when they did not have set plans for the city they were moving to. Angie returned from Florida precisely because she did not have a good life there: her aunt refused to lend her money, she didn't find a job, and she didn't make friends or acquaintances, instead spending her time in a small room by herself. Yet she still yearned to leave Port City and was certain that she wanted to move back to Florida, or to Minnesota. Curtis also dreamed of going as far away from Port City as possible: "I wanna go to Virginia, anywhere away from here. I don't want nothing to do with Port City, I got my boy in Florida but that's it. I gotta figure something out though." I asked him why Virginia or Florida, and it turned out that those were the only two places where someone he knew had managed to go. He explained, "Once I'm out of here I know everything will start going the right way for me. For now, just looking at the bright side."

We were at work one day when Curtis asked me to elaborate on "exactly what" I did at UConn. I explained that I was a student and taught classes while pursuing my doctoral degree.

CURTIS: Oh, that's nice. I think I wanna to be a computer mechanic. I wanna be on baseball scholarship, but depends on how I play though. I gotta start applying for college and scouts will start coming soon, so I'm stressed.

RANITA: Where do you wanna go?

CURTIS: Florida! The team here at Port City is good, we win matches, so I'm nervous!

RANITA: Why Florida?

CURTIS: It's either going to be Florida or Virginia... My boy that's gonna play for the MLB, that's about it in Florida, but I'm gonna start saving up from now till after I graduate and yeah, I ain't trynna be out here any longer.

Curtis and a friend bought plane tickets and left for Florida a little while after Curtis graduated. They crashed at a friend's place (Curtis's friend's cousin who was also friends with Curtis, according to Curtis) and looked for work. Curtis often phoned to complain about how hard it was to find a job or make friends, but he was also excited and proud. Curtis and his friend were planning to start attending a community college in the spring. However, they were unable to find work or a place to stay after their host refused to let them remain in his house, so they returned to Port City. Curtis came back enthusiastic about enrolling at the local community college but said that he wanted to start working first, in order to save some money. He enrolled in two classes at Port City Rivers Community College but proceeded to fail them over several semesters.

When I began my fieldwork, I was uncertain as to why the youth would leave their homes to move to cities where they often became homeless and could not find jobs, leaving their friends and family behind. Of course, one reason is that this desire to leave a small, boring town is fairly common, along with the idea that teenagers should leave their parents to attend college. Leaving Port City was a well-established mobility symbol. For them, the city also embodied their poverty and represented their misfortune. Their popular desire to move to Florida was perhaps based on the fact that immigrants from Puerto Rico, the Dominican Republic, Honduras, and other Latin American countries see Florida as a destination to be near others like them. Because many of the youth had family members in Florida and many of their neighbors, friends, and peers visited their own family members in Florida, it was a place the youth knew could be reached.

The college degrees and white-collar jobs the youth worked toward were often distant and uncertain possibilities, so they frequently settled for more immediate, certain, and available symbols of mobility and success. But it required spending the money they earned through the dead-end, frontline service jobs (in which they invested at the cost of college). This may seem to suggest a problem at the individual level, with the youth failing to give up short-term gratification for long-term gain. But there are more accurate ways to understand this. We need to guard against falling into the trap of imagining these youth as completely rational units who only think in utilitarian terms. It is quite human to seek enjoyment and status from everyday life and the pressures to prove our worth through everyday interactions are exceedingly high. But we also need to look beyond individual effort to assess institutions as well. Economically marginalized children continually struggle to perform well in middle-class institutions like schools and colleges even when they devote as much, if not more, time to their academics. For the Port City youth, thus, the problem was more than mere lack of time for academic endeavors, and their investment in temporary markers of class was not the only thing precluding them from becoming upwardly mobile. As we have seen throughout these chapters, institutions were failing them at a much deeper level.

In the absence of more instrumental measures of social mobility such as a college degree, white-collar job, and income, the youth attempted to perform class, in racialized ways, through symbols such as their taste in food, wine, and entertainment. Doing so allowed youth to perform a socially mobile identity. Their practices also demonstrate the power of middle-class cultural symbols to travel across neighborhoods, and the anxieties they can cause as marginalized youth try to perform them.

9 Dismantling the "At Risk" Discourse

The Making of a Teenage Service Class is my best attempt at documenting the experiences of the youth of Port City. My hope is that I have captured the complexities of their lives and their trajectories to adulthood. As they prepared to transition to adulthood, the youth navigated various relationships and contexts in their lives, including sibling ties, romantic and sexual relationships, schools, and workplaces. The ways in which youth navigated relationships and institutions, structured by the realities of economic marginalization, shaped outcomes that seemed to facilitate upward social mobility while also holding them back. As they transitioned to adulthood, seemingly working toward college degrees and white-collar jobs, youth were left to manage irreconcilable choices, making their transition different than that of the privileged, middle-class U.S. American adolescent.

Marginalized individuals can employ middle-class cultural capital and connections to obtain differential socioeconomic mobility and go beyond their parents' educational and occupational positions. For example, nine percent of students from the most economically marginalized segments of society in the United States acquire a college degree, and about one-third of U.S. Americans have managed to climb to a higher income class during the last half century.[1] Individuals living in similar neighborhoods may

221

have different outcomes—for example, some young people have jobs while others do not, and some young people are invested in education while others become pregnant or involved in criminal activities (while these are overwhelmingly portrayed, in simplistic ways, as exclusive outcomes, they are not).[2] Among the black and Latino / a youth of Port City, too, there were a variety of educational and occupational trajectories along with the everyday experiences of poverty. Some of the youth applied to and were accepted by four-year universities, others crafted plans for transferring from community colleges to four-year universities, and one was even invited to interview with a Harvard alumna. Some of these youth more strongly denounced drugs, gangs and violence, and early parenthood—constructing these as roadblocks to their mobility plans—than others. These differences can be partially explained by the youth's specific intersectional location in the social structure, and the access to resources such location allowed them, as well as by random events. Some of the youth in my study accessed more resources than others because of their older siblings, and some denounced drugs or parenthood in an attempt to either model or not model the behaviors and outcomes of their friends and siblings. Some of the youth's parents were recent immigrants with very limited familiarity with institutions, and others had stricter control over them, allowing youth differential access to resources. Some of the youth happened to find individuals who took a personal interest in their academic and occupational careers, while others grew thicker skins and pursued help despite enduring the anxieties that came with navigating middle-class institutions.[3]

Nonetheless, I decided against singularly pursuing and centering analyses that would situate these differential educational and occupational habits, practices, and trajectories among the youth in my study, even after investing considerable intellectual labor to highlight such differences. Individual and family practices among Port City youth did not indicate arrangements that would seem to lead to upward socioeconomic mobility; to the contrary, most of the practices, limited by systems of education and structures of the labor market, eventually led to low-wage frontline service jobs.[4] By the end of my time in Port City, none of the youth had achieved what they had set out to do—they had drifted from the path they had expected to follow after high school graduation. They either quit college to fully enter the frontline service industry or started to devote more and more time to their minimum-wage work at the cost of higher education; yet they also continued to foster high educational and occupational expectations. Many of the youth wondered why, despite delaying childbirth and avoiding other behaviors that are deemed destructive, despite having graduated from high school and participated in institutions of higher education, and despite fiercely embracing the achievement ideology, they had not moved very far beyond their parents' occupational achievements. They wondered why their lives did not look drastically different, in terms of their jobs, homes, and economic standing, than the lives of their peers who entered early parenthood, did not go to college, dealt drugs, or got into trouble at school.

In this study, I have highlighted the nuanced ways, and mechanisms and processes, through which the open-access educational system intersects with the service economy to lock economically marginalized black and brown youth into low-wage jobs.[5] Institutions and organizations pathologize their bodies and culture through a risk discourse, leaving youth to redefine mobility as avoiding risk behaviors that are consequences of classist and racist systems to begin with. Port City youth thus continued to construct an identity for themselves as socially mobile individuals, owing precisely to their rejection of drugs, gangs, violence, and early parenthood as well as their participation in higher education.

"Progressive liberals" critique the militarization of police, mass incarceration, drug policies, and the stratified reproductive system. Yet, while issues such as drugs, gangs, violence, and teen pregnancy may be urgent for marginalized youth, continuing to focus on them to understand the causes and consequences of marginalization still fosters an individualistic discourse where ultimately modifying individual behavior or local cultures (such as drugs, gangs, violence, and teen parenthood) would break the cycle of poverty. The constraints that youth who are not part of the negative outcome statistics confront in achieving educational and occupational mobility challenge U.S. American individualism. The youth in my study reproduced their parents' class positions despite their investment in school, the labor market, and bourgeois heteronormativity because these inherently middle-class institutions failed them. I have demonstrated how these institutions functioned in ways that allowed youth to give meaning to their life and hold on to their aspirations, while gradually reinforcing their social positions and hegemonic ideologies. In this final chapter, then, I will briefly revisit the age-old structure / agency dilemma, before turning to a call to rethink the "at risk" framing of marginalized youth—as potential parents, drug users and dealers, gang members, and perpetrators of violence—that often shapes both public policies and the experiences of the youth. I conclude with a discussion about what we can do at the local level to facilitate youth's transition to college and their retention once they are there, arguing for a need to provide sustained support in the face of persistent marginalization.

Some readers might question whether those in my study undermine popular stereotypes of black and brown urban youth—that is, disinterested in school, early parents, gang members, or drug dealers—because most of them were young women. But I contend gender alone does not explain the complex reality that I observed. While it is the case that marginalized women's unemployment rates are falling even as male unemployment rates continue to escalate, and girls outdo boys in schools in marginalized communities, economically marginalized black and brown girls are still overwhelmingly subjected to negative portrayals and understood as participating in "risky" behaviors.[6] Portrayals of economically marginalized young women of color also continue to focus on teen parenthood, gang membership, violence, and drug use.[7] Other portrayals simply ignore their trajectories and lives in favor of highlighting young men's marginalization.

STRUCTURE AND AGENCY

A 2007 survey conducted by the Pew Research Center revealed that almost two-thirds of Americans embrace the idea that the United States is a meritocratic society where individuals can get ahead if they work hard to nurture their talents; in other words, that individuals are primarily responsible for their situations. Social scientists, however, demonstrate how the social class of an individual's parents as well as the individual's race and gender leads to unequal educational and occupational outcomes. A subgroup of scholars also acknowledge that there exist "categorical differences in groups" and that the "differences that do exist across society cohere into patterns recognizable as social classes."[8] In other words, structural location shapes individual and group behaviors and practices in ways that seem to cohere as social classes. In brief, social structure impacts individual outcomes through cultural frames. This is a quintessentially Bourdieusian framework—*habitus* develops through early socialization within the family that results in habits and tastes (in music, food, etc.), which then seem natural, shaping *capital* through access to different types and degrees of connections and skills that are drawn upon in various settings and deployed in *fields* or institutions such as schools and workplaces that have rules (but are also shaped by actors and hence are somewhat flexible), resulting in a structure of domination.[9]

Poverty, therefore, directly shapes possibilities of educational and occupational mobility.[10] The youth in my study were born into economically and racially marginalized families. Their parents did not have college degrees and sometimes did not even have high school diplomas, and the youth held minimum-wage jobs and lived in marginalized neighborhoods. As the youth transitioned to adulthood, they entered new institutions, including high schools, nonprofit organizations, and workplaces. They developed connections and relationships with friends, romantic and sexual partners, employers, nonprofit workers, and volunteers, and they engaged in new leisure and extracurricular activities such as going to the movies, restaurants, and community meetings as well as joining dance or sports teams. Oftentimes, these connections, resources, and skills did not come naturally to the youth and led to stress and anxiety, as well as tensions within their families and peer groups, but nevertheless these seemed valuable in the various middle-class institutional settings the youth entered and led to moments of cultural and social rupture as the youth were able to successfully break into elite locations, such as Sandra's interview at Harvard and Ashley's introduction to sushi.[11] How can we understand this relationship between the privileged and the marginalized?

Earlier scholars have proposed the concept of an "inner-city street culture" that embodies "a complex and conflictual web of beliefs, symbols, modes of interaction, values, and ideologies that have emerged in opposition to exclusion from mainstream society" to understand the relationship between the "middle class" and economically and racially marginalized "inner-city" residents.[12] This culture offers an alternative way for U.S.

Americans who are politically and geographically isolated from the mainstream in inner-city enclaves to acquire respect—but this inner-city street culture is then partially responsible for the marginalization of its participants. However, these scholars also note that the majority of those who live in political and ecological isolation do not participate in the so-called "street culture." In fact, like the Port City youth, most youth routinely interact with middle-class actors and "mainstream" society. The Port City youth, for example, went to school and engaged with school personnel, they frequently came into contact with their employers, they interacted with their college professors, and they participated in programs such as Public Allies or other nonprofit programs whose employees and volunteers often came from middle-class backgrounds. These interactions were not regular, deep, or sustained, but rather fleeting and fragmented. It is this relationship between the marginalized and the middle class that I hope to have highlighted in this book.

For the Port City youth, the process of engaging in mobility projects involved piecing together a wide range of resources available through interactions with middle-class actors, as well as families, friends, and neighbors, to solve the mobility puzzle. The youth's regular interactions with middle-class actors shape their everyday experiences and worldviews. These interactions then question the overemphasis on isolated local cultures in understanding social reproduction of poverty. I don't mean to overemphasize structuralist perspectives or neglect the agency of culture. What my observations do conclusively speak to are the hardships endured by those who attempt to break into middle-class institutions and the challenges their mobility project brings, and the need to look beyond cultural practices through which individuals shape how they experience marginalization by larger systemic forces. This narrow focus on highlighting and understanding the "oppositional" cultures of the marginalized, albeit as a consequence of structure and in order to dispel myths about the marginalized, leaves ample room for overemphasizing "risk behaviors" such as teen parenthood, drug use, gang membership, and violence as the explanatory factors for the social reproduction of poverty.

Drawing attention to marginalized youth's embracement of achievement ideology and bourgeois heteronormativity and their attempts to access and perform middle class does not necessarily posit them as passive, unreflexive compliers, for, as I have pointed out throughout the book, their own struggles are hardly lost on them and they are often highly cognizant of their marginalization; it allows us to rethink what has become the default way to tackle the structure/agency dilemma—namely, the overwhelming representation of risk behaviors as acts of resistance that then become a destructive impetus. This representation has produced dominant stereotypes as well as popular contemporary ethnographic studies of marginalized youth that highlight drugs, gangs, violence, and teen pregnancy as their hallmark. The majority of young people who live and attend schools in poor urban neighborhoods do not become pregnant, go to jail, or drop out of school in order to sell drugs. Additionally, avoiding pregnancy does not greatly alter chances of socioeconomic mobility among marginalized women; the overpolicing of marginalized communities often shapes the youth's school-to-prison pathway; and various mechanisms work to undermine educational performance among marginalized students.[13] Although it is crucial to focus on these arguably negative aspects of marginalized youth's lives, many marginalized youth are high-performing students who are nevertheless unlikely to complete college and often do not even pursue it, according to recent quantitative analyses.[14]

Port City youth's interactions within middle-class institutions, however, raise an important question: Will these moments of rupture collectively grant the youth access to middle-class jobs, or at least jobs that pay more and are more upwardly mobile than their parents' jobs? Bourdieusian analyses would dictate that since the slots at the top are limited, access to higher education among marginalized youth will simply lead to other means of sorting individuals. This is also what the majority of quantitative scholars of higher education tell us: While the number of community colleges has multiplied and four-year universities have expanded, educational inequality has not been affected because the types of higher educational institutions students attend afford them unequal opportunities.[15]

Because these young men and women were still in their early to mid-twenties when my study ended, we can't know for sure what will happen to them, but their stories to date strongly suggest that their educational and occupational trajectories will not eventually lead to socioeconomic mobility through college degrees and white-collar jobs. Indeed, the

struggles almost all of the youth faced as they attempted to achieve socioeconomic mobility, despite their individual levels of commitment and
preparation, are very telling regarding their marginalization by middle-
class institutions. Moreover, the youth's haphazard educational trajectories will negatively impact their chances of obtaining white-collar jobs,
since attending community college lowers their chances of graduating and
increases the number of years required to graduate.[16] In addition, working multiple jobs is likely to negatively affect educational performance.[17]
Finally, some of the youth had already transitioned to low-wage work during my study, even as they retained their hope of acquiring a college
degree. Many studies have demonstrated that contemporary economically
marginalized adults continue to struggle in low-wage, unstable service
jobs well into their thirties, moving in and out of work and education and
"deferring their dreams" indefinitely.[18] In addition, although sometimes
the youth left or postponed college for obvious reasons such as a lack of
scholarships and loans, one might question whether they voluntarily
invested less in college to work more hours because they thought that
their job jived well with a class at the college, or simply because they suc-
ceeded better in low-wage jobs than in the middle-class institutions of
higher education. Both forces were at play. All in all, the youth failed to
reach the point in their educational careers they had hoped for and were
not enrolled in the types of educational institutions they were targeting by
following all the rules, which suggests that the ways their educational and
occupational trajectories were shaping up seem less likely to allow for
socioeconomic mobility. Clearly, the situation is far from simple. Complex
political-economic structures, history, individual actors, and culture all
intersect to render simplistic, all-encompassing solutions to socioeconomic inequality ineffective.

RETHINKING THE AT-RISK FRAMEWORK

Youth who do not contribute to the negative statistics but nevertheless
continue to face barriers to obtaining educational and occupational
opportunities bring into stark relief the problematic centrality of citing
individual behaviors such as drug use and dealing, gang membership,

early parenting, and so forth as explanations for the social reproduction of poverty. It would be beneficial for scholars and policy makers to help modify public discourse on marginalized youth as being "at risk" for outcomes like drugs, gang, violence, and early parenthood and to acknowledge these youth as agentic individuals with educational and occupational plans rather than construct all marginalized youth as problems to be solved. This would allow policy makers not to stereotype marginalized youth and generalize about their needs, but instead to acknowledge the complexities of their lives.[19] This will also prevent important resources from being diverted to policing marginalized youth's bodies instead of facilitating their educational and occupational mobility.

It would also be helpful for scholars to move beyond investigating and describing youth who are involved in drugs, gangs, violence, and young parenthood and instead question how these are constructed as "at risk" behaviors in ways that deem all marginalized youth to be constellations of potential problem behaviors to correct—as well as how these perceptions of youth as "at risk" shape the everyday experiences of all youth in a racist, classist, and patriarchal society.[20] For example, organizations in Port City invested in nonviolence training for all the youth and worked to prevent alcohol and drug abuse as well as early parenthood, when what many youth needed instead was help with their college applications. While progressive scholars, policy makers, and individuals claim that these negative behaviors are consequences of marginalized youth's social locations, they continue to believe that correcting them through broad interventions is fruitful. For example, many sociologists who agree that an individual's race, class, and gender influence their educational and occupational opportunities nevertheless often explain this relationship by pointing to the rejection of middle-class values and habits such as investment in higher education and delaying childbirth.

I have challenged this view here by shifting the focus from individuals who reject achievement ideologies and middle-class orientations to youth who, having grown up in marginalized families, strive to access middle-class status. As the youth of Port City demonstrate, some of the attempts to perform middle-class status, such as eating certain food, drinking wine, or leaving certain neighborhoods, are more readily achievable, and others, such as deferring childbirth, are used to indicate future prospects of educational and occupational opportunities. Because longer-term investments in middle-class institutions such as performing well in college or acquiring white-collar work are harder to achieve, they are more amenable to being delayed. Taken together, the youth claimed a socially mobile identity through their practices, etiquettes, dispositions, and habits.

The youth in my study illustrate that drugs, gangs, violence, and early pregnancy—widely accepted explanations for the social reproduction of poverty and the focus of the majority of policies and academic and public debates—are not, in fact, an exhaustive or adequate explanation of this phenomenon. This is not to say that drugs and violence do not present pressing issues requiring policy interventions—drug use and violence among any youth should be understood as a problem and worthy of intervention. But my observations reveal that youth who play by the widely accepted "rules of the game"—by avoiding drugs, gangs, and parenthood and focusing on education—are still unable to move beyond their parents' educational and economic positions. In fact, this continuing focus, by organizations and institutions, on preventing risk behaviors creates further impediments for the youth by reinforcing racist and classist discourse and diverting already scant resources.

The youth of Port City, as well as their families and teachers and members of their community, all assumed that if they stayed clear of drugs and gangs, postponed parenthood, did their homework, and went that extra mile, they could indeed surpass their parents' educational and occupational levels. What is more, the youth in my study internalized these responsibilities and invested in higher education while working multiple jobs and going hungry. They also marginalized their peers who failed to behave in accordance with the widely accepted formula for socioeconomic mobility. They were frequently perplexed and disillusioned that their efforts did not readily yield the outcomes they hoped for, yet they clearly still bought into the basic premise, as witnessed by the fact that when their peers resisted the formula—for example, by having children or rejecting schooling—the youth interpreted this as the cause of their marginalization.

Targeting "risk behaviors" through policy interventions does not challenge larger political-economic structures and racist and classist ideologies—making it a more "palatable" way for many scholars and policy makers to approach the marginalization of black and brown youth. Recently CNN reported that the state where Port City is located spent roughly $13,000 to educate each secondary school student and about $49,000 to keep an inmate in jail. Local organizations, institutions, and community members also focus on these issues. Drug use and violence among youth are the consequences of larger structural problems related to poverty and discrimination, rather than their causes. In addition, socioeconomically marginalized youth are disproportionately punished—in terms of both the number who are punished and the punishment that is exacted—for using the same amounts of drugs as their privileged counterparts.[21] The war on drugs is couched in racist discourses and ideologies.[22] Similarly, violence is posited as an "inner city" problem, with black and brown youth brutally murdering other black and brown youth, while in 2015 alone, police brutality was responsible for killing a thousand civilians across the country.[23] Scholars before me have recognized mass incarceration as a national problem in the United States.[24] Additionally, as I have argued in chapter 4, and as others also argue, early parenting is constructed as a social problem through racialized and classed processes and mechanisms that idealize bourgeois heteronormativity at the cost of other ways of forming families. Indeed, several scholars have argued that postponing parenthood does not reap the same benefits for marginalized youth as it does for their privileged counterparts.[25] In sum, to focus on issues constructed as risk behaviors through racialized and classed discourses is to ignore larger and deeper structural race, class, and gender inequalities.

WHAT'S WRONG WITH SERVICE JOBS?

Readers will notice my despair over youth investing more in frontline low-wage service jobs than in higher education. Some readers may ask: Well, what is wrong with service jobs? Do we all have to become marine biologists, prestigious culinary chefs, or radiologists? The obvious answer is: No. The modern "myth" of success, and what it should entail, is a subject that goes well beyond the scope of this chapter or book. Of course we can find happiness and fulfillment through different ways of life, different careers, and different life goals. We are also suited for different things, simplistically put. Moreover, all types of works should be valued. No one should be stigmatized, or thought of as less capable, because they serve at McDonald's instead of performing surgery.[26]

The question that concerns me is one of equal opportunities. Many youth in my study wanted to pursue college but were forced to work for the minimum wage in jobs they did not want to build a career around. Moreover, even if they wanted these jobs, low-wage jobs are not as stable, protected, and well paying as they were in the manufacturing era as companies continue to hire a disposable labor force to maximize profit.[27] The youth who enter the low-wage frontline service economy thus face the prospect of being stuck in those jobs for life without opportunities for within-job mobility, job security, the support of labor unions, or the opportunity to build careers. In addition, the paychecks from the jobs the youth acquired failed to guarantee basic dignities such as stable homes, food security, clothing, and so forth. These jobs sometimes required them to work more than ten hours a day, seven days a week, often while they were attempting to pursue higher education. Even if we respect our barista or McDonald's cashier and assume that they are bright young people, such respect alone will not guarantee them living wages, square meals, or stable homes—although granting respect to those performing these jobs could contribute to the larger conversation around providing everyone with livable wages.

The service economy has yielded opportunities for many individuals without higher educational degrees; for example, the malleable definition of expertise has given rise to a self-care industry where people are able to build careers as specialized service providers: trainers, life coaches, and the like. Yet such opportunities are unavailable to the economically and racially marginalized, as those who are able to afford the services of the self-care industry are mainly affluent people who are also likely to use the services of other white and/or middle-class people. Recall that when Sandra decided to open a clothing line and Cassy wanted to become a masseuse, their clients were other marginalized members of the Port City community. Sought-after frontline service jobs that provide living wages, labor unions, and opportunities for mobility could value the intricate skills that the youth who work these jobs cultivate and employ; as sociologist Katherine Newman argues in *No Shame in My Game: The Working*

Poor in the Inner City, workers in these jobs have to cultivate dexterity, patience, and communication skills, among others, and these are valuable skills that are indeed transferable from one job to another, and thus can provide a route for upward mobility.

SUSTAINED SUPPORT: POLICY RECOMMENDATIONS

In the face of a larger, complex racial history, global and local economic forces, and deep-seated race, class, and gender structures, prejudice, and discrimination, policy recommendations seem like a daunting task. Several long-standing systematic and coherent policy recommendations by social scientists speak to the structure of education, family practices, public assistance, housing security, health, and more. In the face of my general pessimism and my desire for deeper change, I want to conclude by offering some insights gathered during my fieldwork that specifically pertain to facilitating the high school–to-college transition and college success for marginalized youth in small cities like Port City. I propose sustained and well-rounded support for the youth throughout their transition. These modest insights, together with those offered by other recent ethnographers of children, youth, and inequality, such as Annette Lareau, Victor Rios, Alice Goffman, Philippe Bourgois, Roberto G. Gonzales, Jamie Fader, and Julie Bettie, among many others, may be especially helpful for local and regional nonprofits and policy makers invested in providing educational opportunities for marginalized youth in their communities.

Various existing programs attempt to provide marginalized students with the type of "concerted cultivation" that middle-class children receive at home.[28] Other programs like Big Brother / Big Sister aim to provide support at school and greater access to higher education.[29] In the same vein of providing broader access to resources that are available to middle-class students through their families and other means, first, we could also support youth through the bureaucratic labyrinth of college admission and transfer processes. For example, the information required for filling out FAFSA forms, such as parents' Social Security numbers and income, was often difficult and sometimes impossible for the youth of Port City to obtain. Some youth postponed the process and others simply gave up. These are youth who already live with a sense of constraint, as Annette Lareau would put it. Moreover, they work multiple jobs and frequently help out with younger siblings. Support with the complex, unfamiliar application process could make the difference between applying for college and postponing it.

The youth confronted similar difficulties around the process of transferring from community colleges to four-year universities. They often had little or no idea as to what was required and how they could go about doing it—and they frequently took haphazard classes without constructing a particular pathway for transferring to a four-year university. The obvious solution is for community colleges to offer more resources that would facilitate this process. At the time of my fieldwork, the state's university and community college systems had developed a transfer program for students after they acquired an associate's degree. Port City Rivers' website contained links and documents detailing the transfer process, dual admissions, and course equivalencies—this is standard practice across states. However, it would also be of benefit if faculty and staff at the community colleges did not assume that all students are well prepared and have the know-how to even ask the right questions, or know the importance of carefully planning to transfer. Furthermore, community colleges and state universities are suffering from massive resource cuts while Ivy Leagues continue to receive state funds.[30]

Additionally, given that all transfer information was available on Port City Rivers' website, it is clear that computers, access to the internet, and the ability to navigate these are key to accessing today's educational system. Simply informing students that transfer information is available on a college website may not be enough to support them. As we become increasingly dependent on technology, we must also recognize that this is middle-class cultural capital and does not come naturally for marginalized youth. Many of the youth did not have computers or internet access at home and some had never used a computer at all, so that when the time came to apply for college these were daunting obstacles. The nonprofits that provided these resources were not prepared to teach the youth to use them. The youth typed at a snail's pace, and sometimes hours would pass before they had typed a single paragraph. Nonprofits and other individuals and institutions looking to support youth's transition to college should be mindful of the fact that the ability to navigate technology with ease is a privilege, one that is almost taken for granted by the middle class today. They ought to provide students with detailed and sustained support for navigating computers and the internet (educational institutions ought to also address this issue). Beyond interacting with college websites, homework is also much easier to do using the internet—but because most of the youth in my study did not have internet access at home, things like looking up an unfamiliar word while completing an assignment at a convenient time was often not an option for them.

Less than 30 percent of students entering community college acquire their associate's degree in three years; moreover, socioeconomically marginalized students are less likely to graduate than their privileged counterparts.[31] Tuition costs rise, books needed for college are expensive, and transportation to and from college and work is often difficult to access, making it harder on marginalized students to continue higher education, even when they may have acquired grants and scholarships.[32] The Pell Grant, which is the main federal aid program for students in the United States, does not cover all college expenses.[33] Moreover, marginalized students often have to choose between school and work, and forgo work in order to attend college classes, and living costs also count toward college expense. It is also considerably harder for economically marginalized undergraduate college students to acquire food stamps or access subsidized housing programs.[34] Moreover, the housing demand is rising, and students need to be twenty-four years or older, caring for dependent children, or veterans to receive support.[35] Thus, while some forms of support may allow marginalized students partial access to institutions of higher education, staying in college means facing a different set of challenges.

A recent study by education scholar Sara Goldrick-Rab and colleagues demonstrates how college students struggle with hunger and housing insecurity. While colleges and universities can support students more thoroughly within the limits of available resources, several other policy initiatives can support college students—and this is my second recommendation.[36] Many of the Port City youth who sought assistance for college admission applications or academic work were battling hunger, illness, family responsibilities, mental illness, eviction, and more. We know that nonprofit organizations and schools and colleges are often not prepared to address these persistent struggles, but they should at least offer the youth more persistent, elaborate, and sustained forms of support. Nonprofit organizations could attempt to provide food for youth who come to access their programs in sensible ways. Nonprofits should also be mindful of the youth's constrained time availability and arrange for transportation to and from these programs, and should also provide long-term support after the youth have enrolled in college.

One such model existed in Port City, where a small nonprofit selected and engaged with a number of youth each year and supported them in their academics starting in high school through the first few years of college. Employees and volunteers at the organization assisted the youth with high school assignments and standardized test preparations, tutored families through FAFSA applications, evaluated their daily well-being, and then remained in contact with the youth, supporting them through the first few semesters of college as needed. The organization recently released data, claiming that almost 95 percent of their students enroll in college right after high school and that almost 85 percent of these students continue on to their second year in college.

Third, current practices that proclaim "college for all" should also rethink the consequences of encouraging under- or unprepared students to attend college, especially when this comes at the cost of enormous debt. There is a general agreement among scholars that a higher educational degree pays off in the labor market and higher education is one of the primary ways in which marginalized students obtain some level of socioeconomic mobility. However, taking haphazard college classes, attending college irregularly, or enrolling in for-profit colleges does not accrue the same level of benefits.[37] School personnel as well as nonprofits may need to rethink practices that urge all students to attend college as a way to better their chances of obtaining socioeconomic mobility.[38]

Inequality grows as well-paying manufacturing jobs continue to disappear, and the public sector is underfunded while white and wealthy people continue to access high-quality schools and other services. Although students from marginalized groups—including women, people of color, and the poor and working classes—have greater access to higher education today, as scholars have argued, many only have access to qualitatively different educational opportunities.[39] Growing access to higher education for women, people of color, and economically marginalized students, who were historically excluded, makes it seem as though the U.S. educational system is open to all, since students are allowed to stay within it longer and longer. However, the truth of the matter is that these students drag their way through community colleges, postponing classes, semesters, and transferring, which demonstrates their persistent faith in upward mobility, even as their dead-end jobs speak to a very different reality.

Numerous scholars before me have poignantly depicted the pain and suffering of the urban poor. But these portrayals, while significant and important, often relegate to the background the less sensational pain and suffering that the majority of marginalized individuals experience on a daily basis—hunger, unstable homes, constant bodily discomfort, anguish surrounding relationships that are overburdened with responsibilities, class and race injuries of navigating middle-class white spaces, frustration connected to an inability to complete homework or to apply to college or for a job, long hours traveling, an inability to rest or invest time and money in leisure, and more. I realize that some might read what I have just written as a hopelessly structuralist reduction of marginalization, and it may very well be, yet the "at risk" framework ignores the experiences of the majority of America's urban youth and provides no foundation for understanding them. A more complete understanding of young urban U.S. Americans can challenge us to rethink our approach to supporting and empowering all youth beyond simply targeting the "risk behaviors" in their communities.

I recognize the complexities of formulating and implementing federal and local long-term policies and programs that will facilitate opportunities for marginalized youth within existing educational institutions and the labor market while also challenging the way these same educational and occupational structures institutionally marginalize these youth. My immediate goal in this book has thus been to document the lives of youth who outnumber those represented in the negative statistics but who are largely ignored in public as well as academic debates—the ones who largely denounce drugs, gangs, violence, and early parenthood and actively pursue educational, social, and economic mobility. These youth are marginalized by dominant discourses that construct all marginalized youth as at risk. In the end, I urge readers to grapple with this question, which I hope I have partially answered in this book: What can those who "play by the rules of the game" tell us about the rules, the game, and the players?

Epilogue

It was nearly a year since I had seen Siete, and she was now twenty years old. She wore a long sleeveless black and blue striped dress made of polyester—Siete was always good at finding fashionable things at low prices. She wore black flip-flops and clutched a small purse. Her hair was held up in a tight bun and she was wearing shiny turquoise and black eye makeup and bright red lipstick. She was one of the most attractive women in the room.

I had returned to Port City to attend, along with some of the Port City youth, a wedding of mutual friends. Siete sat somberly and, despite her attractiveness, with an aura of weariness beyond her years at a round table with her older sister Ashley, their mother and her boyfriend, and Ashley's new boyfriend John. When I finally caught Siete's eye from the far end of the room, I felt as though her face lit up with nostalgia and relief as we approached each other.

SIETE: What's going on? You been gone long, so much happened! I didn't even know you were comin'! Ashley don't tell me nothin'!

RANITA: So good to see you! What you been up to?

SIETE: Oh, nothin', just working and putting in mad hours, you know! The usual, trynna make some money. I wanna go to college again and move up in the world, you know.

When Ashley saw us talking, she hurried over and we hugged and said hello. Ashley and I had become very close during the three years I spent in Port City, and we have been in regular touch since I left Port City, now almost four years ago.

ASHLEY: [speaking loudly and in jest] Las Vegas! We gotta go up there and make some money, you know what I'm sayin'? [A throaty laugh followed.] We got money now, we in the phone business, all three of us!

RANITA: Oh you're still in Electronic Limited?

SIETE: Yeah, I'm there too, but I'm trynna go to college, you know, 'cause that's what I wanna do though, like be in the medical profession like a nurse or like the person who does them things when your kid is about to be born! But I had to stop at Port City Rivers, though, 'cause there, like, I needed to work for now, 'cause I'm trynna make some money though, but I wanna go back.

ASHLEY: [seeming to want to end the college conversation] Yeah, ask Ranita how you wanna do all that, she know everything.

RANITA: What happened to the clothing business thing you were doing with Sandra, by the way? She still into it, right? [Siete had joined Sandra and the other original founders for a little while, and then had left and rejoined a few times according to the information I gathered.]

SIETE: Nah, I left that though. 'Cause like she be trynna do everything differently, like her way, and I wasn't into it no more. 'Cause we doin' it for our friend, you know, 'cause he was real good at it, but now she [Sandra] is not doin' how we started though.

RANITA: Oh, really?

ASHLEY: [raising her eyebrows] Oh yeah, I didn't tell you nothin' about it, but she [pointing to Siete] was gonna take off with this ghetto-ass nigga and about to move to Florida and then he got someone pregnant. . . . Yeah, Siete was about to take off. That's why she stopped at Port City Rivers and got into it with Sandra too.

SIETE: [breaking in with embarrassment] No, that's not the only reason, you don't know nothin' about the whole thing, alright? Don't just be sayin' shit to her. Ima tell you later, but like I thought I was gonna go there [Florida] and start college, you know, 'cause like I just wanna get outta this place. Anyway, Ima come up there and see you in Vegas. I really wanna go there, though, and make mad money.

ASHLEY: Yeah, she's gonna come see you, she saved some money this year too. . . . Oh, you met John yet, though? We living together now. I think I love him, he is mad nice and all and he works at Electronic Limited. We gonna get married soon, once we move to like a nicer house or something 'cause he got some money saved up. That's why I can't come down to Vegas now, 'cause I'm trynna save up too, you know.

RANITA: Are you still taking classes at Port City Rivers, though?

ASHLEY: [appearing to be irritated by my question] Nah, not for now, it's not for me maybe, you know. 'Cause this job's nice, though, and they pay me more than other jobs I worked at. I need money.

John walked up to us in the meantime and shook my hand. "Yeah, I heard about you" was the only thing he said during the next hour as we stood and chatted. But he patiently remained with the three of us, and Ashley rested her head on his shoulder every once in a while and held his hands when she spoke of a future together.

I asked about their other sister, Betsy, and inquired why she had not come for the wedding. "She didn't wanna come. 'Cause like she was working and everything and you know her stomach pain and whatnot, and she takin' care of our nephews too, 'cause Maria and Johnny, they went to this barbeque," Siete replied.

I spent two days in Port City with Ashley and her family. I did not get to see the other youth I had spent three years with. Some of them had left the city, but most of them still lived there. Some of them texted me that they would come over to Ashley's house to say hello, but they didn't show up. Many of them later apologized for having missed me due to work, school, or other obligations.

I left Port City to take a faculty position in Las Vegas. When I announced that I was leaving, most of the youth shrugged it off. Ashley said, "Oh, good for you! I wanna leave too." Then, later, after I left and had not returned for a few months, she said, "Damn, you gone forreal. It never hit me." The youth assumed that I, like many of their peers, was attempting to

acquire status by "leaving the place." I often long to be back in Port City—
sometimes I think maybe it is the magic of Port City that brings the youth
back—and if it is not magic, perhaps it's the feeling of home. Almost all of
the youth made—and continue to make—plans to visit me, but no one has
visited yet. Angie often asks me, "What's out there [in Las Vegas]? Is it
cheap? Maybe I'll move up there if you find me a job."

Notes

CHAPTER 1. THE MOBILITY PUZZLE AND
IRRECONCILABLE CHOICES

1. Scholars and activists are increasingly using the more gender-inclusive term Latinx. I contemplated using it to refer to the young people in my book. However, during the course of my fieldwork between 2010 and 2013 Latinx was not as widely used, and the youth in my study referred to themselves as Latina/o. It is to capture their voice that I decided to use Latina/o

2. In other publications, I have used a different pseudonym for Port City.

3. Brock 2010; Nielsen 2015; Rosenbaum 2001.

4. See Hochschild 1995 for a discussion of the ideological underpinnings and complexities of the "American dream."

5. Scholars have criticized the "at risk" discourse as it draws upon racialized, gendered, and classed narratives that are based on the cultural deficit model. This model problematizes individuals, families, and communities instead of targeting social structure. See Swadener and Lubeck 1995; Swadener 1995; Fine 1995. See also Valencia 1997; Menchaca 1997.

6. Sociologists challenge narratives that posit these risk behaviors as a consequence of individual or cultural failure, but nonetheless highlight risk behaviors as emblematic of urban poverty. Scholars argue that marginalized youth respond to blocked opportunity structures by making active choices in their everyday lives such as revering teen motherhood, drugs, gangs, and violence, and rejecting

academic goals and work ethics. These choices often cohere into a local culture that is oppositional to mainstream culture, and this culture then becomes partially responsible for holding youth back. For examples, see Bourgois 1995; Anderson 1999; Dohan 2003.

7. See, for example, Victor Rios's (2011) work on the "the youth control complex." Rios underlines how black and Latino men are policed from an early age because they are deemed at risk of becoming violent, dangerous, and difficult. See also Ferguson 2000, Paulle 2013, and Goffman 2014 on this issue. Black and Latina women are also policed as potential teen mothers; see Ray forthcoming.

8. See Fields 2008, Garcia 2009, and Barcelos and Gubrium 2014 on dominant discourses around black and brown youth's sexualities.

9. Garland 2001.

10. See Perry and Morris 2014 for the impact of the culture of control on all students.

11. See Hochschild 1983 and Leidner 1993 for emotional labor. See Williams and Connell 2010 on aesthetic labor. For the flexible nature of emotional and aesthetic labor, see also George 2008.

12. The institutions and organizations young people engage with provide specific resources, but they consistently conceal the meaning of, or provide confusing information regarding, youth's participation in community college and low-wage work. See Auyero and Swistun (2009: 144) for how institutional actors produced a "labor of confusion" to conceal information about a toxic environment from marginalized residents living near petrochemical compounds in Argentina. See also Bourdieu 2001. The youth in my study did not realize the profound implications of attending community college, such as their greatly lowered chances of timely graduation (see Goldrick-Rab 2006; Rosenbaum 2001; Schneider and Stevenson 2000).

13. Cohen [1972] 2011; Ward 1995; Garot 2010; Western 2006.

14. Smith 2001; Wilson 1996 (on disappearance of low-wage work); Jayaraman 2013.

15. Newman 1999; Alexander, Bozick, and Entwisle 2008.

16. See National Center for Education Statistics 2013. See also Alon 2009.

17. Esping-Andersen 1999.

18. Rosenbaum 2001.

19. Brock 2010.

20. Rosenbaum 2001. Widespread enrollment also benefits for-profit and private universities, where marginalized students incur the most educational debt; see Cottom 2017. See also Tuchman 2009.

21. But see Bettie 2003 and McRobbie 2000 with regard to how girls rejected school.

22. Esping-Andersen 1999; Jayaraman 2013.

23. Jayaraman 2013; MacDonald and Sirianni 1996. While complex and decentralized labor markets offer both opportunities and constraints, scholars

warn us about the dangers of romanticizing the industrial economy by ignoring the conditions under which stable employment was obtained; see Smith 2001.

24. Chen 2015.

25. Chen 2015; NELP 2013.

26. Jayaraman 2013.

27. Steensland 2008; Wacquant 2008; Desmond 2016; Western 2006; Saltman 2007.

28. Ingraham 2015.

29. Jiang, Granja, and Koball 2017.

30. Wilson 1987, 1996; Jencks and Mayer 1990; Coleman 1988.

31. See Wilson 2010.

32. Hays (1994) outlines the general murkiness of the concepts of structure, culture, and individual agency in the social sciences. Poverty scholarship has been influenced by the complexities of these concepts. As I show, contemporary poverty scholars recognize the interrelated nature of structure, culture, and agency.

33. See Bourdieu 1979.

34. For example, social disorganization theory contends that lack of social resources and residential instability in disadvantaged neighborhoods leads to weaker social ties and therefore decreased social control; for example see Shaw and McKay [1942] 1969. Diminished social control weakens local institutions and diminishes opportunities for educational and occupational success; see Sampson, Morenoff, and Earls 1999. Social isolation theory, on the other hand, argues that poor neighborhoods are disconnected from mainstream society and hence have access to neither material resources nor networks of the middle class; see Wilson 1987.

35. This local culture, according to Willis (1977), was sexist and racist and established working-class white masculinity through oppressive and dominating relations with women and with men of Asian and West Indian descent. Willis claimed that this was a creative process that challenged the social reproduction of class: The youth exercised a level of autonomy by recognizing and rejecting the ideological mystifications of schooling, including opportunity and career choice, and aspiring instead to take up factory jobs. In the United States, sociologist Jay MacLeod (1987) documented the relationship between individual agency and race and class structures through variations in responses to poverty. Observing two groups of young men (one majority white and one majority black) in a public housing project, MacLeod found differences in their work, school, and family experiences, as well as their aspirations and expectations. The young men interpreted and responded to the constraints of poverty differently. The black boys embraced the achievement ideology and imagined that the end of state-sponsored racial exploitation would open up new opportunities for them. The white boys, on the other hand, rejected school altogether, imagining that they

were set up to fail. Despite varying aspirations as well as everyday educational practices, however, none of the young men achieved socioeconomic mobility.

36. Lewis 1966: xlv.

37. Liebow 1967; Valentine 1968; Rainwater 1970.

38. See Rodríguez-Muñiz 2015. Perspectives on intergenerational transmission of poverty subsided somewhat when other researchers, such as sociologists Peter Blau and Otis Duncan (1978), did not find evidence supporting the argument that intergenerational socioeconomic mobility was lacking among all marginalized groups.

39. Sociologist William Julius Wilson renewed the focus on culture with his theories on the "underclass" and intergenerational welfare dependency. Wilson argued that the decline in well-paying manufacturing jobs and the out-migration of the middle class from cities led to the growth of an "underclass." The job decline led to a decrease in the marriageable pool of men, which then led to single-parent households, and the out-migration weakened important socializing institutions such as the church, thus isolating the poor from middle-class networks. Wilson's model underlined the intersection of structure and culture: demographic changes socially isolate the inner-city poor, which affects their family and community lives. His ideas about neighborhood isolation were particularly popular among scholars because he identified key structural factors that restricted upward mobility and led to the creation of an "underclass."

40. See the review by Small, Harding, and Lamont 2010. See also Carter 2003, 2005; Harding 2010; Small 2004.

41. In a relatively recent article, sociologist Stephen Vaisey (2009: 1687, 88) draws on Ann Swidler's "toolkit" theory of culture to argue for a "dual process model." In this model, actors are motivated mostly by profoundly internalized "schematic processes," which is akin to Pierre Bourdieu's ideas around *habitus*. Yet, actors are prone to deliberate over their actions, and justify them, when necessitated by the requirements of social interaction. This "theoretical heuristic," Vaisey argues, is useful for understanding the causes and consequences of actions. To understand people's choices and motivations for actions, Vaisey states, we must access individuals' "unconscious cognitive processes," and this is not readily accessible through post-fact interviews when actors attempt to make sense of their actions. For example, if we ask marginalized youth why they became pregnant or why they skipped their college classes in favor of work, their responses might not necessarily reflect the deep and unconscious processes that motivated their actions. Vaisey suggests that forced-choice surveys where actors choose from a given set of responses to a particular situation will draw from people's "practical consciousness" and knowledge, and thereby provide a better window into the culture-action connection.

I go beyond documenting the cognitive processes involved in everyday decision making by examining the embodied experiences of making a decision at any given moment. I document, in situ, as people make everyday decisions related to school, work, family, and romance as they experience hunger, eviction, illness, and other predicaments of poverty. Under the constraints of poverty, actions can be understood as shaped by cultural meanings, skills necessary to complete a particular action, as well as embodied experiences related to poverty at the moment of action. For example, in my study, the youth's decision to complete their homework was often determined by whether or not they were hungry, or in emotional distress because of an untreated family illness or impending housing eviction. The decision to skip work or school was embedded in exhaustion from working eighteen hours and spending long hours navigating public transportation. Decisions within intimate ties were also enacted out of feelings of love. Decisions to drop college classes were influenced by feelings of embarrassment from falling behind. Actions were then interpreted and justified through identities that individuals constructed by drawing on available cultural meanings that define social mobility as a consequence of individual grit.

42. See, for example, Anderson 1999; Bourgois 1995; Edin and Kefalas 2005.

43. Contreras 2012.

44. Small, Harding, and Lamont 2010. See also Duneier, Hasan, and Carter 1999. In a similar vein, in her 2013 book, *Falling Back: Incarceration and Transitions to Adulthood among Urban Youth*, Jamie Fader avoids pathologizing culture by highlighting the process through which structural context shapes the complex lives of young men who become entangled with the criminal justice system.

45. Along with focusing on "risk behaviors," existing studies also write about the poor in isolation from the middle class. In a recent article summarizing trends in poverty studies, sociologist Michael Rodríguez-Muñiz (2015) calls them "ontological myopia[s]" characterized by a narrow focus on economically marginalized communities and their cultures, and specific topics of inquiry. Rodríguez-Muñiz points out that such narrow focus may work to reinforce stigmas, and fail to recognize how material structures shape culture by ignoring the various actors and institutions with which the poor interact regularly and which perpetually and relationally shape their marginalization. A few recent ethnographers such as Matthew Desmond (2016) and Victor Rios (2011) have outlined this relational nature of poverty and social mobility, showing how marginalization is a process, and not a bounded phenomenon, that is shaped through interactions with larger structures. Rios outlines how mass incarceration shapes a "youth control complex" that marginalized youth of color must navigate in their everyday life, and Desmond demonstrates the exploitative process through which profit-mongering institutions and individuals evict marginalized tenants out of their homes, thus further undermining individuals and communities.

46. See Wacquant 2009 for how the U.S. state responded to rising social insecurity through heightened criminalization of the marginalized.

47. See Rios 2015.

48. Maura Kelly, in her working paper "Introduction to Feminist Research in Practice," describes feminist research as reflexive, mindful of the situated nature of knowledge production and the power embedded within it, having policy implications for targeting inequality and drawing on intersectional feminist scholarship.

49. Ray 2016.

50. Although empirical evidence establishes that avoiding childbirth does not facilitate mobility among already marginalized youth, teen pregnancy has been problematized ubiquitously. See Geronimus 1997; Luker 1997.

51. I broadly characterize the Port City youth as the working poor (for a discussion of the "working poor," see Newman 1999). The youth and their families either received government assistance or earned minimum wage at different points during my study. It was not feasible for me to utilize nuanced definitions of class, drawing on contemporary neo-Weberian and neo-Marxist empirical studies, to categorize the Port City youth and their families. I also believe that a thorough analysis of the same is not essential to developing or expanding the central theses of this book. I acquired informed verbal consent from the youth, as required by the University of Connecticut's Institutional Review Board, to ascertain complete anonymity and protect any chance of identification. I also have changed minor details (that do not in any way impact my analyses and conclusions) to further protect their identity.

52. See Desmond 2012.

53. Without a doubt, I have benefited from their life stories much more than they have from mine. This particular point should not distract from the fact that I was still the fieldworker.

54. Naples 1996.

55. Clifford 1986.

56. As I have presented and discussed this work in various avenues, many have rightly asked me to specifically reflect on my class position as I theorized about the lives of the youth. To point out succinctly my position in the class system has been harder than I thought, mainly because the class structure of the United States does not reflect the realities of India. Growing up, my father started as a municipal judge and climbed the ladder to eventually become a high court judge in India (this was after I had settled in the United States). My mother was a homemaker. My parents had not inherited wealth. The daily realities of my upbringing in many ways resembled that of the youth. For instance, we boiled hot water and added it to a bucket to shower in the winter—it was much later that we had an apartment with a source that would provide direct hot water to the tap. We lived in modest rented homes and used nonluxurious and tiresome public transportation for most of my life in India. Eventually my parents bought a modest apartment and then upgraded. In college, we all photocopied chapters of books we had to read—libraries did not have the books and buying books published by Western presses with Indian rupees was not feasible.

These are some examples that highlight the complexities of classed experiences in India. Perhaps, they allowed me to empathize with the bodily experiences of exhaustion due to the long hours spent in public transportation or the exhaustion that comes from small things, like going from place A to B or acquiring a book, requiring intense effort. On the other hand, I grew up as a nonpracticing Hindu in a state that oppresses Muslims, and in India, I did not fear the police—until I was a teenager when, in situations where I was alone, I began to fear all unknown men for their potential as sexual predators—through experience, advice, and learning about police violence against Indian women.

57. There are real benefits to "fitting in" within a community. This can eliminate quite a few mishaps and obstacles. For accounts of trials of researchers who have a harder time "fitting in," see Bourgois 1995; Goffman 2014.

58. But also see Emerson 2001 on the impossibility of becoming a true "insider."

59. Several contemporary ethnographers point to the often unwelcome focus on the ethnographers as a distraction from a sociological account, which ought to be the central focus of our work. For example, see Desmond 2016; Bettie 2003. However, this does not discount genuine concerns over representation of the marginalized.

60. Bettie 2003: 25–26.

61. Readers may wish to consult Bettie 2003 for a summary of the debates.

62. See Halle 1984 and Liebow 1967.

CHAPTER 2. PORT CITY RISING FROM THE ASHES

1. For an exception, see the ethnographic study by Timothy Black (2009) based in a small city called Springfield in the northeastern United States.

2. See Crandall 1993; Jacobs [1961] 1992.

3. See Kneebone and Garr 2011.

4. See Scotti 2004.

5. Healey 2012.

6. I do not cite the study here because its title identifies Port City.

7. Whalen and Vázquez-Hernández 2005.

8. Glasser 1997.

9. See Greene [1942] 1968.

10. See U.S. Congress, Office of Technology Assessment 1992.

11. See Brown-Saracino 2010 on gentrification debates.

12. In Port City, the two casinos were the largest employers, followed by a drug manufacturer, hospitals, military base, and power plants (in that order).

13. See Brown-Saracino 2010 for types of gentrifiers including preservationists.

14. U.S. Census Bureau, 2015.

15. See for example De Haymes, Vidal, Kilty, and Segal 2000.

16. See Calderón (1992) for a discussion of the terminology "Hispanic" and "Latino."

17. The food cooperative was the only food store owned by members in the larger metropolitan area, and the only grocery store in Port City. The coop claimed to only carry "organic and natural foods." The coop also partnered with local farmers and "natural foods vendors." The coop claimed to "support the local community" by providing "whole, natural foods and wares" and "produce, dairy, meat, plants, breads, frozen foods, spices, art, and crafts." I do not refer to the website to protect confidentiality.

18. Public schools are required to administer standardized achievement tests so as to receive federal funding, and states have their own tests. See Guinier (2015) for insights on the classed and racialized nature of standardized tests.

19. Romo and Schwartz 1993.

20. See report by Brown and Hugo Lopez 2010.

CHAPTER 3. SIBLING TIES

1. Bourgois 1995.

2. Ashley initially lived with her mother and three other sisters. But their older sister Maria moved in and out of the house and also lived with her boyfriend. Ashley's mother took in two of her sister's children after her sister passed away.

3. As per Habitat for Humanity's official website, Bank of America and Habitat for Humanity have collaborated for over twenty-five years in order to facilitate "neighborhood revitalization" on a global scale. The program started as a housing sponsorship program back in 1990 and transformed into an elaborate partnership. Their website also states that Bank of America has now invested around $26 million as well as employee volunteers (35,000 hours per year) to facilitate affordable housing for economically marginalized families. Such programs exist alongside a profitable housing market that renders many low-income families homeless and leads to high eviction rate; see for example Desmond 2016.

4. I would like to note to the reader that it is worthwhile to move away from simplistic analyses of events like this one. When I point out issues such as domestic violence or parents' apparent inability to provide for / protect their children, I do not theorize these as individual failures, cultural traits, simply as causes of or the results of poverty, or even the central story of poverty. I do not wish to explain these in any such racialized and classed ways. Rather, my larger argument is that families are complex, and domestic abuse is not relegated to economically or racially marginalized families alone but is also experienced by the privileged— how this is covered, understood, or addressed is classed and racialized. Feminist

scholars have long theorized domestic abuse as a complex phenomenon related to power rather than simply something that is the cause or consequence of racial and economic marginalization (see Anderson 2005 for one overview).

5. Despite the wide recognition of theories that embrace the pivotal function of kinship ties while idealizing their strength in the lives of the urban poor (for example see Stack 1974; Newman 1999), significant scholarship provides contrary evidence. In fact, scholars argue that the families and networks of the poor have high levels of mistrust and hostility, which makes daily survival even harder (for example see Roschelle 1997; Desmond 2012). In this chapter I will reconcile these paradoxical understandings.

6. See Giordano 2003.

7. For example see Lareau 2003; Edin and Lein 1997. See also Newman and Massengill 2006 for a review.

8. The poor are likely to have higher numbers of siblings. For example, 60 percent of children born to new parents (who were in their mid-twenties) in the Fragile Families and Child Wellbeing study had at least one half-sibling at the time of their birth (see for example Child Trends 2009).

9. See Giordano 2003.

10. Owing to their economic and social disadvantages, youth were often regularly compelled to rely on their intimate ties for a variety of necessary resources. For example see Edin and Lein 1997. See also Nelson 2000.

11. The importance of siblings does not invalidate the fact that the "filial bond" is a socially constructed, idealized concept, nor does it undermine the work of the many scholars who have depicted and problematized the role of blood-related kin versus fictive kin in surviving the constraints of poverty. For example see Stack 1974; Lomnitz 1977.

12. I theorized sibling ties, exchange, and intimacy, drawing on this research, in another publication (Ray 2016), and part of this chapter appears in the same article.

13. Sibling relations have been traditionally understudied in the urban poverty literature. Statistical analyses conceptualize the role of sibling ties, in industrialized societies such as the United States, as discretionary and insignificant in shaping families' functionality; for example see Conger and Little 2010. Such studies, however, do not reflect the experiences of those growing up under the constraints of poverty; see for example Lareau 2003.

14. See for example Rios 2011; Goffman 2014.

15. On the issue of exchange and intimacy, see Zelizer 2005. Zelizer's analysis of economic exchange and intimate ties begins by challenging two ideas commonly held by sociologists: the inevitability of firm boundaries between economic activity and intimate relationships in order to preserve social harmony, and the "nothing but" assumption where intimacy and economy are reduced to single explanations such as market activity or power relations. Alternatively, Zelizer argues for the "connectedness" of these two worlds. In every context of

social life, actors perform relational work by connecting economic exchange with intimate relations, thus building "democratic, compassionate caring economies" (p. 303). Situating economic exchanges within the framework of actual social relations, Zelizer demonstrates how personal meanings are produced through economic exchanges; for example, people use various forms of exchanges including gifts, various types of compensation, or payments that are both defined by and structure their relationships with one another. Thus, Zelizer suggests that exchange and intimate relationships, usually considered to be "hostile worlds," are in fact "connected" and complementary worlds that are not at odds with one another. My observations show how relational work may become complicated under the constraints of poverty.

16. I also extend Desmond's arguments in "Disposable Ties" (2012), which offer a convincing argument suggesting that the enactment of kinship ties under the constraints of poverty may entail several obstacles and that ties with strangers may be a viable response to the missing kinship ties of the urban poor. While Desmond's work explores how evicted tenants access immediate and pressing resources through strangers in the absence of kin support, my longitudinal ethnographic observations reveal how kin members are often obligated to exchange resources, and how obligatory exchanges influence their relationships.

CHAPTER 4. RISKY LOVE

1. Historically, urban ethnographers have paid detailed attention to the romantic and sexual relationships of economically and racially marginalized youth. These scholars largely understood romance among people in marginalized communities through the lens of mutual exploitation, focusing on teen pregnancy and early childbirth outside of wedlock (for example see Hannerz 1969; Liebow 1967). They explain that poor young men of color engage in transient sexual encounters to establish their manhood or acquire material goods (for example see Anderson 1999). Marginalized women gain material objects, future financial security, a child who may help them gain adult status (for example see Kaplan 1997), and a welfare check. A new generation of urban poverty scholars now theorizes cultural heterogeneity to emphasize an important point of variation in outcomes among the poor. These scholars, such as Harding (2007), argue that poor youth in marginalized neighborhoods confront a heterogeneous array of cultural frames that are both "ghetto specific" and "mainstream," which they use to inform their sexual behaviors and romantic relations. For example, whether one frames pregnancy as a means of obtaining adult status ("ghetto specific" frame) or an obstacle to attaining social mobility ("mainstream" frame) influences their decisions regarding childbirth. While existing urban ethnographies focus on how class positions impact romantic and sexual experiences of

marginalized youth, by drawing on the works of reproductive justice scholars and scholarship on everyday feminism, I analyze their experiences as a site for the reproduction of race, class, and gender structures.

2. See Barcelos and Gubrium 2014.

3. To provide a space for the voices of young mothers, a growing body of scholars are theorizing how young girls (mostly pregnant or parenting) themselves negotiate dominant raced and classed narratives that construct their sexualities as "risky" (for example see Barcelos and Gubrium 2014).

4. See Ferber 2007.

5. This fact likely reflects, at least in part, an unprecedented nationwide decline in teen pregnancy among marginalized youth. For teen pregnancy rates consult National Center for Health Statistics 2013.

6. The bourgeoning field of reproductive justice (see Luna and Luker 2013), situated within women-of-color feminism, in fact, questions the way that teen pregnancy is constructed as inherently and ubiquitously problematic by academics, policy makers, and the media. Scholars adopting the reproductive justice framework also highlight a particular sociohistorical process through which teen pregnancy became culturally and economically unacceptable. They argue that privileging a heterosexual middle-class transition to adulthood, where childbirth comes after economic independence and marriage, reflects a racialized and classed construction of economically marginalized black and Latina women's sexuality (Bettie 2003; Fields 2008; García 2009, 2012; Ward 1995; Lawlor and Shaw 2002; Lopez 2008; Luker 1997; Mann 2013; Fuentes, Bayetti Flores, and Gonzalez-Rojas 2010; Roberts 1998). See also Cohen 2010.

7. Stacey (1990) offers the concept of "gender strategies" to understand how women appropriate feminist ideologies in their daily lives. In her research, Aronson (2008) finds that as young women transition to adulthood they employ feminist ideals to "give meaning to their experiences through perspectives absorbed from the women's movement" (p. 57); and while young women from marginalized communities may often be indifferent to the label feminist, they incorporate feminist ideologies in their daily lives, and support them (see also Edin and Kefalas 2005).

8. I explore the concept of *identity of distance* in further detail in another publication (Ray forthcoming), and part of this chapter and arguments appear in the same article.

9. See Centers for Disease Control and Prevention (n.d.).

10. See Mann 2013.

11. See for example Barcelos and Gubrium 2014.

12. See also Barcelos and Gubrium 2014.

13. Geronimus 2003.

14. See Mann 2013.

15. "The rod" is a form of birth control. It is a thin, flexible plastic implant, which is inserted directly under the skin of the upper arm. It prevents pregnancy for approximately three years.

16. The privileged also attempt to hold on to, or improve, their class position through partnership; see Hamilton and Armstrong 2009.

17. See for example several works on the state of the gender revolution, including Hamilton and Armstrong 2009; Gerson 2009; Lamont 2013.

18. See Lamont 2013; Gerson 2009. Researchers have recently begun to focus on the ways in which women attempt to reconcile these contradictory cultural messages. Hamilton and Armstrong (2009: 593) demonstrate how an emerging "hookup" culture on college campuses provides opportunities for middle-class women to engage in sexual and romantic relations without long-term commitment (albeit not without stigmatization), thus enabling them to focus on their careers. They also found that marginalized women attending college refrain from participating in the "hookup" culture because they find it alien to their relationship orientation, which is characterized by a relatively rapid transition to marriage and adulthood. Thus, marginalized women attempt to pursue relationships and careers simultaneously rather than successively.

19. Lindholm 1998: 247.

20. Erdmans and Black (2015) show how unsafe neighborhoods, systemic gender inequality, and economic marginalization shape routes to early parenthood. More importantly, in documenting stories about school dropouts or sexual abuse, Erdmans and Black highlight that there are no typical routes that link these life experiences. For example, many young mothers go on to perform well academically.

CHAPTER 5. SAVED BY COLLEGE

1. See Goyette 2008; Reynolds et al. 2006.

2. See Rosenbaum 2001.

3. See Cottom 2017; Levine 2001.

4. Melanie Jones Gast (2016: 13) shows how school personnel attempted to foster a "college-going culture," providing material support through career center, workshops, and presentations to support college preparation, as well as symbols like college posters. Yet, the mass production of "college for all" norm without sustained support did not meet the manifold and unique needs of more marginalized students.

5. A process that Pierre Bourdieu theorized by abandoning the dialectics of coercion and consent.

6. In the meantime, various mechanisms gradually lower students' educational expectations—a process some scholars call "cooling out." For example see Clark 1960; see also Rosenbaum 2001.

7. See for example Sharot 2011.

8. For more on the relationship between educational (and occupational) aspirations and expectations, see Cheng and Starks 2002; Downey, Ainsworth, and Qian 2009; Hanson 1994; see also Domina, Conley, and Farkas 2011.

9. Other scholars show how young women hold on to their aspirations for higher education by constructing them as part of the moral self as well as a practical necessity for better jobs. Given that aspirations then become a moral imperative, young people find it hard to give them up even in the face of the reality that a higher educational degree is unachievable, and participation in community college allows for the persistence of aspirations (Nielsen 2015). See also Deterding 2015.

10. See Kupchik and Monahan 2006.

11. For example see Goffman 2014. See also Western 2006; Black 2009.

12. See Rios 2011 and Ferguson 2000.

13. See Perry and Morris 2014.

14. I inquired about Evelyn's performance and reputation from other students and a few teachers. They all verified that she had improved her academic performance drastically. I do not know whether exactly nine teachers wrote her letters of recommendation, but I saw her communications with five teachers who agreed to write letters for her.

15. See Western 2006; Kupchik and Monahan 2006.

16. See also Goffman 2014.

17. See Baird, Burge, and Reynolds 2008; Rosenbaum 2001; Schneider and Stevenson 2000.

18. See Stevens 2009 on the complex admission processes that colleges employ.

19. I originally thought this was a major accomplishment and a step toward admission to Harvard. Later, personal communication with a Harvard alumnus (who conducts admissions interviews) revealed that the process is less clear. He informed me that the significance of the interview depends on the number of alumni available to conduct interviews in a particular area.

20. Enrolling primarily in two-year colleges is known to lower a student's chances of graduating with a bachelor's degree (see for example Kalogrides and Grodsky 2011). See also Bozick 2007.

21. See Alexander, Bozick, and Entwisle 2008.

CHAPTER 6. THE MAKING OF A TEENAGE SERVICE CLASS

1. Slightly modified to protect anonymity. Also, descriptions of jobs I directly quote in the book come from actual listings of available jobs on various websites. I do not identify the exact websites or companies to protect confidentiality.

2. See also Silva 2013 on the transition to adulthood in the contemporary United States.

3. See for example Newman 1999.

4. The types of low-wage jobs the youth held involved the deployment of what Arlie Hochschild (1983) calls "emotional labor." Emotional labor requires workers to engage in face-to-face interaction, through emotion management, with customers. Beyond the idea of inevitable and complete alienation of (low-wage) service workers from their emotions, several influential studies have effectively demonstrated how frontline workers such as servers in restaurants and fast-food chains autonomously customize their interactions and work environment, assign meanings to their jobs—often outside the control of management—and navigate routinization as a way to manage unpleasant work interactions (Paules 1991; Liedner 1993; Sherman 2007; Bolton and Boyd 2003). The service industry also involves more nuanced understandings of expertise and skills (George 2008). Emotional labor is also deeply racialized and gendered (Harvey Wingfield 2009).

5. Chen 2015.

6. Jayaraman 2013.

7. Even though women make up less than half of the total U. S. workforce, two-thirds of almost 20 million low-wage workers (defined by hourly wage of $10.10 or less) are women (see National Women's Law Center 2014). Women of color with low levels of education have been concentrated in low-wage service jobs at higher rates than men and more privileged women for decades. However, overall organization of low-wage work has transformed drastically as 80 percent of all workers in the United States are now part of the service industry; additionally, the precariousness of the service industry has further affected marginalized women (Smith 2001). Further, understanding the school-to-work transition of economically marginalized women of color is especially crucial now because recent studies report that among women without a college education, women of color find it harder to accrue labor force attachment in the early years of transitioning from school to work. These early years in the labor market have crucial implications for wage growth over lifetime, and women of color fail to catch up with their white counterparts (Alon and Haberfeld 2007).

8. In Port City, the two casinos were the largest employers, followed by a drug manufacturer, hospitals, military base, and power plants (in that order).

9. See Appelbaum et al. 2003 for how employer cost-cutting strategies foster stiffer competitions for low-wage jobs.

10. See Kasinitz and Rosenberg (1996) for the importance of networks in getting access to or being excluded from low-wage jobs. The authors also highlight the role of place and race discrimination in shaping access to low-wage work.

11. See for example Lamont 2002.

12. See Wherry 2008. Purchases or expenditures of the economically marginalized are perceived as reckless, foolish, and impulsive acts. Politicians, the media, and many American citizens regularly question the consumption habits

of the marginalized, criticizing their irresponsible budgeting in the face of dire poverty.

13. Others have also conceptualized money spending as a mode of status attainment. Writing about youth from a Chicago neighborhood, Pattillo (1999) stated how young men and women were targets of mass marketing efforts, using their bodies and accessories as ways of marking status. Women painted their fingernails and men bought expensive Nike shoes.

14. Scholars have recently begun to make influential contributions in theorizing the social meanings of everyday and ordinary economic behaviors; see Zelizer 2011. See also Wherry 2008.

15. Bolton and Boyd 2003.

16. It could certainly be that Cassy did not need to enroll in college in order to connect her interest in psychology with her work and find meaning and passion in her work. Yet, her enrollment in college definitely shaped how she imagined her work and her future as a psychologist. If she had not enrolled in college classes, Cassy may have found it harder to convince herself, and others, that her job was directly aligned with her interest in psychology, and that she was on a path to one day having a white-collar career as a psychologist.

17. See for example George 2008.

CHAPTER 7. INTERNALIZING UNCERTAINTY

1. See Desmond 2016 for a detailed treatment of eviction.

2. Journalists have recently started writing about hunger among college students. Social scientist Sara Goldrick-Rab has conducted some preliminary research on the topic; see for example Goldrick-Rab and Broton 2015. However, ethnographers of urban poverty in the United States have not documented and analyzed the centrality of hunger as an everyday experience of poverty. Most U.S. Americans imagine hunger as a distant reality that only occurs in the "developing" world under the conditions of absolute poverty. Yet, hunger and food insecurity is present in the United States; see McMillan 2012. See also "The New Face of Hunger," a story by McMillan in *National Geographic Magazine*. Over the past two decades, many urban neighborhoods have become "food deserts" as middle-class families moved to the suburbs and supermarket chains abandoned marginalized neighborhoods; see for example Short, Guthman, and Raskin 2007. Researchers have found that not only are supermarkets scant in marginalized neighborhoods, but the price of food is also higher than in wealthier neighborhoods; see for example Hendrickson, Smith, and Eikenberry 2006; Curtis 1997. In the conclusion, I will discuss the importance of tackling food insecurity and hunger when talking about access to higher education.

3. Desmond 2015.

4. DiBlasio 2014.

5. Tavernise 2014.

6. See Herzfeld 1992.

7. What makes for a fulfilling life? Predictability or unpredictability? It seems there are several articles on the subject featured in popular media every week, some asking us to manage time well for a fulfilling life and others urging us to go with the flow and avoid routine. Here, I don't want to engage with questions around what makes for a fulfilling life—what I intend to convey is that those living in poverty have to learn that their life may drastically change at any given moment, unlike the middle class whose days, months, and sometimes years tend to be heavily organized; see for example Lareau 2003.

8. Ethnographies can benefit by not centering the life and feelings of the fieldworker when presenting the experiences and realities of a given community. Yet, many realities become perceptible when an ethnographer can empathize with the community. Throughout the book, I attempt to keep from centering myself, and my own "feelings," as I became part of the lives of sixteen youth. However, it is worthwhile to mention that certain experiences only became perceptible to me because I could imagine and had experienced the embodied feelings—such as symbolic homes, uncontrollable circumstances, etc. At other times, I had to reimagine to empathize. Here, and in a few other places, I describe my own feelings as a way to allude to how and why I started thinking about a particular theme (in this case, how youth manage reminders of death). On a different yet related note, I debated between revealing my presence as the center of a story and making myself an invisible part of it by disguising my presence (by replacing myself with a "friend"). I decided not to do that in order to indicate to the reader that I was present during a particular event in an attempt to not confuse the reader about how I gathered the data. For example, when I gave Angie a ride to the airport one early morning, if I related the story as a friend offering her the ride, readers may have wondered how I gained access to the details of the night. I took elaborate notes right after conversations I wanted to record in great detail and transcribed them the same night. The majority, if not all, conversations where long quotes are presented were recorded.

9. Ethnographers cannot know why people do things. We can only describe what people do, and how they go about doing it. Here, for example, Evelyn may not have applied to colleges and universities for a variety of other reasons, which my observations do not allow me to explain. I know that she did apply to universities on the East Coast and not to universities on the West Coast. Evelyn told me that the fear of sudden death is one of the main reasons she does not apply to universities far away. Through other observations, I note how death is prominent in the lives of the youth, and thus, Evelyn's story, with the caveats of not knowing what the truth is (if there is at all a single and ultimate truth), fits into the larger theme.

10. See for example Fábrega, Jr. 1997.

11. While this may seem like a futile way to navigate illness and uncertainty and make decisions, our conception of logic and rationality is nothing but socially constructed reality. For example, while we now think that certain traditional ways of curing illness were illogical, there are modern cures that do not work as well. This is not to say that tarot cards cure illness or are "logical" ways to make decisions, but rather, I want to stress that we must always question the nature and construction of social reality. In the absence of other ways to deal with uncertainty, Ashley and her family found solace in tarot cards. See also Conrad and Barker 2010.

12. See Yoshikawa, Aber, and Beardslee 2012; Kataoka, Zhang, and Wells 2002.

13. However, we must note the social construction of mood disorders; see for example Horwitz 2011.

14. See Gary 2005 for a discussion of the stigma surrounding mental health-care among marginalized people.

15. See Saguy 2013 for a discussion of how and why weight is linked with health.

16. See Brand 2012.

17. Sen 1981.

18. Journalists have been writing about hunger as a pervasive issue among college students in the United States. For example, see Bahrampour 2014; Mckenna 2015.

19. In her 2015 book *The Power of the Past: Understanding Cross-Class Marriages*, Jessi Streib finds that while the ability to manage uncertainty and be spontaneous is a valuable skill, it does not pay off in middle-class institutions such as school and professional careers.

CHAPTER 8. UNCERTAIN SUCCESS

1. Merton 1957.

2. See also Gouldner 1957; Hannerz 1990. Recent scholars demonstrate how marginalized young adults use enrollment, or plans to enroll, in higher educational institutions to indicate their moral worth; for example, see Nielsen 2015.

3. See Bettie 2003 for a related discussion on the subject.

4. Bourdieu 1977, 1979, 1986. See also Bourdieu and Passeron 1977.

5. See also Frye 2012 on the construction of socially mobile identity among girls. See chapters 1 and 9 herein for more on cultural production theory directly.

6. Bettie 2003.

7. Many ethnographers and scholars of poverty often construct the economically marginalized as residing on an island. While some scholars argue that

"values" and "ideals" found in marginalized communities are nothing but extensions of middle-class orientations (see for example Contreras 2012 for a recent ethnography that draws on this idea; further discussion can be found in chapters 1 and 9 herein), the relationship between the privileged and the economically marginalized is often undertheorized. Desmond (2016) discusses eviction as a context where poverty can be understood in relationship to wealth. However, I discuss what everyday cross-class interactions, common among the youth, look like, and how they shape aspirations, opportunities, and performance of class.

8. See Sennett and Cobb [1972] 1993.

9. See Armstrong and Hamilton 2013 for an interesting discussion on the attractions of the "party pathway" among college students. The community college kids I spent time with also somewhat bought into the "college life," which partially included fun parties.

10. Hotel parties were a common weekend activity among the Port City youth. The young people acquired alcohol, usually from older siblings, and brought drinks and marijuana to a rented hotel room at a local casino (they each contributed money to pay for the room). These parties usually included about ten to fifteen youth in a room, drinking, spending time, and engaging in sexual activity, including intercourse. I was only invited to a hotel party once, when Curtis mentioned I could come, but Lexus quickly warned me against going. She exclaimed: "I don't know [if] you wanna go! It's like nigga be making out and having sex at every corner of the room! If you got no boo and you not into putting your tongue into someone's throat, you better stay out of it."

11. See Khan 2012 for a discussion on multiculturalism and class in contemporary U.S. society.

12. For discussions on the relationship between food choices and socioeconomic status and the social construction of food as a class indicator, see Bourdieu 1979.

13. See Hill 1998 on marginalizing linguistics to preserve white supremacy. See also hooks 1992.

14. See Gilliom 2001.

CHAPTER 9. DISMANTLING THE "AT RISK" DISCOURSE

1. See Pell Institute for the Study of Opportunity in Higher Education and University of Pennsylvania Alliance for Higher Education and Democracy 2015 for information on income and college enrollment.

2. See Newman 1999. See also Elliott et al. 2006.

3. Harding (2007) attempts to explain variable outcomes among marginalized youth. Bettie (2003) also discusses working-class girls who perform well in high school.

4. See Lareau 2003, where everyday practices inside the family cohere in a pattern to warrant investigation of class differences in childrearing practices.

5. Other recent scholars have come to similar conclusions. For example, in *Lives in Limbo: Undocumented and Coming of Age in America* (2015), Roberto G. Gonzales also finds that structural limits (that is, the denial of access to legal citizenship in the United States) locks youth—whom he followed for more than a decade—into the bottom of the economy irrespective of their educational pathways.

6. Murnane 2013. See also Lopez 2003.

7. See for example Jones 2009; Chesney-Lind and Hagedorn 1999 (an entire collection of works and theoretical underpinnings for understanding female gangs); Kaplan 1997.

8. Lareau 2003: 236.

9. See Bourdieu 1979, 1990.

10. For a comprehensive review of the topic, see Small and Newman 2001.

11. See Bettie 2003.

12. Bourgios 1995: 8.

13. I discussed these issues in previous chapters.

14. See Hoxby and Avery 2013.

15. Alon 2009; Lucas 2001.

16. See chapter 5.

17. Perna 2010.

18. Silva (2013) found that poor and working-class men and women continue to drift between higher education and work well into their thirties. See also Alexander, Bozick, and Entwisle 2008.

19. See Barcelos and Gubrium 2014.

20. See Swadener and Lubeck 1995; Swadener 1995; Fine 1995.

21. Moore and Elkavich 2008.

22. See Alexander 2010.

23. Swaine and Laughland 2015.

24. Liptak 2008.

25. See for example Geronimus 1997.

26. See Bronson 2014.

27. Jayaraman 2013.

28. See policy recommendations in Lareau 2003.

29. See Anderson 2015.

30. See Deboer 2017.

31. Bailey and Dynarski 2011.

32. Goldrick-Rab, Broton, and Eisenberg 2015.

33. Goldrick-Rab and Kendall 2014.

34. Lower-Basch and Lee 2014.

35. U.S. Department of Housing and Urban Development, Office of Policy Development and Research 2015.

36. Goldrick-Rab, Broton, and Eisenberg 2015.

37. See Cottom 2017.

38. See Domina, Conley, and Farkas 2011; Rosenbaum 2011; Cottom 2017.

39. Lucas 2001.

Bibliography

Alexander, Karl, Robert Bozick, and Doris Entwisle. "Warming Up, Cooling Out, or Holding Steady? Persistence and Change in Educational Expectations after High School." *Sociology of Education* 81, no. 4 (2008): 371–96.

Alexander, Michelle. *The New Jim Crow: Mass Incarceration in the Age of Colorblindness.* New York: New Press, 2010.

Alon, Sigal. "The Evolution of Class Inequality in Higher Education: Competition, Exclusion, and Adaptation." *American Sociological Review* 74, no. 5 (2009): 731–55.

——— and Yitchak Haberfield. "Labor Force Attachment and the Evolving Wage Gap between White, Black, and Hispanic Young Women." *Work and Occupations* 34, no. 4 (2007): 369–98.

Anderson, Elijah. *Code of the Street: Decency, Violence, and the Moral Life of the Inner City.* New York: W.W. Norton, 1999.

Anderson, Kristin L. "Theorizing Gender in Intimate Partner Violence Research." *Sex Roles* 52, no. 11 (2005): 853–65.

Anderson, Nick. "The New College Admissions Coalition: Is It Really about Access?" *Washington Post*, October 5, 2015. www.washingtonpost.com /news/grade-point/wp/2015/10/05/the-new-college-admissions-coalition-is-it-really-about-access/?utm_term=.c75760ee5627

Appelbaum, Eileen, Annette Bernhardt, and Richard J. Murnane. "Low-Wage America: An Overview." In *Low-Wage America: How Employers Are Reshaping Opportunity in the Workplace*, edited by Eileen Appelbaum,

Annette Bernhardt, and Richard J. Murnane, 1–29. New York: Russell Sage Foundation, 2003.

Armstrong, Elizabeth A., and Laura T. Hamilton. *Paying for the Party: How College Maintains Inequality.* Cambridge, MA: Harvard University Press, 2013.

Aronson, Pamela. "The Markers and Meanings of Growing Up: Contemporary Young Women's Transition from Adolescence to Adulthood." *Gender and Society* 22, no. 1 (2008): 56–82.

Auyero, Javier, and Débora Alejandra Swistun. *Flammable: Environmental Suffering in an Argentine Shantytown.* New York: Oxford University Press, 2009.

Bahrampour, Tara. "More College Students Battle Hunger as Education and Living Costs Rise." *Washington Post,* April 9, 2014. www.washingtonpost .com/local/more-college-students-battle-hunger-as-education-and-living-costs-rise/2014/04/09/60208db6-bb63-11e3-9a05-c739f29ccb08_story. html?utm_term=.bc747647c919

Bailey, Martha J., and Susan M. Dynarski. "Gains and Gaps: Changing Inequality in U. S. College Entry and Completion." National Bureau of Economic Research Working Paper no. 17633, 2011. Accessed December 20, 2015. www.nber.org/papers/w17633

Baird, Chardie L., Stephanie W. Burge, and John R. Reynolds. "Absurdly Ambitious? Teenagers' Expectations for the Future and the Realities of Social Structure." *Sociology Compass* 2, no. 3 (2008): 944–62.

Barcelos, Christie A., and Aline C. Gubrium. "Reproducing Stories: Strategic Narratives of Teen Pregnancy and Motherhood." *Social Problems* 61, no. 3 (2014): 466–81.

Bettie, Julie. *Women without Class: Girls, Race, and Identity.* Berkeley: University of California Press, 2003.

Black, Timothy. *When a Heart Turns Rock Solid: The Lives of Three Puerto Rican Brothers On and Off the Streets.* New York: Pantheon Books, 2009.

Blau, Peter M., and Otis D. Duncan. *The American Occupational Structure.* New York: John Wiley, 1978.

Bolton, Sharon, and Carol Boyd. "Trolley Dolly or Skilled Emotion Manager? Moving On from Hochschild's Managed Heart." *Work, Employment and Society* 17, no. 2 (2003): 289–308.

Bourdieu, Pierre. "Cultural Reproduction and Social Reproduction." In *Power and Ideology in Education,* edited by Jerome D. Karabel and Albert H. Halsey, 487–511. New York: Oxford University Press, 1977.

———. *Distinction: A Social Critique of the Judgment of Taste.* Cambridge, MA: Harvard University Press, 1979.

——. "The Forms of Capital." In *Handbook of Theory and Research for the Sociology of Education,* edited by John G. Richardson, 241–58. New York: Greenwood, 1986.

——. *The Logic of Practice.* Stanford, CA: Stanford University Press, 1990.

——. *Masculine Domination.* Translated by Richard Nice. Stanford, CA: Stanford University Press, 2001.

—— and Jean-Claude Passeron. *Reproduction in Education, Society and Culture.* London: Sage, 1977.

Bourgois, Philippe. *In Search of Respect: Selling Crack in El Barrio.* New York: Cambridge University Press, 1995.

Bowles, Samuel, and Herbert Gintis. *Schooling in Capitalist America.* New York: Basic Books, 1976.

Bozick, Robert. "Making It through the First Year of College: The Role of Students' Economic Resources, Employment, and Living Arrangements." *Sociology of Education* 80, no. 3 (2007): 261–85.

Brand, Peggy Zeglin. *Beauty Unlimited.* Bloomington: Indiana University Press, 2012.

Bridges, Khiara. *Reproducing Race: An Ethnography of Pregnancy as a Site of Racialization.* Berkeley: University of California Press, 2011.

Brock, Thomas. "Young Adults and Higher Education: Barriers and Break-throughs to Success." *Future of Children* 20, no. 1 (2010): 109–32.

Bronson, Brittany. "Your Waitress, Your Professor." *New York Times,* December 18, 2014. www.nytimes.com/2014/12/19/opinion/your-waitress-your-professor .html?_r=0

Brown, Anna, and Mark Hugo Lopez. "Mapping the Latino Population, by State, County and City." *Pew Research Center Hispanic Trends,* 2010. Accessed December 25, 2015. www.pewhispanic.org/2013/08/29/mapping-the-latino-population-by-state-county-and-city/

Brown-Saracino, Japonica. *A Neighborhood That Never Changes: Gentrification, Social Preservation, and the Search for Authenticity.* Chicago: University of Chicago Press, 2010.

——. "Overview: The Gentrification Debates." In *The Gentrification Debates: A Reader,* edited by Japonica Brown-Saracino, 1–18. Metropolis and Modern Life series. New York: Routledge, 2010.

Calderón, José. "'Hispanic' and 'Latino': The Viability of Categories for Panethnic Unity." *Latin American Perspectives* 19, no. 4 (1992): 37–44.

Carter, Prudence L. "'Black' Cultural Capital, Status Positioning, and School Conflicts for Low-Income African American Youth." *Social Problems* 50, no. 1 (2003): 136–55.

——. *Keepin' It Real: School Success beyond Black and White.* Oxford: Oxford University Press, 2005.

Centers for Disease Control and Prevention. "About Teen Pregnancy." N.d. www.cdc.gov/teenpregnancy/about/reduced-disparities-birth-rates.htm

Chen, Michelle. "Five Myths about Fast-Food Work." *Washington Post*, April 10, 2015. www.washingtonpost.com/opinions/five-myths-about-fast-food-work /2015/04/10/a62e9ab8-dee0-11e4-a500-1c5bb1d8ff6a_story.html?utm_term= .c2b265045fd9

Cheng, Simon, and Brian Starks. "Racial Differences in the Effects of Significant Others on Students Educational Expectations." *Sociology of Education* 75, no. 4 (2002): 306–27.

Chesney-Lind, Meda, and John M. Hagedorn, eds. *Female Gangs in America: Essays on Girls, Gangs, and Gender.* Chicago: Lake View Press, 1999.

Child Trends. *Charting Parenthood: A Statistical Portrait of Fathers and Mothers in America.* Washington, DC: Child Trends, 2009. https:// childtrends-ciw49tixgw5lbab.stackpathdns.com/wp-content/ uploads/2013/03/ParenthoodRpt2002.pdf

Clark, Burton R. "The 'Cooling Out' Function in Higher Education." *American Journal of Sociology* 65, no. 6 (1960): 569–76.

Clifford, James. "Introduction: Partial Truths." In *Writing Culture: The Poetics and Politics of Ethnography*, edited by James Clifford and George E. Marcus, 1–27. Berkeley: University of California Press, 1986.

Cohen, Cathy J. *Democracy Remixed: Black Youth and the Future of American Politics.* New York: Oxford University Press, 2010.

Cohen, Stanley. *Folk Devils and Moral Panics: The Creation of the Mods and Rockers.* New York: Routledge, [1972] 2011.

Coleman, James S. "Social Capital in the Creation of Human-Capital." *American Journal of Sociology* 94, Suppl. (1988): S95–120.

Collins, Patricia Hill. *Black Feminist Thought: Knowledge, Consciousness, and the Politics of Empowerment.* Boston: Unwin Hyman, 1990.

Conger, Katherine J., and Wendy M. Little. "Sibling Relationships during the Transition to Adulthood." *Child Development Perspectives* 4, no. 2 (2010): 87–94.

Conrad, Peter, and Kristin K. Barker. "The Social Construction of Illness Key Insights and Policy Implications." *Journal of Health and Social Behavior* 51, no. 1 (2010): 67–79.

Contreras, Randol. *The Stickup Kids: Race, Drugs, Violence, and the American Dream.* Berkeley: University of California Press, 2012.

Cottom, Tressie McMillan. *Lower Ed: The Troubling Rise of For-Profit Colleges in the New Economy.* New York: New Press, 2017.

Crandall, Robert W. *Manufacturing on the Move.* Washington, DC: Brookings Institution Press, 1993.

Curtis, Karen A. "Urban Poverty and the Social Consequences of Privatized Food Assistance." *Journal of Urban Affairs* 19, no. 2 (1997): 207–26.

De Haymes, Maria Vidal, Keith M. Kilty, and Elizabeth A. Segal. *Latino Poverty in the New Century: Inequalities, Challenges, and Barriers*. New York: The Haworth Press, 2000.

Deboer, Freddie. "Inequality University." *Jacobin*, May 22, 2017. www .jacobinmag.com/2017/05/yale-university-connecticut-state-budget-cuts

Desmond, Matthew. "Disposable Ties and the Urban Poor." *American Journal of Sociology* 117, no. 5 (2012): 1295–335.

———. "Unaffordable America: Poverty, Housing, and Eviction." *Fast Focus* 22 (2015): 1–6.

———. *Evicted: Poverty and Profit in the American City*. New York: Crown, 2016.

Deterding, Nicole M. "Instrumental and Expressive Education College Planning in the Face of Poverty." *Sociology of Education* 88, no. 4 (2015): 284–301.

DiBlasio, Natalie. "Hunger in America: 1 in 7 Rely on Food Banks." *USA Today*, August 17, 2014. www.usatoday.com/story/news/nation/2014/08/17/hunger-study-food/14195585/

Dohan, Dan. *The Price of Poverty: Money, Work, and Culture in the Mexican American Barrio*. Berkeley: University of California Press, 2003.

Domina, Thurston, AnneMarie Conley, and George Farkas. "The Link between Educational Expectations and Effort in the College-for-All Era." *Sociology of Education* 84, no. 2 (2011): 93–112.

Downey, Douglas B., James W. Ainsworth, and Zhenchao Qian. "Rethinking the Attitude-Achievement Paradox among Blacks." *Sociology of Education* 82, no. 1 (2009): 1–19.

Duneier, Mitchell, Hakim Hasan, and Ovie Carter. *Sidewalk*. New York: Farrar, Straus, and Giroux, 1999.

Edin, Kathryn, and Maria Kefalas. *Promises I Can Keep: Why Poor Women Put Motherhood before Marriage*. Berkeley: University of California Press, 2005.

——— and Laura Lein. *Making Ends Meet: How Single Mothers Survive Welfare and Low-Wage Work*. New York: Russell Sage Foundation, 1997.

Elliott, Delbert S., Scott Menard, Bruce Rankin, Amanda Elliott, William Julius Wilson, and David Huizinga. *Good Kids from Bad Neighborhoods: Successful Development in Social Context*. New York: Cambridge University Press, 2006.

Emerson, Robert. *Contemporary Field Research: Perspectives and Formulations*. Long Grove, IL: Waveland Press, 2001.

Erdmans, Mary Patrice, and Timothy Black. *On Becoming a Teen Mom: Life before Pregnancy*. Berkeley: University of California Press, 2015.

Esping-Andersen, Gøsta. *Social Foundations of Postindustrial Economies*. Oxford: Oxford University Press, 1999.

Fábrega, Horacio, Jr. *Evolution of Sickness and Healing.* Berkeley: University of California Press, 1997.

Fader, Jamie J. *Falling Back: Incarceration and Transitions to Adulthood among Urban Youth.* New Brunswick, NJ: Rutgers University Press, 2013.

Ferber, Abby L. "The Construction of Black Masculinity: White Supremacy Now and Then." *Journal of Sport and Social Issues* 31, no. 1 (2007): 11–24.

Ferguson, Ann Arnett. *Bad Boys: Public Schools in the Making of Black Masculinity.* Ann Arbor: University of Michigan Press, 2000.

Fields, Jessica. *Risky Lessons: Sex Education and Social Inequality.* New Brunswick, NJ: Rutgers University Press, 2008.

Fine, Michelle. "The Politics of Who's "at Risk." In *Children and Families "at Promise": Deconstructing the Discourse of Risk,* edited by Beth Blue Swadener and Sally Lubeck, 76–95. New York: State University of New York Press, 1995.

Frye, Margaret. "Bright Futures in Malawi's New Dawn: Educational Aspirations as Assertions of Identity." *American Journal of Sociology* 177, no. 6 (2012): 1565–624.

Fuentes, Liza, Verónica Bayetti Flores, and Jessica Gonzalez-Rojas. *Removing Stigma: Towards a Complete Understanding of Young Latinas' Sexual Health.* New York: National Latina Institute for Reproductive Health, 2010. http://latinainstitute.org/sites/default/files/NLIRH-HPWhite-5310-F2.pdf

Garcia, Lorena. "Now Why Do You Want to Know about That? Heteronormativity, Racism, and Sexism in the Sexual (Mis)education of Latina Youth." *Gender and Society* 23, no. 4 (2009): 520–41.

———. *Respect Yourself, Protect Yourself: Latina Girls and Sexual Identity.* New York: New York University Press, 2012.

Garland, David. *The Culture of Control: Crime and Social Order in Contemporary Society.* Chicago: University of Chicago Press, 2001.

Garot, Robert. *Who You Claim: Performing Gang Identity in School and on the Streets.* New York: New York University Press, 2010.

Gary, Faye A. "Stigma: Barrier to Mental Health Care among Ethnic Minorities." *Issues in Mental Health Nursing* 26, no. 10 (2005): 979–99.

Gast, Melanie Jones. "'You're Supposed to Help Me': The Perils of Mass Counseling Norms for Working-Class Black Students." *Urban Education* (2016): 1–27. http://journals.sagepub.com/doi/pdf/10.1177/0042085916652178

George, Molly. "Interactions in Expert Service Work: Demonstrating Professionalism in Personal Training." *Journal of Contemporary Ethnography* 37, no. 1 (2008): 108–31.

Geronimus, Arline T. "Teenage Childbearing and Personal Responsibility: An Alternative View." *Political Science Quarterly* 112, no. 3 (1997): 405–30.

————. "Damned if You Do: Culture, Identity, Privilege, and Teenage Childbearing in the United States." *Social Science and Medicine* 57, no. 5 (2003): 881–93.

Gerson, Kathleen. *The Unfinished Revolution: How a New Generation Is Reshaping Family, Work, and Gender in America.* New York: Oxford University Press, 2009.

Gilliom, John. *Overseers of the Poor: Surveillance, Resistance, and the Limits of Privacy.* Chicago: University Of Chicago Press, 2001.

Giordano, Peggy. "Relationships in Adolescence." *American Sociological Review* 29, no. 1 (2003): 257–81.

Glasser, Ruth. *Aqui Me Quedo: Puerto Ricans in Connecticut: Los Puertorriquenos en Connecticut.* Middletown: Connecticut Humanities Council, 1997.

————. "From "Rich Port" to Bridgeport: Puerto Ricans in Connecticut." In *The Puerto Rican Diaspora: Historical Perspectives,* edited by Carmen Whale and Víctor Vázquez-Hernández, 174–99. Philadelphia: Temple University Press, 2005.

Goffman, Alice. *On the Run: Fugitive Life in an American City.* Chicago: University of Chicago Press, 2014.

Goldrick-Rab, Sara. "Following Their Every Move: An Investigation of Social-Class Differences in College Pathways." *Sociology of Education* 97, no. 1 (2006): 67–79.

———— and Nancy Kendall. "Redefining College Affordability: Securing America's Future with a Free Two Year College Option." *F2CO.* Madison: Wisconsin HOPE Lab, 2014. www.luminafoundation.org/files/resources/redefining-college-affordability.pdf

———— and Katharine Broton. "Hungry, Homeless and in College." *New York Times,* December 4, 2015. www.nytimes.com/2015/12/04/opinion/hungry-homeless-and-in-college.html?_r=0

————, Katharine Broton, and Daniel Eisenberg. "Hungry to Learn: Addressing Food and Housing Insecurity among Undergraduates." Madison: Wisconsin HOPE Lab, 2015. www.wihopelab.com/publications/Wisconsin_HOPE_Lab_Hungry_To_Learn.pdf

Gonzales, Roberto G. *Lives in Limbo: Undocumented and Coming of Age in America.* Berkeley: University of California Press, 2015.

Gouldner, Alvin W. "Cosmopolitans and Locals: Toward an Analysis of Latent Social Roles." *Administrative Science Quarterly* 2, no. 3 (1957): 281–306.

Goyette, Kimberly A. "College for Some to College for All: Social Background, Occupational Expectations, and Educational Expectations over Time." *Social Science Research* 37, no. 2 (2008): 461–84.

Greene, Lorenzo Johnston. *The Negro in Colonial New England, 1620–1776.* New York: Atheneum, [1942] 1968.

270   BIBLIOGRAPHY

Guinier, Lani. *The Tyranny of the Meritocracy: Democratizing Higher Education in America.* Boston: Beacon Press, 2015.

Halle, David. *America's Working Man: Work, Home, and Politics among Blue-collar Property Owners.* Chicago: University of Chicago Press, 1984.

Hamilton, Laura, and Elizabeth Armstrong. "Gendered Sexuality in Young Adulthood: Double Binds and Flawed Options." *Gender and Society* 23, no. 5 (2009): 589–616.

Hannerz, Ulf. *Soulside: Inquiries into Ghetto Culture and Community.* New York: Columbia University Press, 1969.

———. "Cosmopolitans and Locals in World Culture." *Theory Culture Society* 7, no. 2 (1990): 237–51.

Hanson, Sandra. "Lost Talent: Unrealized Educational Aspirations and Expectations among U. S. Youths." *Sociology of Education* 67, no. 3 (1994): 159–83.

Haraway, Donna. "Situated Knowledges: The Science Question in Feminism and the Privilege of Partial Perspective." *Feminist Studies* 14, no. 3 (1988): 575–99.

Harding, David J. "Cultural Context, Sexual Behavior, and Romantic Relationships in Disadvantaged Neighborhoods." *American Sociological Review* 72, no. 3 (2007): 341–64.

———. *Living the Drama: Community, Conflict, and Culture among Inner-City Boys.* Chicago: University of Chicago Press, 2010.

Harding, Sandra. *Objectivity and Diversity: Another Logic of Scientific Research.* Chicago: University of Chicago Press, 2015.

Harvey Wingfield, Adia. "Racializing the Glass Escalator: Reconsidering Men's Experiences with Women's Work." *Gender and Society* 23, no. 1 (2009): 5–26.

Hays, Sharon. "Structure and Agency and the Sticky Problem of Culture." *Sociological Theory* 12, no. 1 (1994): 57–72.

Healey, Richard G. "Railroads and Immigration in the Northeast United States 1850–1900." *Geography Compass* 6, no. 8 (2012): 455–76.

Hendrickson, Deja, Chery Smith, and Nicole Eikenberry. "Fruit and Vegetable Access in Four Low-Income Food Deserts Communities in Minnesota." *Agriculture and Human Values* 23, no. 3 (2006): 371–83.

Herzfeld, Michael. *The Social Production of Indifference: Exploring the Symbolic Roots of Western Bureaucracy.* Chicago: University of Chicago Press, 1992.

Hill, Jane H. "Language, Race, and White Public Space." *American Anthropologist* 100, no. 3 (1998): 680–89.

Hochschild, Arlie Russell. *The Managed Heart: Commercialization of Human Feeling.* Berkeley: University of California Press, 1983.

Hochschild, Jennifer L. *Facing Up to the American Dream: Race, Class, and the Soul of the Nation*. Princeton, NJ: Princeton University Press, 1995.

hooks, bell. *Black Looks: Race and Representation*. Boston: South End Press, 1992.

Horwitz, Allan V. "Creating an Age of Depression: The Social Construction and Consequences of the Major Depression Diagnosis." *Society and Mental Health* 1, no. 1 (2011): 41–54.

Hoxby, Caroline, and Christopher Avery. "The Missing 'One-Offs': The Hidden Supply of High-Achieving, Low-Income Students." Brookings Papers on Economic Activity, 2013. Accessed October 30, 2014. www.brookings.edu /~/media/projects/bpea/spring-2013/2013a_hoxby.pdf

Ingraham, Christopher. "If You Thought Income Inequality Was Bad, Get a Load of Wealth Inequality." *Washington Post*, May 21, 2015. www .washingtonpost.com/news/wonk/wp/2015/05/21/the-top-10-of-americans-own-76-of-the-stuff-and-its-dragging-our-economy-down/?utm_term= .26e379dc3876

Jacobs, Jane. *The Death and Life of Great American Cities*. New York: Vintage, [1961] 1992.

Jayaraman, Saru. *Behind the Kitchen Door: The People Who Make and Serve Your Food*. Ithaca, NY: ILR Press, 2013.

Jencks, Christopher, and Susan E. Mayer. "The Social Consequences of Growing Up In a Poor Neighborhood." In *Inner-City Poverty in the United States*, edited by Laurence Lynn Jr. and Michael McGeary, 111–86. Washington, DC: National Academy Press, 1990.

Jiang, Yang, Maribel R. Granja, and Heather Koball. "Basic Facts about Low-Income Children: Children under 18 Years, 2015." National Center for Children in Poverty, 2017. www.nccp.org/publications/pdf/text_1170.pdf

Jones, Nikki. *Between Good and Ghetto: African American Girls and Inner City Violence*. New Brunswick, NJ: Rutgers University Press, 2009.

Kalogrides, Demetra, and Eric Grodsky. "Something to Fall Back On: Community Colleges as a Safety Net." *Social Forces* 89, no. 3 (2011): 853–77.

Kaplan, Elaine Bell. Not *Our Kind of Girl: Unraveling the Myths of Black Teenage Motherhood*. Berkeley: University of California Press, 1997.

Kasinitz, Philip, and Jan Rosenberg. "Missing the Connection: Social Isolation and Employment on the Brooklyn Waterfront." *Social Problems* 43, no. 2 (1996): 180–96.

Kataoka, Sheryl H., Lily Zhang, and Kenneth B. Wells. "Unmet Need for Mental Health Care among U.S. Children: Variation by Ethnicity and Insurance Status." *American Journal of Psychiatry* 159, no. 9 (2002): 1548–55.

Kelly, Maura. Working paper. "Introduction to Feminist Research in Practice."

Khan, Shamus R. *Privilege: The Making of an Adolescent Elite at St. Paul's School*. Princeton, NJ: Princeton University Press, 2012.

Kneebone, Elizabeth, and Emily Garr. "The Landscape of Recession: Unemployment and Safety Net Services across Urban and Suburban America." *Brookings Institute, Metropolitan Opportunity Series*, 2011. www.brookings.edu/wp-content/uploads/2016/06/0331_recession_garr.pdf

Kupchik, Aaron, and Torin Monahan. "The New American School: Preparation for Post-Industrial Discipline." *British Journal of Sociology of Education* 27, no. 5 (2006): 617–31.

Lamont, Ellen. "Negotiating Courtship: Reconciling Egalitarian Ideals with Traditional Gender Norms." *Gender and Society* 28, no. 2 (2013): 189–211.

Lamont, Michèle. *The Dignity of Working Men: Morality and the Boundaries of Race, Class, and Immigration*. Cambridge, MA: Harvard University Press, 2002.

Lareau, Annette. *Unequal Childhoods: Class, Race, and Family Life*. Berkeley: University of California Press, 2003.

Lawlor, Debbie A., and Mary Shaw. "Too Much Too Young? Teenage Pregnancy Is Not a Public Health Problem." *International Journal of Epidemiology* 31, no. 3 (2002): 552–53.

Levine, Arthur. "Privatization in Higher Education." In *Privatizing Education: Can the Marketplace Deliver Choice, Efficiency, Equity, and Social Cohesion?*, edited by Henry Levin, 133–50. Boulder, CO: Westview Press, 2001.

Lewis, Oscar. *La Vida: A Puerto Rican Family in the Culture of Poverty—San Juan and New York*. New York: Random House, 1966.

Liebow, Elliott. *Tally's Corner: A Study of Negro Street Corner Men*. Boston: Little, Brown, 1967.

Leidner, Robin. *Fast Food, Fast Talk: Service Work and the Routinization of Everyday Life*. Berkeley: University of California Press, 1993.

Lindholm, Charles. "Love and Structure." *Theory, Culture and Society* 15, no. 3 (1998): 243–63.

Liptak, Adam. "U.S. Prison Population Dwarfs That of Other Nations." *New York Times*, April 23, 2008. www.nytimes.com/2008/04/23/world/americas/23iht-23prison.12253738.html

Lomnitz, Larissa Adler. *Networks and Marginality: Life in a Mexican Shantytown*. New York: Academic Press, 1977.

Lopez, Iris. *Matters of Choice: Puerto Rican Women's Struggle for Reproductive Freedom*. New Brunswick, NJ: Rutgers University Press, 2008.

Lopez, Nancy. *Hopeful Girls, Troubled Boys: Race and Gender Disparity in Urban Education*. New York: Routledge, 2003.

Lower-Basch, E., and H. Lee. *SNAP Policy Brief: College Student Eligibility*. Washington, DC: Center for Law and Social Policy, 2014. www.clasp.org/resources-and-publications/publication-1/SNAP_College-Student-Eligibility.pdf

Lucas, Samuel R. "Effectively Maintained Inequality: Education Transitions, Track Mobility, and Social Background Effects." *American Journal of Sociology* 106, no. 6 (2001): 1642–90.

Luker, Kristin. *Dubious Conceptions: The Politics of Teenage Pregnancy.* Cambridge, MA: Harvard University Press, 1997.

Luna, Zakiya, and Kristin Luker. "Reproductive Justice." *Annual Review of Law and Social Science* 9 (2013): 327–52.

MacDonald, Cameron Lynne, and Carmen Sirianni. "The Service Society and the Changing Experience of Work." In *Working in the Service Society,* edited by Cameron Lynne MacDonald and Carmen Sirianni, 1–27. Philadelphia: Temple University Press, 1996.

MacLeod, Jay. *Ain't No Makin' It: Leveled Aspirations in a Low-Income Neighborhood.* Boulder, CO: Westview Press, 1987.

Mann, Emily. "Regulating Latina Youth Sexualities through Community Health Centers: Discourses and Practices of Sexual Citizenship." *Gender and Society* 27, no. 5 (2013): 681–703.

Mckenna, Laura. "The Hidden Hunger on College Campuses." *Atlantic,* January 14, 2015. www.theatlantic.com/education/archive/2016/01/the-hidden-hunger-on-college-campuses/424047/

McMillan, Tracie. *The American Way of Eating: Undercover at Walmart, Applebee's, Farm Fields, and the Dinner Table.* New York: Scribner, 2012.

McRobbie, Angela. "The Culture of Working-Class Girls." In *Feminism and Youth Culture,* 2nd ed., edited by Angela McRobbie, 44–66. New York: Routledge, 2000.

Menchaca, Martha. "Early Racist Discourses: Roots of Deficit Thinking." In *The Evolution of Deficit Thinking: Educational Thought and Practice,* edited by Richard R. Valencia, 13–40. New York: Routledge, 1997.

Merton, Robert K. *Social Theory and Social Structure.* New York: Free Press, 1957.

Moore, Lisa D., and Amy Elkavich. "Who's Using and Who's Doing Time: Incarceration, the War on Drugs, and Public Health." *American Journal of Public Health* 98, no. 5 (2008): 782–86.

Murnane, Richard J. "U.S. High School Graduation Rates: Patterns and Explanations." National Bureau of Economic Research Working Paper no. 18701, 2013. Accessed June 15, 2015. www.nber.org/papers/w18701

Naples, Nancy A. "A Feminist Revisiting of the Insider / Outsider Debate: The 'Outsider Phenomenon' in Rural Iowa." *Qualitative Sociology* 19, no. 1 (1996): 83–106.

National Center for Education Statistics (NCES). *Digest of Education Statistics,* 2013. Accessed February 1, 2016. https://nces.ed.gov/programs/digest/

National Employment Law Project (NELP). *Going Nowhere Fast: Limited Occupational Mobility in the Fast Food Industry.* Data Brief, July. New

York: NELP, 2013. https://nelp.3cdn.net/84a67b124db45841d4_
   00m6bq42h.pdf

National Women's Law Center (NWLC). *Underpaid and Overloaded: Women in
   Low-Wage Jobs.* Washington, DC: NWLC, 2014. www.nwlc.org/sites/default
   /files/pdfs/final_nwlc_lowwagereport2014.pdf

Nelson, Margaret. "Single Mothers and Social Support: The Commitment to,
   and Retreat from, Reciprocity." *Qualitative Sociology* 23, no. 3 (2000):
   291–317.

Newman, Katherine S. *No Shame in My Game: The Working Poor in the Inner
   City.* New York: Knopf and Russell Sage Foundation, 1999.

——— and Rebekah Peeples Massengill. "The Texture of Hardship: Qualitative
   Sociology of Poverty, 1995–2005." *Annual Review of Sociology* 32 (2006):
   423–46.

Nielsen, Kelly. "'Fake It 'til You Make It': Why Community College Students'
   Aspirations 'Hold Steady.'" *Sociology of Education* 88, no. 4 (2015): 265–83.

Pattillo, Mary E. *Black Picket Fences: Privilege and Peril among the Black
   Middle Class.* Chicago: University of Chicago Press, 1999.

Paules, Greta F. *Dishing It Out: Power and Resistance among Waitresses in a
   New Jersey Restaurant.* Philadelphia: Temple University Press, 1991.

Paulle, Bowen. *Toxic Schools: High-Poverty Education in New York and
   Amsterdam.* Chicago: University of Chicago Press, 2013.

Pell Institute for the Study of Opportunity in Higher Education and University
   of Pennsylvania Alliance for Higher Education and Democracy. "Indicators
   of Higher Education Equity in the United States." 2015. Accessed November
   15, 2015. www.pellinstitute.org/downloads/publications-Indicators_of_
   Higher_Education_Equity_in_the_US_45_Year_Trend_Report.pdf

Perna, Laura W. "Understanding the Working College Student." *American
   Association of University Professor Publications,* 2010. Accessed October 25,
   2011. www.aaup.org/article/understanding-working-college-student#.
   VCYd9itdVbx

Perry, Brea L., and Edward W. Morris. "Suspending Progress: Collateral
   Consequences of Exclusionary Punishment in Public Schools." *American
   Sociological Review* 79, no. 6 (2014): 1067–87.

Rainwater, Lee. *Behind Ghetto Walls: Black Families in a Federal Slum.*
   Chicago: Aldine Transaction, 1970.

Ray, Ranita. "Exchange and Intimacy in the Inner City: Rethinking Kinship
   Ties of the Urban Poor." *Journal of Contemporary Ethnography* 45, no. 3
   (2016): 343–64.

———. "Identity of Distance: How Economically Marginalized Black and Latina
   Women Navigate Risk Discourse and Employ Feminist Ideals." *Social
   Problems,* Forthcoming.

Reynolds, John, Michael Steward, Ryan Macdonald, and Lacey Sischo. "Have Adolescents Become Too Ambitious? High School Seniors' Educational and Occupational Plans, 1976–2000." *Social Problems* 53, no. 2 (2006): 186–206.

Rios, Victor. *Punished: Policing the Lives of Black and Latino Boys.* New York: New York University Press, 2011.

———. "Decolonizing the White Space in Urban Ethnography." *City and Community* 14, no. 3 (2015): 258–61.

Roberts, Dorothy. *Killing the Black Body: Race, Reproduction, and the Meaning of Liberty.* New York: Vintage, 1998.

Rodríguez-Muñiz, Michael. "Intellectual Inheritances: Cultural Diagnostics and the State of Poverty Knowledge." *American Journal of Cultural Sociology* 3, no. 1 (2015): 89–122.

Romo, Frank, and Michael Schwartz. "The Coming of Post-Industrial Society Revisited: Manufacturing and the Prospects of a Service-Based Economy." In *Explorations in Economic Sociology,* edited by Richard Swedberg, 335–73. New York: Russell Sage Foundation, 1993.

Roschelle, Anne. *No More Kin: Exploring Race, Class, and Gender in Family Networks.* Thousand Oaks, CA: Sage, 1997.

Rosenbaum, James E. *Beyond College for All: Career Paths for the Forgotten Half.* New York: Russell Sage Foundation, 2001.

———. "The Complexities of College for All: Beyond Fairy-tale Dreams." *Sociology of Education* 84, no. 2 (2011): 113–17.

Saguy, Abigail C. *What's Wrong with Fat?* New York: Oxford University Press, 2013.

Saltman, Kenneth J. *Capitalizing on Disaster: Taking and Breaking Public Schools.* New York: Routledge, 2007.

Sampson, Robert J., Jeffrey D. Morenoff and Felton Earls. "Beyond Social Capital: Spatial Dynamics of Collective Efficacy for Children." *American Sociological Review* 64, no. 5 (1999): 633–60.

Scheper-Hughes, Nancy. *Death without Weeping: The Violence of Everyday Life in Brazil.* Berkeley: University of California Press, 1993.

Schneider, Barbara, and David Stevenson. *The Ambitious Generation: America's Teenagers, Motivated but Directionless.* New Haven, CT: Yale University Press, 2000.

Scotti, Rita A. *Sudden Sea: The Great Hurricane of 1938.* Boston: Back Bay Books, 2004.

Sen, Amartya. *Poverty and Famines: An Essay on Entitlement and Deprivations.* Oxford: Clarendon Press, 1981.

Sennett, Richard and Jonathan Cobb. *The Hidden Injuries of Class.* New York: W. W. Norton [1972] 1993.

Sharot, Tali. "Major Delusions: Why College Graduates Are Irrationally Optimistic." *New York Times*, May 14, 2011. www.nytimes.com/2011/05/15/opinion/15Sharot.html

Shaw, Clifford Robe, and Henry Donald McKay. *Juvenile Delinquency and Urban Areas: A Study of Rates of Delinquency in Relation to Differential Characteristics of Local Communities in American Cities.* Chicago: University of Chicago Press, [1942] 1969.

Sherman, Rachel. *Class Acts: Service and Inequality in Luxury Hotels.* Berkeley: University of California Press, 2007.

Short, Anne, Julie Guthman, and Samuel Raskin. "Food Deserts, Oases, or Mirages? Small Markets and Community Food Security in the San Francisco Bay Area." *Journal of Planning Education and Research* 26, no. 3 (2007): 352–64.

Silva, Jennifer M. *Coming Up Short: Working-Class Adulthood in an Age of Uncertainty.* New York: Oxford University Press, 2013.

Small, Mario L. *Villa Victoria: The Transformation of Social Capital in a Boston Barrio.* Chicago: University of Chicago Press, 2004.

——— and Katherine Newman. "Urban Poverty after the Truly Disadvantaged: The Rediscovery of the Family, the Neighborhood, and Culture." *Annual Review of Sociology* 27, no. 1 (2001): 23–45.

———, David Harding, and Michèle Lamont. "Reconsidering Culture and Poverty." *Annals of the American Academy of Political and Social Science* 629, no. 1 (2010): 6–27.

Smith, Dorothy E. *The Everyday World as Problematic: A Feminist Sociology.* Boston: Northeastern University Press, 1987.

Smith, Vicki. *Crossing the Great Divide: Worker Risk and Opportunity in the New Economy.* Ithaca, NY: Cornell University Press, 2001.

Stacey, Judith. *Brave New Families: Stories of Domestic Upheaval in Late Twentieth Century America.* New York: Basic Books, 1990.

Stack, Carol B. *All Our Kin: Strategies for Survival in a Black Community.* New York: Harper and Row, 1974.

Steensland, Brian. *The Failed Welfare Revolution: America's Struggle over Guaranteed Income Policy.* Princeton, NJ: Princeton University Press, 2008.

Stevens, Mitchell L. *Creating a Class: College Admissions and the Education of Elites.* Cambridge, MA: Harvard University Press, 2009.

Streib, Jessi. *The Power of the Past: Understanding Cross-Class Marriages.* New York: Oxford University Press, 2015.

Swadener, Beth Blue. "Children and Families 'at Promise': Deconstructing the Discourse of Risk." In *Children and Families "at Promise": Deconstructing the Discourse of Risk,* edited by Beth Blue Swadener and Sally Lubeck, 17–49. New York: State University of New York Press, 1995.

———— and Sally Lubeck. "The Social Construction of Children and Families "at Risk": An Introduction." In *Children and Families "at Promise": Deconstructing the Discourse of Risk*, edited by Beth Blue Swadener and Sally Lubeck, 1–15. New York: State University of New York Press, 1995.

Swaine, Jon, and Oliver Laughland. "Number of People Killed by US Police in 2015 at 1,000 after Oakland Shooting." *Guardian*, November 16, 2015. www.theguardian.com/us-news/2015/nov/16/the-counted-killed-by-police-1000

Tavernise, Sabrina. "Number of Americans without Health Insurance Falls, Survey Shows." *New York Times*, September 16, 2014. www.nytimes.com/2014/09/16/us/number-of-americans-without-health-insurance-falls-survey-shows.html?_r=0

Tuchman, Gaye. *Wannabe U: Inside the Corporate University.* Chicago: University of Chicago Press, 2009.

United States Census Bureau. *American FactFinder: Census Report, 2015.* Accessed February 1, 2016. http://factfinder.census.gov/faces/nav/jsf/pages/index.xhtml

United States Congress, Office of Technology Assessment. "After the Cold War: Living with Lower Defense Spending." OTA-ITE-524. Washington, DC: United States Government Printing Office, 1992.

United States Department of Housing and Urban Development, Office of Policy Development and Research. "Barriers to Success: Housing Insecurity for U.S. College Students." Housing Report, 2015. Accessed February 1, 2016. www.huduser.gov/portal/periodicals/insight/insight_2.pdf

Vaisey, Stephen. "Motivation and Justification: A Dual-Process Model of Culture in Action." *American Journal of Sociology* 114, no. 6 (2009): 1675–715.

Valencia, Richard R. "Conceptualizing the Notion of Deficit Thinking." In *The Evolution of Deficit Thinking: Educational Thought and Practice*, edited by Richard R. Valencia, 1–12. New York: Routledge, 1997.

Valentine, Charles A. *Culture and Poverty: Critique and Counter-Proposals.* Chicago: University of Chicago Press, 1968.

Wacquant, Loïc. *Urban Outcasts: A Comparative Sociology of Advanced Marginality.* Cambridge, MA: Polity Press, 2008.

————. *Punishing the Poor: The Neoliberal Government of Social Insecurity.* Durham, NC: Duke University Press, 2009.

Ward, Martha C. "Early Childbearing: What Is the Problem and Who Owns It?" In *Conceiving the New World Order: The Global Politics of Reproduction*, edited by F. D. Ginsburg and R. Rapp, 140–57. Berkeley: University of California Press, 1995.

Western, Bruce. *Punishment and Inequality in America.* New York: Russell Sage Foundation, 2006.

Whalen, Carmen, and Víctor Vázquez Hernández. *The Puerto Rican Diaspora: Historical Perspectives*. Philadelphia: Temple University Press, 2005.

Wherry, Frederick F. "The Social Characterizations of Price: The Fool, the Faithful, the Frivolous, and the Frugal." *Sociological Theory* 26, no. 4 (2008): 363–79.

Williams, Christine L., and Catherine Connell. "Looking Good and Sounding Right: Aesthetic Labor and Social Inequality in the Retail Industry." *Work and Occupations* 37, no. 3 (2010): 349–77.

Willis, Paul. *Learning to Labour: How Working Class Kids Get Working Class Jobs*. New York: Columbia University Press, 1977.

Wilson, William J. *The Truly Disadvantaged: The Inner City, the Underclass, and Public Policy*. Chicago: University of Chicago Press, 1987.

———. *When Work Disappears: The World of the New Urban Poor*. New York: Knopf, 1996.

———. "Why Both Social Structure and Culture Matter in a Holistic Analysis of Inner-City Poverty." *Annals of the American Academy of Political and Social Science* 629, no. 1 (2010): 200–19.

Yoshikawa, Hirokazu, J. Lawrence Aber, and William R. Beardslee. "The Effects of Poverty on the Mental, Emotional, and Behavioral Health of Children and Youth: Implications for Prevention." *American Psychologist* 67, no. 4 (2012): 272–84.

Zelizer, Viviana A. *The Purchase of Intimacy*. Princeton, NJ: Princeton University Press, 2005.

———. *Economic Lives: How Culture Shapes the Economy*. Princeton, NJ: Princeton University Press, 2011.

Index